Translated Documents of Greece and Rome

E. Badian and Robert K. Sherk, Editors

VOLUME 4

Rome and the Greek East to the death of Augustus

Rome and the Greek East to the death of Augustus

EDITED AND TRANSLATED BY
ROBERT K. SHERK

*Professor of Classics, State University
of New York at Buffalo*

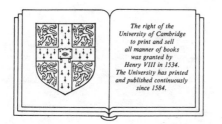

The right of the
University of Cambridge
to print and sell
all manner of books
was granted by
Henry VIII in 1534.
The University has printed
and published continuously
since 1584.

CAMBRIDGE UNIVERSITY PRESS

CAMBRIDGE
LONDON NEW YORK NEW ROCHELLE
MELBOURNE SYDNEY

Published by the Press Syndicate of the University of Cambridge
The Pitt Building, Trumpington Street, Cambridge CB2 1RP
32 East 57th Street, New York, NY 10022, USA
296 Beaconsfield Parade, Middle Park, Melbourne 3206, Australia

First published 1984

Printed in Great Britain at the University Press, Cambridge

Library of Congress catalogue card number: 83-1833

British Library Cataloguing in Publication Data
Sherk, Robert K.
Rome and the Greek East. – (Translated Documents of
Greece and Rome; 4)
1. Rome – History – Sources
I. Title II. Series
937'.008   DG13
ISBN 0 521 24995 3 hard covers
ISBN 0 521 27123 1 paperback

Translated Documents of Greece and Rome

SERIES EDITORS' INTRODUCTION

Greek and Roman history has always been in an ambivalent position in American higher education, having to find a home either in a Department of History or in a Department of Classics, and in both it is usually regarded as marginal. Moreover, in a History Department the subject tends to be taught without regard to the fact that the nature of the evidence is, on the whole, very different from that for American, English, or French history, while in a Classics Department it tends to be viewed as a 'philological' subject and taught by methods appropriate to Greek and Latin authors. Even on the undergraduate level the difference may be important, but on the graduate level, where future teachers and scholars, who are to engage in original research, are trained, it becomes quite clear that neither of these solutions is adequate.

One problem is the standard of proficiency that should be required in Greek and Latin – both difficult languages, necessitating years of study; and few students start the study, even of Latin, let alone Greek, before they come to college. The editors recognize that for the student aiming at a Ph.D. in the subject and at advancing present knowledge of it there can be no substitute for a thorough training in the two languages. Nevertheless, they believe that it is possible to extend serious instruction at a high level to graduate students aiming at reaching the M.A. level and to make them into competent teachers. It is also possible to bring about a great improvement in the standard of undergraduate courses not requiring the ancient languages – courses that instructors themselves usually find unsatisfactory, since much of the source material cannot be used.

In order to use this material, at both graduate and serious undergraduate levels, the instructor must, in fact, be able to range far beyond the standard authors who have been translated many times. Harpocration, Valerius Maximus, and the *Suda* are often necessary tools, but they are usually unknown to anyone except the advanced scholar. Inscriptions, papyri, and scholia can be baffling even to the student who does have a grounding in the ancient languages.

It is the aim of the series to supply that need for translations of materials not readily available in English. The principal historical authors (authors like Livy and Plutarch) are not included; they are easy enough to find in adequate translations, and the student will have to read far more of them than could be provided in a general source book. References to important passages in the works of those authors have been given at suitable points, but it is assumed that the instructor will direct the student's reading in them. While doing that reading, the student will now be able to have at his side a comprehensive reference book. Occasionally a passage from an otherwise accessible author (not a main historical source) has been included, so that the student may be spared the temptation of failing to search for it. But most of the material collected in this series would be hard for him to find anywhere in English, and much of it has never been translated at all.

Such translations of documentary sources as exist (and there are some major projects in translation among them, e.g. in the field of legal texts, which are intended to be far more than source books for students) tend to be seriously misleading in that they offer continuous texts where the original is (so often) fragmentary. The student cannot be aware of how much actually survives on the document and how much is modern conjecture – whether quite certain or mere guesswork. This series aims at presenting the translation of fragmentary sources in something like the way in which original documents are presented to the scholar: a variety of type fonts and brackets (which will be fully explained) have been used for this, and even though the page may at first sight appear forbidding to one unaccustomed to this, he will learn to differentiate between text and restoration and (with the instructor's help and the use of the notes provided) between the dubious, the probable, and the certain restoration. Naturally, the English can never correspond perfectly to the Greek or Latin, but the translation aims at as close a correspondence as can be achieved, so that the run of the original and (where necessary) the amount surviving can be clearly shown. Finer points of English idiom have deliberately been sacrificed in order to produce this increased accuracy, though it is hoped that there will be nothing in the translation so unnatural as to baffle the student. In the case of inscriptions (except for those with excessively short lines) line-by-line correspondence has been the aim, so that the student who sees a precise line reference in a modern work will be able to find it in the translation.

Translation is an art as well as a science; there are bound to be differing opinions on the precise interpretation and on the best rendering of any given passage. The general editors have tried to collaborate with volume editors in achieving the aims outlined above. But there is always room for improvement, and a need for it. Suggestions and corrections from users of the series will always be welcome.

The general editors sincerely hope that the present series will make a major contribution to raising the standard of ancient history teaching in the U.S.A. and, indeed, wherever English is the medium of instruction, and that it will help to convey to students not fully proficient in Greek or Latin, or even entirely ignorant of those languages, some of the immediacy and excitement of real (as distinct from textbook) history. Perhaps some will be encouraged to develop their skill in the two languages so as to go on to a fuller understanding of the ancient world, or even to professional study of it.

Harvard University   E.B.
State University of New York at Buffalo   R.K.S.

CONTENTS

Volume Editor's Introduction   xiii
Abbreviations   xv
Symbols   xviii
  1 Roman mercenary commander of the Ptolemaic garrison on Crete, 217–209 BC   1
  2 Treaty between Rome and the Aetolian League, 212 or 211 BC   1
  3 M. Aemilius Lepidus and his alleged guardianship of the Boy King Ptolemaios V
    Epiphanes, 201/200 BC   2
  4 Letter of T. Quinctius Flamininus to Chyretiai, 197–194 BC   4
  5 Lampsakos honors its citizen Hegesias, 196/195 BC   4
  6 Statues and other honors for T. Quinctius Flamininus in the East, 196 BC
    and after   7
  7 King Eumenes of Pergamum and the war against King Nabis, 195 BC   8
  8 Letter of the praetor M. Valerius Messalla to the city of Teos, 193 BC   9
  9 The Delians honor P. Cornelius Scipio Africanus, c. 193 BC   10
 10 Delos seeks to renew friendship with Rome, c. 192 BC   11
 11 Troops of the Achaean League aid the Romans against the Gauls, 192 or
    122 BC   11
 12 Letter of Manius Acilius Glabrio to the Delphians, 190 BC   11
 13 Participation of the Achaeans in the battle of Magnesia, 190 BC   12
 14 Letter of L. Cornelius Scipio and his brother to Herakleia in Karia, 190 BC 13
 15 Two letters from the praetor Spurius Postumius and a decree of the senate,
    189 BC   14
 16 Letter of a consul (C. Livius Salinator?) to the Delphians, 189/188 BC   15
 17 Decree of Elateia honoring the Stymphalians, c. 189 BC   16
 18 The Lycian League and its celebration of the festival of the goddess Roma,
    c. 180 BC   17
 19 Letter to the Delphian Amphictiones about King Perseus, 171/170 BC   18
 20 Decree of the senate concerning Koroneia, 171 or 170 BC   20
 21 Two decrees of the senate on affairs at Thisbai, 170 BC   20
 22 Argos honors Gnaeus Octavius, 170 BC   22
 23 An Athenian with the Roman army at the battle of Pydna, 168 BC   23
 24 Statue of L. Aemilius Paullus placed on a pillar erected previously for King
    Perseus, 168/167 BC   24
 25 Treaty between Rome and Kibyra, first half of second century   24
 26 Envoys from Teos to Rome oppose the encroachment of King Kotys on the
    territory of Abdera, c. 166 BC   25
 27 Romans admitted to the Samothracian Mysteries, second and
    first centuries BC   26

Contents

28 Decree of the senate concerning the Sarapieion at Delos, *c.* 164 BC   27

29 A letter of King Attalus II of Pergamum to the priest in Pessinus, *c.* 159 BC   28

30 Treaty between King Pharnakes I of Pontos and the city of Chersonesos, 155 BC   29

31 Testament of Ptolemaios VIII Euergetes II, leaving his kingdom of Cyrene to the Romans, 155 BC   30

32 Decree of the senate concerning Ariarathes and the city of Priene, *c.* 155–154 BC or soon afterwards   31

33 Treaty between Rome and Methymna, 154 BC or later   32

34 A letter of the praetor M. Aemilius and a decree of the senate concerning Magnesia and Priene, *c.* 150 BC or earlier   33

35 Destruction of Corinth and new Roman regulations for Greece, 146 BC   34

36 The builder of the Via Egnatia in Macedonia, *c.* 146–143 BC   36

37 Conclusion of a letter by a Roman magistrate to the Dionysiac Artists, after 146 BC   36

38 Decree of the senate concerning Narthakion and Melitaia, 140 BC or earlier   37

39 Decree of Pergamum on citizenship after the death of Attalus III, 133 BC   39

40 Decree of the senate concerning the death of King Attalus III, probably 133 BC   40

41 The cult of the goddess Roma in Miletus, *c.* 130 BC   41

42 Manius Aquillius constructs the first Roman roads in Asia, 129–126 BC   43

43 The city of Bargylia supplies troops in the war against Aristonicus, 129 BC   43

44 Decree of Pergamum to celebrate its friendship and alliance with Rome, *c.* 129 BC   45

45 Decree of the senate concerning Pergamene land, probably 129 BC   47

46 Samos honors Gnaeus Domitius Ahenobarbus, 129–126 BC   48

47 Roman negotiatores (businessmen) in the Greek East, second/first century BC   49

48 Lete honors M. Annius, quaestor, 119 BC   51

49 Decree of the senate concerning Phrygia, 119 (?) or 116 BC   53

50 Letter of Q. Fabius Maximus to the city of Dyme, perhaps 115 BC   54

51 Epidauros honors one of its prominent citizens, 112/111 BC   55

52 M. Minucius Rufus honored by Delphi, 110–106 BC   56

53 Decree of the senate and a treaty with Astypalaia, 105 BC   56

54 M. Antonius transports his fleet across the isthmus of Corinth, 102 or 101 BC   58

55 Piracy law(s) from Delphi and Knidos, 101/100 BC   59

56 The rise of Mithridates and his war against the Romans, 100–87 BC   66

57 Letter of Q. Mucius Scaevola to Ephesus, 98–93 BC   68

58 The Organization of Peoples and Tribes in Asia, early first century BC   69

59 Exemption of sacred territory from the revenue contracts of the publicans, 89–87 BC   70

59a Plarasa-Aphrodisias decides to aid the Romans against Mithridates, 88 BC   70

59b Letter of Q. Oppius to Plarasa-Aphrodisias after the war against Mithridates, 85/84 BC   71

60 Chaeremon of Nysa, friend of the Romans, enemy of Mithridates, 88/87 BC   72

61 Ephesus declares war against Mithridates, 86/85 BC   73

62 Two letters of Sulla concerning the Dionysiac Artists, *c.* 84–81 BC   74

Contents

63 A letter of Sulla to Stratonikeia, followed by a second letter introducing a
   decree of the senate concerning that city, 81 BC   75
64 A letter of Cn. Cornelius Dolabella to Thasos, 80 BC   78
65 Decree of the Koinon of Asia, 80–48 BC   80
66 Decree of the senate concerning three Greek naval captains, 78 BC   81
67 P. Servilius Vatia in Cilicia and Isauria, 78–75 BC   83
68 Murder of publicans in Herakleia in Pontos, 74 BC   84
69 C. Salluvius Naso honored for his actions against Mithridates, 74/73 BC   84
70 Oropos and the publicans, 73 BC   85
71 Roman naval actions during the Third Mithridatic War, 72–69 BC   87
72 Antonian law concerning Termessus Maior in Pisidia, 72 or 68 BC   89
73 Greek city of Mesambria in Thrace placed under a Roman officer, 71 BC   92
74 Roman businessmen, Roman officials and the debts of a Greek city, 71 BC   93
75 The Greek East honors Pompey the Great, 67–62 BC   95
76 Envoys from Tragurion in Dalmatia meet Julius Caesar in Aquileia, 56 BC   96
77 Letter of a Roman official to the conventus (judiciary centers) of the province
   of Asia, 51 or c. 29 BC   96
78 The city of Dionysopolis, King Burebista, and the Romans, 49 or 48 BC   98
79 Statues of Julius Caesar dedicated in the Greek East after Pharsalus, 48 BC
   or later   99
80 Julius Caesar makes concessions to Pergamum, 48/47 BC   101
81 P. Servilius Isauricus restores to Pergamum its ancestral laws and its
   democracy, 46–44 BC   102
82 Envoys from the city of Chersonesos to Julius Caesar and the senate in
   Rome, 46 BC   102
83 A letter of Caesar with a copy of a decree of the senate concerning Mytilene,
   46/45 BC   103
84 Greek cities honor Brutus the tyrannicide, 44/43 BC   104
85 Letter of M. Antonius to the Koinon of Asia concerning the Association of
   Victorious Athletes, 42/41 or 33/32 BC   105
86 Letters of Octavian concerning Seleukos of Rhosos, 42–30 BC   106
87 Letter of Octavian to Plarasa-Aphrodisias concerning documents relevant
   to the city's status, 39/38 BC   109
88 M. Antonius gives foreign territory to Cleopatra, who commemorates the
   event by adopting a second era, 37/36 BC   110
89 Coinage of Antonius and Cleopatra, 34/33 BC(?)   111
90 Worship of Isis by a Roman officer, his son and friends, 32 BC   112
91 Letter of Octavian to the city of Mylasa, 31 BC   112
92 Octavian dedicates his camp overlooking the promontory of Actium, 29 BC   113
93 Dedication of C. Cornelius Gallus, first Roman prefect of Egypt, 29 BC   114
94 Preparations in Egypt for a military expedition, after 30 BC   114
95 Legal decision by Augustus and Agrippa, and a governor's letter to Kyme,
   27 BC   115
96 An earthquake at Tralles in Asia, and help from Augustus, 26 BC   117
97 Two decrees of the senate and a treaty with Mytilene, 25 BC   118
98 M. Vipsanius Agrippa and Julia in the Greek East, 16–13 BC   120

Contents

99 Greek translation of funeral oration given by Augustus for Agrippa, 12 BC   122

100 Letter of Augustus to the Alexandrians and the proceedings of an embassy,
10/9 BC   123

101 A new calendar for the province of Asia in honor of Augustus, 9 BC   124

102 Five edicts of Augustus and a decree of the senate, 7/6 and 4 BC   127

103 Letter of Augustus to Knidos, 6 BC   133

104 Gaius, son of Augustus, is honored at Sardis, 5 BC   134

105 Oath of loyalty sworn in Paphlagonia to Augustus and his descendants, 3 BC   135

106 Roman legionaries guard the government grain during its transportation
down the Nile to Alexandria, 2 BC   136

107 Restoration of sacred writings to the archives of Nysa, 1 BC   137

108 Letter of a governor of Asia concerning a point of law, c.AD 4/5   138

109 Greek athletic contests named in honor of Augustus and his family, c. AD 5   139

110 Early Roman organization of mines and quarries in Egypt, AD 11   140

111 Minutes of an audience in Rome given by Augustus with his Advisory
Board to envoys from Alexandria, AD 13   141

112 Augustus sets up the final report of his accomplishments in the Greek East,
c. AD 12–14   142

Glossary   145

Appendixes
I Roman names   154
II Roman consuls   155
III Greek and Roman chronology   161

Indexes
I Personal names   164
II Gods and goddesses   169
III Geographical names   169
IV Subjects and terms   172
V Translated passages   178

VOLUME EDITOR'S INTRODUCTION

The involvement of Rome in Greek affairs toward the end of the third century, the victory over Macedon and then the Roman annexation of Macedon, Greece and Asia produced conditions that transformed the intellectual, social and political nature of the Roman ruling class. So important was this transformation that special attention must be given to it, and it was felt that a separate volume would be necessary to illustrate the many political and diplomatic actions that were so much a part of it. Like the other volumes of the series this one will supply translations of materials not readily available in English, but references to important passages in authors like Polybius or Livy will be given at the appropriate places. The basic intent of the translations has been to express the exact meaning of the original Latin or Greek and to preserve the 'feel' of the original documents and facilitate the checking of references by a conscious effort to maintain line-by-line precision. At times the nature of the Latin or Greek languages has made it impossible, or at least exceedingly difficult, to preserve such line-by-line translation, and therefore a certain amount of manipulation of English grammar or style has been necessary. The result is often contrary to natural English idiom. It is hoped that students of ancient history who use this book will be stimulated to that more intensive study of the original languages so vital to advanced research. It is also hoped that scholars will find in these pages a convenient collection of documents and materials that will make their own researches less time-consuming.

The bibliographies attached to each document are not designed to be exhaustive, but to direct the reader to those books and articles which are the most useful and authoritative and which, in turn, will lead him to previous discussions. As for the documents themselves, the sheer mass of material for inclusion in this volume is so great that the selective process made it necessary to omit many that should have been included, if space had been available. But publisher's restraints had to be followed, and only at the last minute there came to hand Joyce Reynolds' *Aphrodisias and Rome*. Partial use of this very important publication was possible only to the extent of adding a few short documents (nos. 59a–b), revising one other (no. 87) and adding a few notices elsewhere.

A word should be added about the original language of the documents in this volume. The reader may assume that it is Greek, except where the notation '(Latin)' alerts him to the contrary. No such distinction is made in the case of ancient authors, since that information will be presumed to be known.

As co-editor of the series, E. Badian has read and re-read with his eagle eye all of the manuscript. His suggestions and corrections have made this a better book than it might otherwise have been. His good judgment and immense knowledge are here given the recognition they deserve. Whatever errors remain are the results of my own carelessness or stubbornness.

ABBREVIATIONS

AAntHung	Acta Antiqua Academiae Scientiarum Hungaricae
Accame, *Dominio*	S. Accame, *Il dominio romano in Grecia dalla guerra acaica ad Augusto* (Rome 1946)
AE	L'Année Épigraphique
AJA	American Journal of Archaeology
AJAH	American Journal of Ancient History
AJP	American Journal of Philology
ANRW	Aufstieg und Niedergang der römischen Welt
Athen. Mitt.	Mitteilungen des deutschen Archäologischen Instituts, Athenische Abteilung
Atkinson, *Historia*	K. M. T. Atkinson, 'Governors of the Province Asia in the Reign of Augustus', *Historia* 7 (1958) 300–30
Badian, *FC*	E. Badian, *Foreign Clientelae (264–70 B.C.)* (Oxford 1958)
Badian, *Publicans*	E. Badian, *Publicans and Sinners* (Ithaca, N.Y. 1972)
Badian, *Studies*	E. Badian, *Studies in Greek and Roman History* (Oxford 1964)
BCH	Bulletin de Correspondance Hellénique
Bengtson, *Strategie*	H. Bengtson, *Die Strategie in der Hellenistischen Zeit* I–III (Munich 1937–52)
Bernand, *Philae*	A. Bernand, *Les inscriptions grecques de Philae* I–II (Paris 1969–)
Bernhardt, *Historia*	R. Bernhardt, 'Der Status des 146 v. Chr. unterworfenen Teils Griechenlands bis zur Einrichtung der Provinz Achaia', *Historia* 26 (1977) 62–73
BGU	Berliner griechische Urkunden (Ägyptische Urkunden aus den Königlichen Museen zu Berlin) (Berlin 1895–)
Bowersock, *Augustus*	G. W. Bowersock, *Augustus and the Greek World* (Oxford 1965)
Briscoe, *Commentary*	J. Briscoe, *A Commentary on Livy (Books XXXI–XXXIII)* (Oxford 1973)
Broughton, *Asia*	T. R. S. Broughton, 'Roman Asia', in T. Frank, *An Economic History of Ancient Rome* IV (Baltimore 1938)
Broughton, *MRR*	T. R. S. Broughton, *The Magistrates of the Roman Republic* I (1951), II (1952), Supplement (1960), published by the American Philological Association
Busolt, *Staatskunde*	G. Busolt, *Griechische Staatskunde*[3] Part I (Munich 1920)
CAH	Cambridge Ancient History
CIL	Corpus Inscriptionum Latinarum
CP	Classical Philology
Daux, *Delphes*	G. Daux, *Delphes au IIe et au Ier siècle* (Paris 1936)
Day, *Athens*	J. Day, *An Economic History of Athens under Roman Domination* (New York 1942)
Degrassi, *Imagines*	Corpus Inscriptionum Latinarum. Auctarium. Inscriptiones Latinae Liberae Rei Publicae: Imagines, ed. A. Degrassi (Berlin 1966)
Dunant-Pouilloux, *Recherches*	C. Dunant and J. Pouilloux, *Recherches sur l'Histoire et les Cultes de Thasos* II: *Études thasiennes* V (Paris 1958)
Durrbach, *Choix*	F. Durrbach, *Choix d'Inscriptions de Délos*, Vol. I in two fascicles (Paris 1921–22)

Abbreviations

Ehrenberg, *State*	V. Ehrenberg, *The Greek State* (Oxford 1960)
FGrHist	F. Jacoby, *Die Fragmente der griechischen Historiker* (Berlin and Leiden 1923–)
FIRA	*Fontes Iuris Romani Antejustiniani* I–III (Rome 1941–3)
Fraser, *Samothrace*	P. M. Fraser, *Samothrace* II.1: *The Inscriptions on Stone* (London and New York 1960)
Gelzer, *Caesar*	M. Gelzer, *Caesar: Politician and Statesman*, trans. P. Needham (Oxford 1968)
GRBS	*Greek, Roman and Byzantine Studies*
Greenidge, *Public Life*	A. H. J. Greenidge, *Roman Public Life* (London 1901)
Hansen, *Attalids*^{2}	E. V. Hansen, *The Attalids of Pergamon*^{2} (Ithaca, N.Y. 1971)
Hatzfeld, *Trafiquants*	J. Hatzfeld, *Les trafiquants italiens dans l'Orient hellénique* (Paris 1919)
Historia	*Historia: Zeitschrift für Alte Geschichte*
Holleaux, *Études*	M. Holleaux, *Études d'Épigraphie et d'Histoire Grecques* I–VI (Paris 1938–)
Hopp, *Untersuchungen*	J. Hopp, *Untersuchungen zur Geschichte der letzten Attaliden* (Munich 1977)
HSCP	*Harvard Studies in Classical Philology*
IC	*Inscriptiones Creticae*
I.Délos	*Inscriptions de Délos*
IG	*Inscriptiones Graecae*
IG Bulg I^2	*Inscriptiones Graecae in Bulgaria Repertae* I^2 (ed. Mihailov)
IGLS	*Inscriptions grecques et latines de la Syrie* (ed. Jalabert and Mouterde)
IGRR	*Inscriptiones Graecae ad Res Romanas Pertinentes* (ed. Cagnat)
I. Ilion	*Die Inschriften von Ilion* (Bonn 1975) (ed. P. Frisch)
I. Lampsakos	*Die Inschriften von Lampsakos* (Bonn 1978) (ed. P. Frisch)
ILLRP	*Inscriptiones Latinae Liberae Rei Publicae* (ed. Degrassi)
ILS	*Inscriptiones Latinae Selectae* (ed. Dessau)
I. Magnesia	*Die Inschriften von Magnesia am Maeander* (Berlin 1900) (ed. Kern)
I. Olympia	*Die Inschriften von Olympia* (Berlin 1896) (ed. Dittenberger and Purgold)
IOSPE	*Inscriptiones Antiquae Orae Septentrionalis Ponti Euxini Graecae et Latinae* (ed. Latyschev)
I. Priene	*Inschriften von Priene* (ed. Hiller von Gaertringen)
JHS	*Journal of Hellenic Studies*
JRS	*Journal of Roman Studies*
Laidlaw, *Delos*	W. M. Laidlaw, *A History of Delos* (Oxford 1933)
Larsen, *Greece*	J. A. O. Larsen, 'Roman Greece', in T. Frank, *An Economic Survey of Ancient Rome* IV (Baltimore 1938)
Larsen, *States*	J. A. O. Larsen, *Greek Federal States* (Oxford 1968)
Magie, *RRAM*	D. Magie, *Roman Rule in Asia Minor* I–II (Princeton 1950)
Mellor, *Worship*	R. Mellor, ΘΕΑ ΡΩΜΗ. *The Worship of the Goddess Roma in the Greek World* (Göttingen 1975)
Meloni, *Perseo*	P. Meloni, *Perseo e la fine della monarchia macedone* (Rome 1953)
Meyer, *Staat*	E. Meyer, *Römischer Staat und Staatsgedanke*^{3} (Zürich and Stuttgart 1964)
Milet	*Milet, Ergebnisse der Ausgrabungen seit dem Jahre 1899* (ed. Wiegand) (Berlin 1906)
Moretti, *IGUR*	L. Moretti, *Inscriptiones Graecae Urbis Romae* I–III (Rome 1968–79)
Moretti, *ISE*	L. Moretti, *Iscrizioni storiche ellenistiche* I–II (Florence 1967 and 1976)

Abbreviations

Nicolet, *L'ordre*   C. Nicolet, *L'ordre équestre à l'époque républicaine (321–43 av. J.-C.)* I (Paris 1966)

OGIS   *Orientis Graeci Inscriptiones Selectae* (ed. Dittenberger)

Ormerod, *Piracy*   H. A. Ormerod, *Piracy in the Ancient World* (London 1924)

PBSR   *Papers of the British School at Rome*

P. Oxy.   *The Oxyrhynchus Papyri*

RDGE   R. K. Sherk, *Roman Documents from the Greek East* (Baltimore 1969)

RE   Pauly-Wissowa-Kroll (ed.), *Real-Encyclopaedie der classischen Altertumswissenschaft*

REA   *Revue des Études Anciennes*

REG   *Revue des Études Grecques*

Reynolds, *Aphrodisias*   J. Reynolds, *Aphrodisias and Rome* (London 1982)

RIDA   *Revue Internationale des Droits de l'Antiquité*

Robert, *Ét. Anat.*   L. Robert, *Études Anatoliennes* (Paris 1937)

Robert, *Hellenica*   L. Robert, *Hellenica. Recueil d'épigraphie, de numismatique et d'antiquités grecques* I– (Paris 1940–)

Robert, *Opera*   L. Robert, *Opera minora selecta* I–IV (Amsterdam 1969–)

Rostovtzeff, *SEHHW*   M. I. Rostovtzeff, *Social and Economic History of the Hellenistic World* I–III (Oxford 1941)

Samuel, *GRC*   A. E. Samuel, *Greek and Roman Chronology* (Munich 1972)

Samuel, *PC*   A. E. Samuel, *Ptolemaic Chronology* (Munich 1962)

SB   *Sammelbuch griechischer Urkunden aus Ägypten* (ed. Preisigke and Bilabel)

Schmitt, *Staatsverträge*   H. H. Schmitt, *Die Staatsverträge des Altertums* III (*Die Verträge der griechisch-römischen Welt von 338 bis 200 v. Chr.*) (Munich 1969)

Schwertfeger, *Bund*   T. Schwertfeger, *Der Achaiische Bund von 146 bis 27 v. Chr.* (Munich 1974)

SDAW   *Sitzungsberichte der deutschen Akademie der Wissenschaften*

SEG   *Supplementum Epigraphicum Graecum*

Sherwin-White, *Citizenship*²   A. N. Sherwin-White, *The Roman Citizenship*² (Oxford 1972)

*SIG*³   *Sylloge Inscriptionum Graecarum*³ (ed. Dittenberger *et al.*)

Sokolowski, *Lois*   F. Sokolowski, *Lois sacrées de l'Asie Mineure* (Paris 1955)

Studia Pontica   *Studia Pontica* III (ed. Anderson, Cumont, Grégoire) (Brussels 1910)

TAM   *Tituli Asiae Minoris*

TAPA   *Transactions of the American Philological Association*

Täubler, *Imperium*   E. Täubler, *Imperium Romanum* (Leipzig 1913)

Tod, *Arbitration*   M. N. Tod, *International Arbitration amongst the Greeks* (Oxford 1913)

Walbank, *Commentary*   F. W. Walbank, *A Historical Commentary on Polybius* I–III (Oxford 1957–79)

Welles, *RC*   C. Bradford Welles, *Royal Correspondence in the Hellenistic Period* (New Haven 1934)

Wilcken, *Grundzüge*   Part 1 of U. Wilcken and L. Mitteis, *Grundzüge und Chrestomathie der Papyruskunde*, Leipzig-Berlin 1912

Wilcken, *Chrestomathie*

Will, *Histoire*   E. Will, *Histoire politique du monde hellénistique (323–30 av. J.-C.)* II (Nancy 1967)

ZPE   *Zeitschrift für Papyrologie und Epigraphik*

SYMBOLS

( )   indicate an explanatory addition to the text.

[ ]   enclose letters or words that no longer stand in the text as it survives, but have been restored by modern scholars.

<>   enclose letters or words thought to have been accidentally omitted on the original document.

[[ ]]   enclose letters or words that were deliberately erased in ancient times.

{}   enclose apparently superfluous letters or words.

| indicates the end of a line in an inscription.

|| indicate the beginning of every fifth line in an inscription.

/   indicates the end of a line of verse.

//   indicate the beginning of every fifth line of verse.

*   indicates the text on which the translation of an inscription or papyrus here given is based.

v   indicates a vacant letterspace on the original document.

vv   indicate that there is more than one letterspace vacant on the original document.

vacat   indicates that an entire line or a space between entire lines was left vacant.

LACUNA indicates that a portion of the document is missing.

Italics   indicate that only a part of the original word is extant on the document.

Spelling

Most of the personal and place names are transliterated directly. However, the names of Greek and Roman authors as well as individuals are given in their familiar English or Latin spelling, and certain place names, more familiar to readers in a Latin spelling, are retained in that spelling, regardless of the language of the document. Latin names will regularly appear in their Latin spelling for the same reason, but the more unusual Greek names will be transliterated. To many 'Aetolia' is more familiar than 'Aitolia', while 'Cibyra' would be no more enlightening than 'Kibyra'. Still, I have not followed a rigid set of rules.

1   Roman mercenary commander of the Ptolemaic garrison on Crete. Between 217 and 209 BC.

Light blue limestone, good lettering of the third century, Itanos.

ILS 9458; **IC* III 4, no. 18 (+ photograph).

S. Spyridakis, *Ptolemaic Itanos and Hellenistic Crete* (Berkeley 1970) 79–81; R. S. Bagnall, *The Administration of the Ptolemaic Possessions outside Egypt* (Leiden 1976) 121–3.

To King Ptolemaios Philopator | and Queen Arsinoe | this well and Nymphaion[1] | (are dedicated by) Lucius, son of Gaius, Roman, garrison-commander.[2]

1 Spyridakis suggests that a water reservoir is meant rather than a sanctuary of the Nymphs.
2 As the commander of a Ptolemaic garrison on Crete, Lucius must have been a mercenary who hired himself out to the Ptolemies. For the date see Spyridakis and Bagnall.

2   Treaty between Rome and the Aetolian League. 212 or 211 BC.

Limestone stele broken at top and bottom, letters of the late third century, Thyrrheion in Akarnania.

G. Klaffenbach, 'Der römisch-ätolische Bündnisvertrag vom Jahre 212 v. Chr.', *SDAW* (1954) no. 1 (+ photographs); *IG* IX[2] 2.241; Schmitt, **Staatsverträge* 3.536; Moretti, *ISE* II 87. Cf. Livy 26.24.1–14; Polybius 9.39.1–3; 18.38.5–9.

A. H. McDonald, *JRS* 46 (1956) 153–7; E. Badian, *Latomus* 17 (1958) 197–211; *idem, FC* 56–7; G. A. Lehmann, *Untersuchungen zur historischen Glaubwürdigkeit des Polybios* (Munster 1967) 10–131, 365–71, 386–90; W. Dahlheim, *Struktur und Entwicklung des römischen Völkerrechts*, Vestigia 8 (Munich 1968) 181–207; R. M. Errington, *The Dawn of Empire* (Ithaca, N.Y. 1972) 113–15; D. Musti in *ANRW* 1.2.1146–51.

[---] *a|gainst* all these (nations?)[1] [--] | let the (League) officials of the
5   Aetolians *do*[2] | as he (it?) wishes to be done. And if any ‖ cities of these nations are captured by the Romans by for|ce, let it be permitted that these cities and their | territories, as far as the Roman People are concerned, | be possessed by the People of the Aetolians. | [Whatever] apart
10   from the city and its territory[3] the Roman‖s capture, let the Romans possess. If any | of these cities are captured by the Romans and Aetolians in com|mon, let it be permitted that these cities and their terri|tories, as far as the People <of the Romans> are concerned, be possessed by the
15   Aetolians. | Whatever they capture (in common) apart from the city, ‖ let them both have in common. If any of these | cities, in regard to the Romans or the Aetolians, capitu|lates or surrenders[4] to them, let it be

1

permitted that these | *men* and cities and their territories, *as far* | as the
20   People of the Romans are concerned, ‖ be received by the Aetolians
[into their] League | [--] autonomous[5] | [--] from the Ro|[mans --] the
peace[6] [--|--]

This is the oldest surviving original of a Roman treaty and the earliest document concerning the public relations of Rome with the Greek East. The phraseology points to a
close translation of the Latin original: e.g. 'the People of the Aetolians' in line 8 renders
the Latin *populus Aetolorum*, a phrase that refers to the Aetolian League in a characteris-
tically Roman way. The Greek translation appears to have been made in Aetolia, since
the dialect used is a form of North-West Greek, while official Roman translations were
in the Hellenistic Koine. It is clear from its terms that the treaty reflects no Roman
desire for territorial expansion, but is aimed solely at prosecuting the war against Philip.
Livy, using Polybius and working within the annalistic framework, has given us an
incomplete summary of the treaty, perhaps even incorporating parts of the preliminary
agreement made in the field by the praetor M. Valerius Laevinus, which would have
been subject to revision for the final draft by the senate.

1 Livy (26.24.11) gives a loose geographical indication of what area in Greece is meant:
   'cities from the border of Aetolia as far as Corcyra'. The epigraphic text at this point,
   just prior to its extant remains, would have given the actual names of the various
   peoples, as seen in the phrase 'all these'. Cf. Polybius 11.5.4.
2 Klaffenbach connected this word with the lacuna in line 2 and restored 'against all
   these let the (League) officials of the Aetolians *make* [war immediately,]' etc.
3 I.e. the movable booty, including the inhabitants who would be enslaved.
4 This phrase has caused great controversy, since the difference between the two Greek
   verbs is not immediately apparent. Some, like Klaffenbach, have attempted to distinguish carefully the one from the other, while others, like Lehmann, believe the difference in the tenses of the two is the significant element. The first is in the present subjunctive, the second in the aorist subjunctive. But the phrase appears merely to reflect
   the traditional legal language of such Latin originals, as Badian (*Historische Zeitschrift*
   208 [1969] 640–1) points out. He suggests that the translator was unwilling to use the
   same Greek verb in two tenses, as he found them in the Latin, and therefore used two
   different words of almost the same meaning in two different tenses. His suggestion is followed here.
5 Apparently such cities that enter the League are to remain autonomous.
6 This seems to refer to what Livy (26.24.12–13) says: 'If the Aetolians made peace with
   Philip they were to add to the treaty that the peace would be ratified if Philip should
   abstain from war against the Romans and their allies and those who were under their
   control; likewise, if the Roman People should make a treaty with the king, they should
   take care that he does not have the right of making war upon the Aetolians and their
   allies.'

3   M. Aemilius Lepidus and his alleged guardianship of the Boy King Ptolemaios V Epiphanes. 201/200 BC.

A: Justin 30.2.8. **B**: Justin 31.1.2. **C**: Valerius Maximus 6.6.1. **D**: Denarius minted in Rome
in 61 BC with legends (Latin). M. H. Crawford, *Roman Republican Coinage* (2 vols, Cambridge 1974) I 443–4, no. 419/2 (Plate LI, no. 419/2). Cf. Livy 31.2.3; 31.18.1; Tacitus
Ann. 2.67.4.

H. Heinen in *ANRW* 1.1.647–50 (favorable to the tradition); W. Huss, *Untersuchungen zur Aussenpolitik Ptolemaios' IV* (Munich 1976) 168–70 (unfavorable).

A. Justin 30.2.8

When the infamy of the (Egyptian) kingdom had been expiated, as it were, by the death of the king[1] (and)[2] by the punishment of the courtesans, the Alexandrians sent envoys to the Romans begging them to accept the guardianship of the orphan (Ptolemaios V) and to watch over the kingdom of Egypt.

B. Justin 31.1.2

Since Ptolemaios (IV) Philopator, king of Egypt, was dead and since his little son was only a few years old and, with his hope of succeeding to the kingdom, had been left as a prize to the members of his household, Antiochus the king of Syria determined to seize Egypt. Thus, when he had invaded Phoenicia and other states of Syria, but which were actually under the rule of Egypt, the senate sent envoys to him to declare that he should keep his distance from the kingdom of the little boy who had been handed over to the senate's trust by the last prayers of his father.

C. Valerius Maximus 6.6.1

When King Ptolemaios (IV) had left the Roman People as guardian to his son, the senate sent M. Aemilius Lepidus, pontifex maximus and twice consul (187 and 175 BC), to Alexandria to undertake the boy's guardianship.

D. Denarius, Crawford, *op. cit.* pp. 443–4, no. 419/2

(Obverse, female head wearing a turreted diadem)	Alexandria.
(Reverse, figure in a toga crowning another figure who wears a chiton)	M. Lepidus Pontifex Maximus Guardian of the king.[3] By decree of the senate.[4]

1 When Ptolemaios IV died in 205 or 204 BC, a bloody struggle arose over the regency, resulting in a serious instability of Egyptian rule. For this palace revolution see Polybius 15.26–34 and Walbank's discussion, *Commentary* II 435ff., and Will, *Histoire* 92–6.

2 This word seems necessary. F. Ruehl, in his edition of Justin of 1886, inserted it into the text, but O. Seel in his edition of 1972 did not admit it.

3 The tableau on this coin clearly refers to the alleged guardianship of M. Aemilius Lepidus back in 201/200 BC. The coin was minted in 61 BC under the direction of his descendant M. Aemilius Lepidus, who was doubtless the future triumvir with Octavian and Antonius.

4 This merely indicates that the senate had given its approval to the minting of the coin.

4   Letter of T. Quinctius Flamininus to Chyretiai. Between 197 and 194 BC.

Stone of white marble, letters of early second century, near the site of Chyretiai in Perrhaibia.

*SIG*³ 593; *RDGE* 33. Cf. Livy 31.41.5; 34.48.2.

RDGE pp. 211–13.

Titus Quinctius, consul of the Romans (198 BC),¹ | to the tagoi² and the city of Chyretiai, greetings. Since in all other matters too | we have made clear our own policy and that of the People of the Romans | which we have
5   toward you in general, we have also wished ‖ in the future to appear in every part to be champions | of what is honorable, in order that in these matters too men may not have (the means) to slan|der us, men who have not been accustomed in accordance with the best principles to con|duct themselves. Whatever properties have been lost by you | in land and
10   buildings, of those (now) belonging to the public (domain) ‖ of the Romans, all of them we give to your city, | in order that also in these matters you may learn our nobility of character | and because in no way at all have we wished to be avaricious, | considering goodwill and concern for our reputation to be of supreme importance. But all those who | have not
15   recovered what belongs to them, ‖ if they notify you and if it is the truth they seem to be sp|eaking, and if you conduct your investigation in accord with my writ|ten decisions, I decide it is just (for their property) to be restor|ed to them. *vv* | *vv* Farewell.

1   From 197 to 194 BC Flamininus was proconsul in Greece and Macedonia, his command being extended from one year to the next. The Greeks, however, continued to call him consul throughout those years.
2   The eponymous magistrates of the city.

5   Lampsakos honors its citizen Hegesias. 196/195 BC.

Two fragments of a stele of white marble, broken at top and bottom, damaged on both sides, common letters of the early second century, Lampsakos in the Troad.

*SIG*³ 591; Frisch, *I. Lampsakos* 4 (+ photograph). Cf. Livy 33.38.1–7; Appian, *Syrian Wars* 2; Polybius 21.13.1–5; Diodorus 29.7.

Holleaux, *Études* V 141–55; E. Bickermann, *Philologus* 87 (1932) 277–99; Magie, *RRAM* II 745–6, n. 35; P. Desideri, *Studi Classici e Orientali* 19–20 (1970–71) 501–6; Frisch, *op. cit.* 15–39.

[-- in | the decrees] written above. [When the Peo|ple sought out] and
appealed with all [ar|dor] to men to volunteer their service, and when
5 they decreed [th||at for those who] undertook embassies on behalf of the
city to | [the Massali]otes and Romans there would be some (form of)
honor from the | [People], and that, when the envoys returned, a *pre|limi-*
nary decree would be passed by the Boule that they would be honored, and
after *some men* were proposed | and would not accept, while some others
10 were actually elected || *and declined under oath* because of the length of the
journey [and | the expense,] Hegesias was proposed. Instead of declining
under | oath [after being elected]¹ and asked by the People, [he thought]
nothing | of the dangers involved in the foreign travel, but | ⌈considered⌉
15 his own affairs [of less importance] than the city's inter||est, and [he
accepted] the embassy. He went abroad, [arri|ved in] Greece and meet-
ing, along with his *fellow* | *envoys*, the Roman commander in charge of |
the fleet, [Lucius (Quinctius Flamininus),²] he recounted to him in
detail that the | People (of Lampsakos), [being kinsmen and] friends of
20 the Roman People, had se||nt [them] to him in order that he (Hegesias)
might request of him and *appe|al* to him, [along with] his fellow envoys,
since we were kinsmen of the [Ro|mans, to take thought] for our city
that he should do [whatever | might seem] advantageous for our People,
for it fell *to them* (the Romans) | [always to guard] the interests of our
25 city because we [ha||ve] kinship with them, (kinship) which [---] |³ and
because of the fact that our brothers are the Massaliotes | [who are
friends] and allies of the Roman People. And | [(the envoys) took care
to] *obtain* fitting answers | to *send back* [to our People.] Because of these
30 answers our People [were] in very high spirits, || [for in these answers]
(the commander) made it clear that he accepted the *relation|ship and*
kinship that we have with the Romans. | [And⁴ he promised that] if he
made friendship or a treaty with anybody, | he would include our city
[in it] and would *stand guard* over (our) | [democracy] and autonomy
35 and *peace*, [and || he would always do what] *he could* to be of service, and
that if anyone [should] | try to cause trouble,] he would not permit it
but would prevent it.

Then [with] his | *fellow envoys* (Hegesias) met with the quaestor attached
to the fleet [--|- and after persuading] him always to be the author of
some good (toward us), | [he received] from him too a letter to [our]
40 People, || [which our People decided] was useful and deposited in [our
pub|lic archives.] Having crossed over [--|---|-] and concerning which
he had the decrees, [he made] | the long and dangerous journey by ship
45 [to Massal]ia *and went* [before || the Six] Hundred,⁵ won them over and
contrived [to | obtain] envoys for the joint embassy with *himself* [on behalf
of | their city] to Rome. Judging it would be helpful, they asked for [and
ob|tained from the] Six Hundred a letter useful [to our Peo|ple to the]

50   People of the Galatian Tolostoagioi.[6] Having crossed [to ‖ Rome with]
his fellow envoys and those who had been sent with | [him from Massa]lia,
he dealt with the senate in company with [them, | and (was present when
the Massaliotes) made known] the goodwill and esteem which [they con-
tinued] *to have* | [toward] them (the Romans), renewed the existing |
55   [friendship with] them, and also explained to them [about us, ‖ that] they
were in fact brothers to our People [and] | had [goodwill (toward us)] *in
accordance with* that kinship. (Hegesias) *himself* explained | [about these
matters] and about the things his People wanted to be done [when | they
had sent off the] embassy, and he appealed to them with his [fellow |
envoys to take thought for] the safety of their other friends and kinsmen,
60   ‖ and to care for our city [because of the | kinship and] friendly relations
existing between us and them and [because of] | the recommendation *made*
for us by the Massal[iotes. And he as|ked] to receive a [letter] useful to our
People. When the *envoys* [earnestly begged (?)] | that we be included [in
65   the ‖ treaty] which the Romans made[7] with *King* [Philip, | the senate (?)]
did include[8] us in the treaty with [the ki|ng, as] even they *themselves* write,
and concerning [all other | matters] the senate *referred* them to [the
Ro|man] consul Titus (Quinctius Flamininus)[9] and to the Ten (Commis-
70   sioners) [in charge of Gre‖ek affairs.] Having come to Corinth with [--|-
and Apo]llodoros, he met with the commander[10] [and the | Ten,] *spoke*
with them about our People and [appea|led with all] ardor for them to
75   care [for us | and to contribute] to the preservation of our city [as au‖tono-
mous] and democratic. Concerning these matters he duly [received | a
favorable decision] and letters to the kings[11] [--| and perceiving that
(these letters) were useful] to them (i.e. our People) he sent them off [--|-
the People,] as it had decreed before [--]

1 This is the restoration in *SIG*[3]. Frisch: '[after being called upon]'.
2 The brother of T. Quinctius Flamininus. Lucius was consul in 192 BC. The senate
   had given him command of the fleet in Greece in 198 BC as well as of the coastal area:
   Broughton, *MRR* I 332.
3 The People of Lampsakos claimed kinship with the Romans because they lived in the
   Troad, from where came Aeneas the legendary founder of the Roman people. Lampsakos and Massilia were also related to each other, for both of them had been colonies of
   Phokaia: Thucydides 1.13.6.
4 'And' in *SIG*[3]. Frisch: 'Just as'.
5 I.e. the Boule of Six Hundred at Massilia.
6 One of the three tribes of the Galatians in Asia Minor. See Strabo 12.5.1. Although the
   Galatians were known as plunderers in Asia Minor, there is no real evidence that the
   Tolistoagioi ever menaced Lampsakos. The reason for the interest of Lampsakos in
   the Tolistoagioi is unknown.
7 The tense is odd. Perhaps 'were making'?
8 Neither Livy nor Polybius mentions Lampsakos in regard to the treaty. Bickermann
   believes that the Lampsakenes did not understand the Roman technical terminology
   and thus mistakenly thought they had been included in the treaty, i.e. actually mentioned by name in it. Desideri thinks the Lampsakenes were in fact mentioned in it.

9 After the battle of Cynoscephalae in 197 BC Flamininus remained in Greece and Macedonia, his imperium extended each year down to 194 BC (cf. above, no. 4, n. 1). With the Ten Commissioners he had concluded the treaty of peace with Philip in 196 BC. The senate had appointed this commission of ten senators to work with him in settling affairs in Greece and in particular to secure freedom for the Greeks: Polybius 18.42 with Walbank's discussion, *Commentary* II 604–8.

10 I.e. Flamininus.

11 Eumenes of Pergamum and Prusias I of Bithynia may be meant.

6 Statues and other honors for T. Quinctius Flamininus in the East. After the declaration of Greek freedom at the Isthmian Games of 196 BC

A: **IG* XII 9.931. Marble base, Chalkis in Euboia. **B**: B. Powell, *AJP* 7 (1903) 40; B. D. Meritt in *Corinth* VIII. 1: *Greek Inscriptions* (Cambridge, Mass. 1931) no. 72 (+ photograph); *SEG* XI 73; **SEG* XXII 214; Moretti, *ISE* I 37. 196/5 BC (?). Limestone plaque, Corinth. **C**: *IG* V 1.1165; *ILS* 8766; **SIG*³ 592. 195 BC or later. Marble (not otherwise described), Gytheion. **D**: **IG* XII 9.233 (cf. Addenda p. 177). Marble fragment, letters of second century, Eretria. **E**: **SIG*³ 616. 189/8 BC. Limestone base, Delphi. Cf. Daux, *Delphes* 593–5, who would push the date back a year or two. **F**: E. Mastrokostas, *REA* 66 (1964) 309–10 (+ photograph); **SEG* XXIII 412. 189/8 BC. Limestone base, Scotussa in Thessaly. Cf. G. Daux, *BCH* 89 (1965) 301–3. **G**: G. Daux, *BCH* 88 (1964) 569–76 (+ photograph); **SEG* XXII 266, lines 13–14, extract from an honorary decree for a citizen named Augis. *C*. 100 BC. Limestone stele with gable, Argos.

Cf. Plutarch, *Flam*. 16–17.

A. *IG* XII 9.931, Chalkis

(On the front)¹ Aristomachos | (son) of Aristokleides, | Amphikrates |
5 (son) of Eurynomos, ‖ (dedicate this statue) to Titus, savior and benefactor, | after they served as gymnasiarchs.

B. *SEG* XXII 214, Corinth

(In honor of) Titus, [(son) of Titus, Quinctius, Roman,] | (by) Aristain[os (son) of Timokades of Dyme,²] | *because of* his excellence [and beneficence] | toward *him* [and the Achaians.]

C. *SIG*³ 592, Gytheion

Titus, (son) of Titus, Quinctius, consul of the Ro|mans,³ (is honored by) the People of the Gytheates, their sa|vior.⁴

D. *IG* XII 9.233, Eretria

[---] to keep holiday and to *sacrifice* | [and to wear a wreath (?)] for the

things that have | [been done[5] -- and to erect (a statue of) Titu]s, consul of the Rom[an|s -- in the temple of Ar]temis [--]

E. *SIG*³ 616, Delphi

[The city] of the Del[phians | (dedicates this statue of) Titus Quinc]tius, [son] of Titus, [Ro|man,] *because of his excellence* [and bene|ficence toward] it, to A[pollo.][6]

F. *SEG* XXIII 412, Scotussa in Thessaly

Praylos (son) of Phoxios | (dedicates this statue of) [T]itus, son of Titus, Quinctius | because of his excellence and goodwill | toward him and toward the city.

G. *SEG* XXII 266, lines 13–14, Argos

. . . and now when there was need for ready cash, upon request he gave without interest ten thousand drachmas | to the hieromnemones and to the treasurer for the festival of the Titeia,[7] etc.

1 On the right and left sides there are remains of a total of seven more names of Greeks from Chalkis.
2 Aristainos was the leader of the Achaian League in 198 BC (Livy 32.19.2), 195 BC (Livy 34.24), and 186 BC (Polybius 22.10.2). He may have made this dedication in his position as head of the League in 196/5 BC. On difficulties in the identification of Aristainos, sometimes called Aristainetos in Polybius and Plutarch, see J. Deininger, *Historia* 15 (1966) 376ff., and R. M. Errington, *Philopoemen* (Oxford 1969) Appendix 4, pp. 276–9, for opposite views.
3 In this context the title does not mean that Flamininus was consul at the moment when the inscription was engraved.
4 Flamininus had freed Gytheion from the domination of King Nabis of Sparta: see Errington, *Philopoemen* 95ff.
5 This document appears to be a decree, and the 'things' done may refer to the victory over Macedon and the proclamation of Greek freedom, especially for Eretria. See Polybius 18.45.5–6; 18.47.10–11; Livy 33.34.10.
6 Flamininus was made a proxenos at Delphi in 189/8 BC (*SIG*³ 585, line 116), which may also be the date for the erection of this statue. On the nature of the statue (not equestrian, as stated in *SIG*³) see F. Chamoux, *BCH* 89 (1965) 220.
7 These 'Games of Titus' continued to be held on into the Roman imperial age: see Plutarch, *Flam.* 16.4. Cf. Bowersock, *Augustus* Chapter 9 and Appendix 1.

7 King Eumenes of Pergamum and the war against King Nabis. 195 BC.

Two bases (A–B) of white marble, Pergamum.

*SIG*³ 595 A–B. Cf. Livy 34.29.4–5; 34.30.7; 34.35.2.

Hansen, *Attalids*² 72–3.

(A)¹ [King Eumenes (II) from] the spoils [obtained from] the expedition |
[which he made with the Roman]s *and* [the other] *allies* against Nabis the
Lakonian, | [who had subjugated the Argiv]es [and the] Me[s]s[e]nians,
(has dedicated) these first-fruits to Athena Nikephoros.²
(B) (This statue of) [King Eu]menes (has been dedicated) *because of* his
excellence | by [those who] sailed [with] *him* | [to Gr]eece, soldiers | [and
5   sailors,] for the war against Nabis ‖ [the Lako]nian.

In 198 BC the city of Argos left the Achaian League and turned to Philip V of Macedon
for protection. Unable to protect it, Philip handed the city over to Sparta. King Nabis of
Sparta supported a most unpopular regime in Argos that continued even after the defeat
of Philip by the Romans in 197 BC. Early in 195 BC Flamininus with a mixed army of
Romans and Greeks marched against Nabis and forced him to accept a peace treaty. Argos
was returned to the Achaian League, but Nabis was left to rule at Sparta.

1 This base is over fifteen feet long.
2 The date when Athena was first called Nikephoros ('Victory Bringer') at Pergamum is
   unknown, but the festival called Nikephoria at Pergamum was probably started by
   Attalus I in the 220s BC: see C. P. Jones, *Chiron* 4 (1974) 184ff.

8   Letter of the praetor M. Valerius Messalla to the city of Teos. 193 BC.

Stone (not otherwise described) found in the ruins of the temple of Dionysos in Teos.

*SIG*³ 601; *IGRR* IV 1557; *RDGE 34.

Magie, *RRAM* I 102–3; *RDGE* pp. 214–16; R. M. Errington, *ZPE* 39 (1980) 279–84.

vv Of the Romans.¹ *vv* | Marcus Valerius, (son) of Marcus, praetor (193
BC), and the | tribunes² and the senate to the Boule and the | People of
5   Teos, greetings. *v* Menippos, from Antiochus the ki‖ng having been sent
to us as envoy and cho|sen also by you to be an envoy for your city, | gave
us your decree and himself in accordance with it | spoke with all enthu-
10   siasm.³ We received the ma|n kindly because of his for‖mer reputation and
his present excell|ence and we listened favorably to the requests he made.
That | we wholly and constantly have attached the highest importance
to | reverence of the gods one can estim|ate from the goodwill we have
15   experienced ‖ on this account from the supreme deity. Not only that, but
for | many other reasons we are convinced that manifest to everyone has
been | our own high respect for the divine. Therefore, because of the|se
things and because of our goodwill toward you and the one who made the

20   request, | the envoy, we judge your city and its terri‖tory to be holy, as it is
now, and inviolable and imm|une from taxation by the People of the
Romans, and as for | honors to the god and privileges to you, we will tr|y to
help increase them, while you carefully maintain, for the | future, your
goodwill toward us. *vv* Farewell.

1   In larger letters, as a heading. This letter was originally only one of a large collection of
documents engraved on stone for public scrutiny in Teos, all of them concerned with
the inviolability of the city and similar matters. Many Greek cities had testified to its
inviolability in writing, and the present letter is the testimony 'Of the Romans'.
2   This is the earliest appearance of the tribunes in the heading of such documents.
3   At this time Antiochus III was not yet an enemy of Rome. For Menippos in Rome as a
representative of the king see Livy 34.57.6ff.; Diodorus 28.15.2ff; Appian, *Syrian Wars* 6.
Holleaux thinks it was only natural at this time for Teos to turn to Menippos to plead its
cause in Rome.

9   The Delians honor P. Cornelius Scipio Africanus.
About 193 BC.

Stele broken at the bottom; above the text, on the left, a crown of leaves, on
the right of it a knotty baton or staff,[1] letters stoichedon,[2] of the second
century, Delos.

*IG XI 4.712 (photograph on Pl. IV); Durrbach, *Choix* 64.

Laidlaw, *Delos* 126–7.

Decreed by the Boule and the People. A[n]|tilakos (son) of Simides made
the motion: since Pub[li|us] Cornelius, son of Publius, Scipio, | Roman,
5   being proxenos and benefactor ‖ of the temple and the Delians, bestows all
ca|re on the temple | and the Delians, it is decreed by the Boule and | the
10   People to crown Publius Corn[e]|lius, son of Publius, Scipio, Roman, ‖ at
the Apollonia[3] with the sacred | crown of laurel; the sacred herald shall |
announce in the theater, when the children's cho|ruses are conducted,
15   the following proclamation: | The People of Delos crown Publius ‖ Cor-
nelius Scipio, Roman, with the sacred crown of laurel because of his good
character | and his piety toward the temple and | his goodwill toward the
People of Delos. | Lysanias (son) of Kaibon put the motion to the vote.

1   The cognomen 'Scipio' is connected with a root meaning 'staff', and it is possible that
the knotty staff was the heraldic emblem of the Cornelii Scipiones. For the connection
between cognomen and emblem see T. Mommsen, *Römische Forschungen* I (Berlin 1864)
44–5, who leaves open the question whether the heraldic emblem produced the cognomen or *vice versa*.
2   See the Glossary *s.v.* Stoichedon.
3   A Delian festival featuring a full program of tragedy, comedy, and musical perfor-
mances.

10   Delos seeks to renew friendship with Rome. About 192 BC (?).
Marble stele with molding, letters of the early second century, Delos.

IG XI 4.756; Durrbach, **Choix* 65.

Durrbach, *Choix* pp. 84–6; Laidlaw, *Delos* 126.

Gods. | Decreed by the Boule and the People. | Telemnestos (son) of Aris-
teides made the mo|tion. Since there have been sent ‖ by the People
envoys | to Rome to renew good | relations [and] | friendship | and con-
5   cerning the *interests* | of our temple and [People, in (?)] ‖ which all their
[zeal and] *en|thusiasm* [--]

**11   Troops of the Achaian League aid the Romans against the
Gauls. 192 BC or 122 BC.**
Limestone base of an equestrian statue, good lettering similar to that of
the second half of the second century, but often squeezed together,
Olympia.

E. Kunze, *Bericht über die Ausgrabungen in Olympia* V (Berlin 1956) 160–4 (+ photograph);
SEG XV 254; Moretti, **ISE* I 60; Schwertfeger, *Bund* 28. Possible dating in 192 BC: Livy
35.22.3–4; 40.2–4. For 122 BC: Orosius 5.13.2; Livy, *Per.* 61; Velleius Paterculus 2.10.2;
39.1; Strabo 4.2.3; Florus 1.37.5.

Kunze, *op. cit.* 160ff. (argues for 122 BC); Moretti, *ISE* pp. 153–4 (argues for 192 BC or a
few years later); Schwertfeger, *Bund* 28–37 (argues for 122 BC); Larsen, *States* 500–1.

Of the Achaians from Patrai, Dyme, Pharai, | Thrious, Heraia,[1] Thel-
phousa, Psophis, | Kleitor, Kynaitha, Kallistai, | Ascheion, Leontion,
5   Tritaia, Aigion, ‖ Aigeira, Pellana, Boura, | Pheneos, Karneia, those who
made an expedition | with Gnaeus Domitius, consul | of the Romans,[2]
against the Gauls (dedicated this statue of) Damon (son) of Alkisthenes |
10   of Patrai, their own commander, because of his excellence, ‖ to Olympian
Zeus.

1 Heraia, Thelphousa, Psophis, Kleitor, Kynaitha, and Pheneos are Arkadian cities.
2 He could be Cn. Domitius L.f. Ahenobarbus, the consul of 192 BC (Broughton, *MRR*
   I 350) who fought against the Boii, or Cn. Domitius Cn.f. Ahenobarbus, the consul of
   122 BC (Broughton, *MRR* I 516) who fought against the Allobroges and Arverni.

**12   Letter of Manius Acilius Glabrio to the Delphians. Early 190
BC.**
Block from the base of an equestrian statue of Acilius Glabrio, Delphi.

SIG[3] 609; **RDGE* 37 A with extracts from B.

P. Roussel, *BCH* 56 (1932) 1–24; *RDGE* pp. 221–4.

[--] is to be *lodging* for our *citizens*. [And do you see to it | that] all these
(regulations) are engraved on a stone stele and displayed in the [temple.
And if any persons cause] *opposi|tion* about the estates or the fruits from
them or the buildings or the [possessions, say|ing they] are theirs, con-
cerning these matters whatever decisions have been made during our
5   presence [let these be legally binding; || as for you,] do you, after appoint-
ing a *tribunal* to handle things properly, settle [the remaining --|-] And
it has been reported to me that there have been secret distributions of
funds to some individuals from these (estates), [as well as sales, the pay-
ment | not] *going* into the public treasury; have regard that nothing similar
happens [in the future. And concerning] | matters relating to the temple,
if (the) Thessalians or any others send envoys, I will try [in Rome (?) with
all] | my power to see to it that your ancestral rights that existed from the
10   beginning will be yours forever, [the] || autonomy of your city and your
temple [kept safe (?)].

(EXTRACTS FROM B)

The lands given to the god | and
to the city:[1] |
    At Hypopleistia |
The (estate) of Androsthen[i]-
5   das the Tolphonian ||
The (estate) of Mikky<l>ion
the Physkeian |

(Eleven other estates follow,
and there are eleven more
estates, at six other locations,
set out in the same way.)

35

Buildings which he[2] gave to the
god and | to the [city:] |
    vacat ||
The (building) of Agelaos the
Naupaktian |
The (building) of Patron the
Tolphonian |

(Forty-four other buildings are
listed, including one bathhouse
belonging to a private individual.)

1   In the period of Aetolian control of Delphi many Aetolians had (illegally?) taken possession of property in and around the city. After the Romans had liberated Delphi
Acilius Glabrio evicted them from the area and restored the land and buildings, listed
here in two columns.
2   That 'he' is Manius Acilius Glabrio and the author of the letter can be seen from
another document (*SIG*[3] 826E, col. 3, line 38) which names him as the Roman who
gave the Delphian land called Nateia back to the Delphians. Nateia is mentioned here
in this list (line 29) as one of the 'lands given to the god and to the city'.

13   Participation of the Achaians in the battle of Magnesia. 190 BC.
Block of bluish white marble, once part of a statue base, Pergamum.

*SIG[3] 606. Cf. Livy 37.18 and 20.

Holleaux, *Études* V 412–16 (*CAH* 8.222–5); Hansen, *Attalids*[2] 79–87.

(This statue of) Att[al]us (son) of King A[tt]alus (I) | (has been erected)
because of his excellence and bravery | and his goodwill toward them | by
the Achaians who crossed over in accordance with their alliance ‖ with
King Eumenes (II), his brother, | in the war fought against Antiochus | and
who joined in Lydia, | by the Phrygius River,[1] in the battle, (and has been
dedicated) to Athena Nikephoros.[2]

5

1 The Battle of Magnesia was fought not far from the confluence of the Phrygius and the
   Hermus: Livy 37.37.9; Strabo 13.5.
2 See above, no. 7, n. 2.

14   Letter of L. Cornelius Scipio and his brother to Herakleia in Karia. 190 BC.

Square block of bluish-white marble broken at the top, letters of early
second century, Herakleia by Mt Latmos.

SIG[3] 618; *RDGE 35.

RDGE pp. 217–18.

[Lucius Cornelius Scipio,] consul of the Romans (190 BC), | [and Publius
Scipio,[1] his] *brother*, to Herakleia's Boule and Peo|ple, [greetings.] We had
a *meeting* with your envoys Dias, Dies, Diony|[sios, --]am[an]der, [Eu]de-
mos, Moschos, Aristeides, (and) Menes, men *fi‖ne* [and good] who gave
us your *decree* and spoke in *accord|ance* with what was recorded in the *decree*,
leaving out nothing | of their *personal devotion*. We are in fact well disposed
toward all the Greeks | and will try, since you have come into our | [pledge
of good faith,[2]] to take all possible care of you and always *to be the authors* of
some good (for you). ‖ We grant to you your freedom just as also | [to the]
other cities which have given us the power of decision (over them), retain-
ing | your right to govern all your affairs [by yourselves] according to your
own laws, | [and in] all other ways we will try to be of service to you and to
be always the [authors] of some good to you. | We also accept from you the
kind acts and ‖ [pledges of good faith] and will ourselves try to omit no
favor toward you in return. | We have *sent* to you Lucius Orbius to care
for your | [city] *and* territory, that nobody may harm you. Farewell.

5

10

15

1 It had long been thought that the author of this letter was the consul of 189 BC, Cn.
   Manlius Vulso, but M. Holleaux (*Strategos Hypatos* (Paris 1918) 131–46, and *Rivista di
   Filologia Classica* 52 (1924) 29–44) saw from his analysis of the historical evidence of the
   period that such could not be the case. He suggested L. Cornelius Scipio. Then G. De
   Sanctis (*Atti dell'Academia di Torino* 57 (1921/22) 242ff.) further suggested that the
   brother Publius might be mentioned in the second line. Holleaux then recognized part

of the word *brother* in that line. The two brothers were also known to have been co-
authors of another letter (to Kolophon: *RDGE* 36).

2 To the Romans this was virtually equivalent to 'since you have surrendered yourselves
to us' and, thus, was often much misunderstood by the Greeks very early in their relations with Roman officials. See Livy 36.28 and Polybius 20.9–10. Cf. *RDGE* pp. 200–1.

15   Two letters from the praetor Spurius Postumius and a decree of the senate. 189 BC for the two letters; the date of the decree is unknown.

Marble stele, now in small fragments; some older fragments, now lost,
are known to us in copies, Delphi.

*SIG*³ 612; Hollcaux, *Études* V 282–3; **RDGE* 1.

Holleaux, *Études* V 249–94; *RDGE* pp. 21–5.

First letter

[Spurius Postumius, son of Lucius, praetor of the Romans (189 BC),
to the magistrates and the city of Delphi, greetings. The | envoys
Boulon, Thrasykles and Orestas, sent by you, spoke about the inviolabi-
lity of the temple and the city and its | territory, and about freedom and
immunity from taxation,] asking that [these be granted to you by the
People of the | Romans. Know therefore that it has been decreed by the
senate that the temple of the Pythian] Apollo [is to be inviolate, that the
5 || city of Delphi and its territory and the Delphians are to be] *autonomous*
and free and *immune from taxation*, [living and administering their govern-
ment | by themselves, and] having dominion over the *sacred* territory and
the sacred harbor, just as [was their] *inherited right* [from the beginning.
That | you might know, I have *decided*] to write to you [about these things.]

Second letter

Spurius Postumius, son of Lucius, praetor of the Romans, to the
League of the Amphictiones, [greetings. The Delphian] *en|voys* Boulon,
Thrasykles and Orestas [spoke] about the inviolability of the temple and
the city and its [territory,] | and about freedom and immunity from taxa-
tion, asking that these be granted to them *by* [the People of the Romans.] |
Know therefore that it has been decreed by the senate that the temple of
5 the Pythian Apollo [is to be inviolate, and] || the city of Delphi and its terri-
tory and the D[elphian]s are to be autonomous and free and [immune
from taxation, liv|ing] and administering their government *by themselves*
and having dominion over the sacred territory [and the sacred] *har|bor*,
just as [was] their inherited right from the beginning. [That] you might
know, I have decided to *write* to you [about these things.]

The decree

On the fourth day before the Nones of May (May 4) [in the Comitium (?) --] *Octavius*, (son) of Gnaeus, *praetor* (?),[1] *con|sulted* the senate. [(Witnesses) present at the] writing were: [--]us, (son) of Publius; Mani[us, (son) of --;] | Gaius Atinius, (son) of Gaius; Tiberius [-- Whereas the] Delphians *spoke* [about their] inviolate [temple, | their] free [and autonomous
5   and tax-immune] city, about this [matter as follows] ‖ it was decreed: just as formerly [the senate --] had decided [--,] it was decreed to [hold to] that [decision.]

Very soon after Manius Acilius Glabrio had freed Delphi from Aetolian control in 191 BC, the senate passed a decree which guaranteed the inviolability of the temple of Apollo and the free and autonomous status of the Delphians. Postumius then sent one letter to the Delphians and another, identical in content to the first, to the Amphictionic League. What we have here are the mutilated remains of those two letters. The first of them can be restored with near certainty by reference to the second.

1 In 168 BC a certain Gnaeus Octavius was praetor: Broughton, *MRR* I 428. He is the Roman honored at Argos in 170 BC: see below, no. 22. However, since only the *nomen* Octavius is extant here, in a very mutilated form, full identification is difficult.

16   Letter of a consul (C. Livius Salinator?) to the Delphians. 189/188 BC.

Block of gray limestone once part of an equestrian statue of Manius Acilius Glabrio (above, no. 12), Delphi.

SIG[3] 611; Holleaux, *Études* V 284–5; **RDGE* 38. Cf. the letters of Spurius Postumius to the Delphians (above, no. 15).

Holleaux, *Études* V 249–86; *RDGE* pp. 226–8.

[Gaius Livius, son of Marcus, (?)[1]] consul of the R[o]m[ans (188 BC) and the] *tri|bunes*[2] and [the] *senate* to the *magistrates* and the *city* of Delphi, [greetings.] | The envoys sent by you, Herys (son) of Eudoros and [D]amo[sthe]|nes (son) of Archelas, gave us the letters and themselves
5   spoke in accordance with ‖ what had been recorded in them, (spoke) with all enthusiasm and of their personal devotion no|thing did they omit. And they made it clear that you had conducted the gymnastic contest | and the sacrifice on our behalf; and the senate turned its attention | to this and passed a decree regarding your former envoys, | Boulon, Thrasykles, and
10   Orestas, who had come to us[3] but on ‖ their return home had been killed, (a decree) to write to Marcus Fulvius, | our commander,[4] that he should see to it that, when for us | the events at Same have turned out favorably,

he seek out the guilty persons and see | to it that they receive the appro-
priate punishment and that the properties of the envoys | be restored, all
15 of them, to their relatives; and it also passed a decree ‖ to write to the
Aetolians about the crimes committed among you, that | for the present
they should seek out all the things that had been taken away from you and
res|tore them to you, and that in the future nothing (similar) should ever
happen; and concerning those who in Delphi are set|tlers, the senate has
allowed you to have the power to evict | whomever you wish and to permit
20 to settle among you those who are pleasing to the ‖ League of the Del-
phians; the replies, given to those who previously to | us had come from
you as envoys,⁵ we have given to the (present envoys), as | they asked us,
and for the future we will try always to be the authors of some good | for the
Delphians because of the god (Apollo) and because of you and because of |
our ancestral custom to revere the gods and to honor them as the cause of
25 a‖ll good things.

1 The restoration of his name rests upon a complicated series of chronological observations: *RDGE* pp. 227–8. The consul must be one of those of 189 or 188 BC.
2 See also no. 8, n. 2.
3 See the letters of Spurius Postumius, above, no. 15.
4 M. Fulvius Nobilior was consul in 189 BC, but his imperium was extended for another
   year to complete the war in Greece: Broughton, *MRR* I 360 and 366.
5 Boulon, Thrasykles, and Orestas, now all dead.

17   Decree of Elateia honoring the Stymphalians.¹ About 189 BC.
Limestone stele, its surface badly scarred, poorly engraved, Stymphalos
in Arcadia.

M. Mitsos, *REG* 59–60 (1946–7) 150–74 (+ photograph); S. Accame, *Rivista di Filologia
Classica* 77 (1949) 217–48; Moretti, *ISE* I 55; *SEG* XXV 445. Cf. Polybius 18.43.1; Livy
32.24.1ff.; Pausanias 10.34.3–4.

A. Passerini, *Athenaeum*, N.S. 26 (1948) 83–95; Accame, *loc. cit.*, and *L'espansione romana in
Grecia* (Naples 1961) 254ff.; G. A. Lehmann, *Untersuchungen zur historischen Glaubwürdigkeit
des Polybios* (Munster 1967) 120–5; G. Klaffenbach, *BCH* 92 (1968) 257–9; Larsen, *States*
238–9, 405–6.

[---|-] and of care [and] *kindheartedness proper* to the [relationship] and |
[--] they (the Stymphalians) received, each into his own home with all
[kind|heartedness (?), and at] public expense they distributed provisions
5 to all (the Elateians) for quite a long time, and of whatever ‖ [there was
need they gave a share (?)] of everything; they let them share in the reli-
gious ceremonies and sacrifices, considering them to be their own | [citi-
zens; and] they marked off a section of their own territory and divided it
among the Elateians, and (made it) im|mune [from all (burdens) for] ten

[years;] and they wrote about all these things upon a bronze stele | [and
erected it in the temple] of Artemis [Braur]onia, omitting nothing of
every *benefaction* | [toward them; and later] again, after some years, when
10   the Romans came to Greece ‖ [with an army (?),] and Manius (Acilius
Glabrio) *was in control* of the territory about [E]lateia,[2] the Stymphalians
sent an embassy t|o [the Achaians that] an embassy should be sent off to
Manius concerning the return of the Elateians to their | [own country, and
when the Achaians] *sent* as envoys Diophanes and Atha[no]kles, and
Manius had conce|ded that the *city* and the *territory* and the laws[3] [should
be restored] to the Elateians, the Elateians [re|mained in Sty]mphalos for
quite some time, *giving no ground for complaint* and in a manner worthy of
15   their ancestors, ‖ [until they could return] to their own land.[4]

1 In 198 BC Elateia in Phokis had been in the hands of Philip V and had then been captured by Flamininus after fierce fighting: Livy 32.24. The Elateians were then driven
   into exile, perhaps by Flamininus (as argued by Accame, Klaffenbach and Briscoe,
   Commentary 214) or else by the Aetolians (Passerini, Lehmann and Larsen). Because of a
   legendary relationship between Elateia and Stymphalos, a city in the mountains of
   Arcadia (Pausanias 8.4), the exiled Elateians found temporary homes in Stymphalos,
   which was a member of the Achaian League.
2 This refers to the arrival of the Romans in 191 BC, the year in which Manius Acilius
   Glabrio was consul, to fight against Antiochus the Great.
3 Klaffenbach recognized this word on a squeeze and it was subsequently confirmed on
   the stone. Former editors: 'slaves'.
4 The text continues on to line 34. Lines 15–34 relate how the Elateians finally returned to
   their own land and decreed to honor the Stymphalians for their past humanitarian
   actions.

18   The Lycian League and its celebration of the festival of the god-
dess Roma. About 180 BC.
Limestone block, broken at the bottom, Araxa in Lycia.

G. E. Bean, *JHS* 68 (1948) 46–56, no. 11 (+ photograph); *SEG* XVIII 570, lines 62–79.

Bean, *loc. cit.*; J. and L. Robert, *REG* 63 (1950) 185–97, no. 183; J. A. O. Larsen, *CP* 51
(1956) 151–70; *idem, States* 241–8; Mellor, *Worship* 36–8.

And when he[1] was sent as en|voy to the envoys from the Romans led by |
65   Appius,[2] and when he was sent a second time as envoy to ‖ the envoys from
the Romans led by Publi|us,[2] he performed both embassies in a manner
worthy | of the People (of Araxa) and the confederation (of the Lycians),[3]
procuring every advantage | for the city; and many other em|bassies he
performed without traveling expenses as a liturgic service; and when the
70   Lea‖gue of the Lycians was celebrating the five-year national festival | to
Roma the goddess manifest,[4] and he was sent as festival-envoy to the | first

five-year festival, he performed the sacrifices, | with those chosen to assist him, in a fine and worthy manner, | and made the journey in a manner
75   worthy of our city ‖ and the confederation; and in the second national festival ce|lebrated by the League for Roma when he was chosen festival-envoy, along wi|th those who had been chosen to assist him he gave an additional gift | [---] in a manner worthy of the | [city ---]

1   I.e. Orthagoras, a citizen of Araxa in Lycia. Our document is a decree of Araxa designed to honor him for his many past services to the city and to the Lycian League. Lines 1–62 list those services in many local wars and diplomatic missions. Although the conclusion of the decree is lost, it would have outlined the nature of the honors to be conferred upon him.

2   The Roman envoys Appius and Publius appear to belong to the commission of ten sena-tors (listed by Livy 37.55.7; cf. Broughton, *MRR* I 363) which was sent out in 189–188 BC to assist Gnaeus Manlius Vulso in implementing the treaty with King Antiochus after the Battle of Magnesia. Among them were Appius Claudius Nero, Publius Cor-nelius Lentulus, and Publius Aelius Tubero.

3   The terms 'confederation' and 'league' of the Lycians both refer to the same organiza-tion, although 'confederation' may refer to the federal citizenship or the body of mem-bers, while 'league' may indicate the federal government or federal state, as Larsen (*CP* p. 168, n. 7) suggests. The Lycian League not only permitted its members to act with strength as a united body but it also played a real political and diplomatic role vis-à-vis Rome and the Hellenistic kingdoms: J. Deininger, *Die Provinziallandtage der römischen Kaiserzeit* (Munich 1965) 69ff.

4   The consecration of a temple to the cult of the deified *Roma* became a recognized symbol of allegiance to Rome, and after the battle of Magnesia the Lycian League was particu-larly anxious to secure the favor of Rome: see Larsen (*CP* pp. 155ff.). The epithet 'mani-fest' may refer to the active intervention of Rome against King Antiochus.

19   Letter to the Delphian Amphictiones about King Perseus. 171/170 BC.

Stele of white marble broken at the right and bottom, damaged at the top and lower left, Delphi.

*SIG*³ 643; G. Colin, *Fouilles de Delphes* III 4.75; *RDGE* 40 B. Cf. Livy 42.11–14; 42.40.1–10; Polybius 22.18.1–8; 25.3.1–4.

Daux, *Delphes* 319–25; P. Meloni, *Perseo e la fine della monarchia macedone*, Annali Univer. Cagliari 20 (Rome 1953) 241–3; *RDGE* pp. 237–9; E. S. Gruen, *AJAH* 1 (1976) 29–60; F. W. Walbank, *Ancient Macedonia* II (Thessaloniki 1977) 81–94.

5   [--|--|-] set over now [--|-] that they [--‖-] to the gods [--|-] you may administer just as it *belongs* [to you. Know first of all, therefore,] | that [Per]seus contrary to what is proper [came with his army to the festival | of the] Pythia;[1] it was [clearly] not right at all [for him to have a share with you] | *either* in the sacrifices or in the games [or in the festal assemblies,
10   since] ‖ he invited in the [barbarians] from across *the* [Danube, who for]

no [worthy | reason] for the enslavement of [Greece had even formerly
been aroused,] | marched against the shrine [at Delphi, intending to
plun|der] and destroy it, and received [from the god fitting punishment.] |
He also transgressed the [treaty] made by his [father, which he himself
15 had renewed;] ‖ the Thracians, our[2] [allies, he defeated; Abrou|p]olis,
whom we had included [in the treaty with Philip (V),] he thr|ew out of
his kingdom;[3] the *envoys,* [who had been sent from the Thebans] | to Rome
about an alliance, [he removed from his path by the treacherous ship-
wreck.] | In addition, he came to such a height of madness [that, consider-
20 ing it of great importance, contrary to the oa‖ths, to do away with] the
freedom [given to you] through [our commanders | by throwing] the
whole (Greek) nation into disorders [and political strife,] he continued to
do [nothing except] | what is base, and, [confounding everything and
courting the masses, | and] destroying the men in positions of leadership,
[he foolishly announced cancellations of debts] | and made revolutions,
25 *revealing* [what hatred he had conceived toward the best ‖ men;] conse-
quently, it happened that the Pe[rrhaibians and Thessalians fell into ter-
rible] | disasters, and the barbarians even *more dreadfully* [set upon them.
And, | eager for a great] war so that, [having caught you] *deprived of aid,* he
might perhaps | enslave [all the Greek] *cities,* [he plotted the murder of
Arthetauros the Illyrian[4] | and dared to lay an ambush for] King Eume-
30 nes, [our friend and ally,] ‖ at the time when in fulfilment of [a vow he
came to Delphi,[5] disre|garding the devotion toward the] god [customarily
practiced] by all those who go there, [and not | observing what protection
your temple] has attained in the eyes of all *men* [among the | Greeks as well
35 as] the barbarians from all [time --|--] you for all the [--‖--] sharing (?)
[--|--] others [--]

Ever since his accession to the Macedonian throne in 179 BC Perseus had taken steps to
strengthen his country, win over the Greeks, form friendly ties with Syria and Bithynia,
and secure the friendship of Rhodes. This deepened Rome's distrust of his motives and
caused his enemy, Eumenes II of Pergamum, to visit Rome in 172 BC in order to denounce
him to the senate (Livy 42.11–14). The senate listened and finally decided on war. The
present document, clearly a letter from some high authority (see n. 2), seems to be a piece
of propaganda designed to win over the Greeks for the coming confrontation with Perseus.
The majority of restorations made in this document are based on the accounts given by
Polybius and Livy, and, thus, verbatim accuracy may not be assumed. Pomtow's restorations in *SIG*[3] differ somewhat from Colin's.

1 The festival of the Pythian Apollo in Delphi is meant.
2 The use of 'our' and 'we' is almost certainly collective for the Romans, although proof is
   lacking, and clearly points to a letter as the format. It would have been addressed to the
   Amphictiones to achieve general distribution to all Greeks.
3 Abroupolis was king of the Sapaei, a Thracian people living on the bank of the Nestos
   River. See Polybius 22.18.2, with the comments of Walbank, *Commentary* III 206.

4 Livy says (42.13.6) that Arthetauros had sent letters to Rome, obviously hostile to Perseus.
5 When Eumenes returned to Greece after addressing the senate early in 172 BC he was struck unconscious by rocks thrown at him from an ambush. Although reported dead, he recovered at Aegina. See Livy 42.15.3ff.

20   Decree of the senate concerning Koroneia. 171 or 170 BC.
Stele of white marble, damaged at the top, bottom and right side, Koroneia in Boiotia.

L. Robert, *Études épigraphiques et philologiques* (Paris 1938) 287–9; *SEG* XIX 374; *RDGE* 3. Cf. the decree of the senate concerning Thisbai, below, no. 21, especially lines 25–31 and 58; Livy 42.46.7–110; 42.63.3; 43.4.11; Polybius 27.5.1–3.

Robert, *op. cit.* 290–2; Meloni, *Perseo* 263ff.; *RDGE* pp. 32–3; R. M. Errington, *Rivista di Filologia e di Istruzione Classica* 102 (1974) 79–86.

[-- whoever] entered into [ou|r friendship before Publius | Li]cinius[1] [brought his army against the] | city of Korone[ia, that they should have
5 control of their land] ‖ and buildings [and things belonging to them;] | concerning this [matter it was decreed as follows:] | that whatever things once [belonged to them | they are to be permitted] to have as their own.
10 [Decreed.] | Likewise, whereas [the same (envoys) spoke] ‖ about the citadel [---][2] to fortify it [---] | except for the [---]

1 P. Licinius Crassus, the consul of 171 BC who was given Macedonia as his province: Broughton, *MRR* I 416.
2 Robert: '[that they should be permitted]'.

21   Two decrees of the senate on affairs at Thisbai. 170 BC.
Marble stele, good lettering of the second century, Thisbai in Boiotia.

SIG[3] 646; *FIRA* I 31; *RDGE* 2. Cf. Polybius 27.5; Livy 42.46.7; 42.63.12.

Meloni, *Perseo* 245ff.; *RDGE* pp. 28–31; J. Deininger, *Der politische Widerstand gegen Rom in Griechenland 217–86 v. Chr.* (Berlin 1971) 164–7.

Quintus Maenius, son of Titus, praetor (170 BC), consulted the sen|ate in the Comitium on the seventh day before | the Ides of October (October 9). At the writing | (the witnesses) present were:[1] Manius Acilius, son of
5 Manius, (of the tribe) Volt[i‖nia;] Titus Numisius, son of Titus. Whereas the This|[bai]ans spoke about the situation among th|em, that they, who in friendship | to us had remained, should be given (advisors) | to whom
10 they could explain the situation among them, about th‖is matter it was decreed as follows: that Quintus | Maenius the praetor should from the senate | select five men who appeared to him in keeping with the interest of

the Repub|lic and his own good faith. Decreed. | On the day before the
15   Ides of October (October 14).[2] (Witnesses) present at the writing ‖ were:
Publius Mucius, son of Quintus; Marcus Clau|dius, son of Marcus;
Manius Sergius, son of Manius. | In like manner whereas the same
(Thisbaians) spoke about their territory | and harbors and revenues and
about mountain lands, whatever of those had | been theirs it was
decreed that they be permitted to possess them, as far as we are con-
20   cerned. ‖ Concerning their magistracies and temples and revenues,
that they | should themselves have legal authority over them, about this
matter it was decreed as follows: | whoever had entered into our
friendship before Gaius Lucre|tius had brought his army against the
city of Thisbai,[3] | that they should have the legal authority for the next
25   ten years. Decreed. ‖ Concerning the territory, buildings and things
belonging to them, whoever | owned any of these, it was decreed that
they should be permitted to possess what had been theirs. | In like
manner whereas the same (Thisbaians) said that | the deserters, being
private (persons and) exiles there, | should be permitted to fortify the
citadel and that they should settle there, just as they explained it, (just
30   so) as fol‖lows it was decreed: that they should settle there and fortify
it.[4] Decre|ed. That the city should be fortified was not decreed. In like
manner whereas the same (Thisbaians) | said that the gold, which they
had collected for a crown in or|der that they might dedicate (this)
crown on the Capitolium, to them, ju|st as they explained it, (i.e.) that
35   (the gold) be restored to them *in order that* this crown on ‖ [the] Capitolium
might be dedicated, just so it was decreed to restore it. In like | manner
whereas the same (Thisbaians) said that the men who are *again*|*st* our
Republic and theirs, | *that* these men should be arrested, about this matter
just as seemed to Quin|tus Maenius the praetor in keeping with the
40   interest of the Republic and his own good ‖ faith, just so it was decreed
that he should act. That those who to other cities had de|parted and
had not come forward into the presence of our commander | should not
return to their rank (in the government?), about this matter to Aulus |
[Ho]stilius the consul (170 BC) it was decreed that a letter should be
sent that about this matter he sh|ould take thought, as might seem to
45   him to be in keeping with the interest of the Republic and ‖ his own
good faith. Decreed. *vv* | In like manner whereas the same (Thisbaians)
spoke about | the trials of Xenopithis and Mnasis, that they should be
expelled from Chalkis, | and of Damokrita, (daughter or wife) of
Dionysios, (that she should be expelled) from Thebes, that these
women should be expelled from those cities | it was decreed, but that
50   they may not return to Thisbai. Decreed. ‖ In like manner whereas they
said that these women had brought vessels with silver | to the comman-
der, about this mat|ter it was decreed to discuss it at a later date in the

presence of Gaius Lucretius. | In like manner whereas the same This-
55   baians declared that concerning grain and olive | oil they had a partner-
ship agreement with Gnaeus Pandosinus,[5] about th‖is matter it was
decreed that if they wish to be assigned judges, to them judges will be
assig|ned. In like manner whereas the same (Thisbaians) spoke about
the | giving of letters to the Thisbaians for Aetolia and Phokis, about this |
60   matter it was decreed that the Thisbaians and Koroneians for Aetolia and
Phok|is, and for whatever other cities they might wish, be given cour‖teous
letters. *vv*

1 After each meeting of the Roman senate a small committee of senators was formed to
   write down in final form the contents of whatever decrees had been passed. The members of such a committee were described simply as those who 'were present at the
   writing', and their names were affixed to each decree as witnesses of its contents and its
   wording. One copy of each decree was deposited in the state archives, the *aerarium
   Saturni*, and another in the temple of Ceres. See *RDGE* pp. 7ff.
2 At the first meeting of the senate to hear the Thisbaians it was found that they needed
   advice and assistance in preparing their requests (October 9). Therefore the praetor Q.
   Maenius was authorized by decree to select a commission of five suitable men to aid
   them. When this had been done, the Thisbaians were presented a second time to the
   senate (October 14) and they made their requests. The senate then voted separately on
   each of them, as presented in lines 16–60.
3 In 171 BC the praetor C. Lucretius Gallus captured Haliartus and marched on Thisbai.
   Thisbai eventually surrendered, was placed under the political control of pro-Roman
   authorities, and witnessed the sale of the local Macedonian partisans into slavery.
4 The 'deserters' were those Thisbaians who had come over to the Roman side during the
   fighting. Apparently they were few in number and now ask permission to fortify themselves on the citadel in Thisbai and live there.
5 He was a Roman businessman with extensive enterprises overseas: Nicolet, *L'ordre* 348.

22   Argos honors Gnaeus Octavius. 170 BC.
Limestone stele with molding at top, broken on left and right, the surface
badly worn, Argos.

P. Charneux, *BCH* 81 (1957) 181–202 (+ photograph); *SEG* XVI 255; Moretti, *ISE* I
42. Cf. Polybius 28.3–5; Livy 43.17.2–10.

Since Gnaeus Octavius, (son) of Gnaeus, Roman,[1] [continues to be] well
disposed | toward the Achaian League and individually toward those
(Achaians) who at any time [make a request of him,] | displaying in every
circumstance his own *affection* [and | goodwill,] and forethought for what
5   is advantageous [to the] ci‖ty and the Achaians, and (since) having been
sent as envoy [with] | *Gaius by* [A]ulus, consul[2] of the Romans, [he has
come] | to call upon the Achaians to preserve their *friendship* [and] | alli-
ance with the Romans, it has been decreed by the People: to *prai|se*
[G]naeus Octavius, (son) of Gnaeus, Roman, for the affection which [he

10   has] ‖ toward the city and the Achaian League; that he is to be | proxenos
of the city and benefactor and *citizen* – he | and his descendants – and he is
to have the right to purchase and own land and house (in Argos), | and
security and immunity (from taxes?) and inviolability both in *war* | and in
15   *peace*, both on land and on sea,[3] and the same *privi‖leges* as those who have
benefited the People the most; and (it is further decreed) to *en|grave* this
decree on a stone stele and erect it *in* | the *temple* of Apollo Lykeios in order
that it may be clear tha|t the People to those who have chosen to be their
benefactors | will render thanks corresponding to the benefits (received);
20   and let the ta‖sk of erecting the stele fall to the strategoi; | and the expense
25   [--|--|--|--‖--] on the fourth (day) of (the month) Apellaios in the [--]

1 Gnaeus Octavius was praetor in 168 and consul in 165 BC. He was assassinated in
Syria in 162 BC in the gymnasium at Laodiceia-on-the-sea by a certain Leptines of that
city: Polybius 31.11.1 and 32.2–3.
2 Aulus Hostilius Mancinus as consul in 170 BC tried at least once in that year to invade
Macedonia from Thessaly, but failed. 'Gaius', the other envoy, is Gaius Popillius
Laenas (consul 172 BC).
3 This is a peculiar assortment of honors, perhaps more for show than for practicality.

23   An Athenian with the Roman army at the battle of Pydna. 168 BC.
Stele of Pentelic marble with top molding, surface badly weathered,
Athens.

B. D. Meritt, *Hesperia* 3 (1934) 18–21 (+ photograph); *idem, Hesperia* 5 (1936) 429–30;
Moretti, *ISE* I 35; *SEG* XXV 118. Cf. Livy 42.55.7ff.; 44.36.8.

B. D. Meritt, *The Athenian Year* (Berkeley 1961) 219–20; Walbank, *Commentary* III 386.

Gods. | In the archonship of Eunikos (169/8 BC), in Attali|s' prytany,
(which was) the twelfth, in which Hierony|mos (son) of Boethos of (the
5   deme) Kephisia was secretary, ‖ on the last day of Skirophorion, on the
nine-|and-twentieth (day) of the prytany,[1] Ekkle|sia in the Peiraios, of the
10   proedroi (the one who) put the matter to the vo|te was *vv* | *vacat* ‖ *vacat*[2] | It
was decreed by the Boule and the People. | Satyros (son) of Satyros of (the
deme) Kol[on]os said: Sin|ce Kalliphanes of (the deme) Phyle cam-
15   paign|ed with the Roma[ns] and (with) Ki‖ng E[u]menes' brothers Atta-
lus and | Athenaios,[3] and, wishing to make | himself useful to his native
city, | was present at the victory that came to the Romans | in Ma[c]ed[o]-
20   nia,[4] and, being full of eagerness him‖self to announce to the citizens the
25   e|vents [---|---|---|---‖---|---|-] with good luck *it is decre|ed* [by the Boule
30   that the men] chosen by lot to be *pro|edroi* [for the] *next* Ekklesia ‖ *should
deliberate* about *these matters*, and the opinion | of the Boule [they should

communicate] to the | *People* that the Boule has decided to praise | [Ka]l-
l[iph]anes (son) of Kalliphanes of (the deme) Phyle | [and to crown him]
35   *with a crown* [of olive branch ‖ because of his goodwill] and eagerness
[---|---|---|--], and the en|graving of this decree is to be done by the sec-
40   retary ‖ -for- the prytany on a stone stele | [and he is to erect] it in the agora
next to the statue | [--] and the expense | [of the engraving and the erection
45   of the] | *stele* is to be paid by the treasurer *of the milita‖ry* fund.
       The Boule | (and) the People | (honor) Kalliphanes | (son) of Kal-
50   liphanes ‖ of (the deme) Phyl[e].[5]

1 These chronological data show that the decree was voted in the Ekklesia on the last day
   of the year 169/8 BC, i.e. early in July. But recently Meritt (*Athenian Year* p. 220) has
   come to believe that the calendar had been retarded by a double intercalation, with
   the result that the first day of the new year 168/7 would begin on August 7. If he is
   right, our decree was passed on August 6, 168 BC, about six weeks after the battle of
   Pydna (see below, n. 4).
2 It was the president of the proedroi who put the question to the vote before the People.
   His name is missing.
3 Livy (42.55.7–8) informs us that Philetaerus, the third brother of Eumenes II, had been
   left in Pergamum to protect the kingdom. See Hansen, *Attalids*[2] 112ff.
4 Livy (44.37.5–9) records that the battle of Pydna took place on the day after a lunar
   eclipse, which modern reckoning has dated to June 21, 168 BC. See Walbank, *Commentary* III 386.
5 The last sentence is inscribed in a crown.

24   Statue of L. Aemilius Paullus placed on a pillar erected previously for King Perseus. 168/167 BC.
Base of a huge marble pillar, Delphi.

ILS 8884; *CIL* I[2] 622; *SIG*[3] 652a; **ILLRP* 323. Cf. Plutarch, *Aem.* 28; Polybius 30.10; Livy
45.27.7.

Rostovtzeff, *SEHHW* II 740 (with Pl. LXXXII).

Lucius Aemilius, son of Lucius, general, took (this pillar) from King
Perseus | and the Macedonians.

25   Treaty between Rome and Kibyra. First half of second century BC.
Limestone fragment, once a part of the anta of a building, letters of the
first half of the second century, Kibyra in Asia Minor.[1]

*OGIS 762.

Magie, *RRAM* I 241–2; II 967–8; Badian, *FC* 295, n. L; Mellor, *Worship* 39–41.

[-- for the] *People of the* [Ro]mans *to do.*[2] And *if anyone* takes the initiative in
waging wa|r against the People of the Romans or transgresses his (exist-
ing) trea|ty (with the Roman People), then the People of Kibyra | shall aid
5 the People of the Romans, as is appropriate, ‖ as far as it may be possible,
in accordance with the treaties and oaths, for the Kibyran | People to do
(so). And if as regards this treaty | the People of the Romans and the
People of Kibyra with mutual | consent wish to add or subtract anything,
as long as with mutual (and) pub|lic consent both of them are willing,
10 they shall be allowed (to do so). And whatever ‖ they add in the treaty,
those things shall be included | in the treaty, and whatever they subtract
from the trea|ty, those things shall be excluded. This treaty on a *bronze* |
tablet they shall engrave and set up in | Rome in the temple of Jupiter
15 Capitolinus and in [Kibyra] ‖ on the base (of the statue) of Roma, the one
of gold which they decreed.[3]

1 Immediately to the east of Karia and adjacent to it, in Asia Minor, was the state of
Kibyratis which included the four main communities of Kibyra, Bubon, Balbura and
Oenoanda.
2 Dittenberger (in *OGIS*) restores 'to remain', but Täubler (*Imperium* 55, n. 2) makes out a
better case for 'to do (so)'. Täubler also restores the preceding part of the treaty to yield
a parallel obligation for the Roman People.
3 The present text, however, was not engraved on a statue base.

26   Envoys from Teos to Rome oppose the encroachment of King Kotys on territory of Abdera. About 166 BC.

Marble slab broken in the middle from top to bottom, letters of the early
second century, Teos.

SIG[3] 656; *IGRR* IV 1558. Cf. Polybius 30.17; Livy 45.42.6ff.

Robert, *Opera* I 320–6; P. Herrmann, *ZPE* 7 (1971) 72–7.

The People of Ab[dera] (honor) | Amymo|n (son) of Epi|kouros, | Mega-
5 thy|mos (son) of Athe|naios. ‖[1] When our People *had* need of an embassy
to | Rome about our country's [territory,] concerning which the king of the
Thracians, | Kot[ys], had delivered a request [to the] *senate* and through
his son[2] | and the envoys whom he sent with him | had laid claim to our
10 ancestral territory, ‖ envoys were selected [by the] People of Teos,[3]
Amy|mon (son) of Epikouros and M[egathym]os (son) of Athenaios,
men | fine and good and *worthy* [of their] country and well disposed
toward | our People, and all their zeal and | enthusiasm did they exercise,
15 and of their [eagerness] nothing did they o‖mit; in the *meetings* that took
place about our | territory they [made use of] all their foresight in order
not to ne|glect any of the things that could *make* the situation *turn out*

favorably, | always proposing the best[4] opinion to bring recovery in our dif-
20 ficulties; | in their embassy to [Rome] on behalf of our ‖ People they suf-
fered both mental and *bodily* distress, | but they met with the Roman
[leading men],[5] winning them | over by their daily [salutation,] and they
induced | the (Roman) patrons[6] of our *country* to come to the | aid of our
People, and when [some[7] (of the Romans)] preferred our antagonist
25 (Kotys) ‖ and stood up in his defense, [by] their exposition of the situation |
and by daily morning-calls at their atri|a[6] (our envoys) won over their
friendship. Concerning [these matters] it was decreed by the Boule and
the Peo|ple of Abdera to *praise* the aforementioned me|n and to summon
30 them to front-[row seats each] year at the Dionysiac fes‖tival as long as
they live, and [to crown them] with a gold crown at the *festival* | while the
herald makes the announcement: 'The People cro|wn with a gold crown
A[mymon (son) of E]pikouros of Teos, becau|se of his excellence and
goodwill toward *them*, [and Me]gathymos (son) of Athenaios of Teos with
a go|ld crown, because of his excellence [and goodwill] toward them'.
(Etc.)[8]

1 This sentence occupies only the first four lines of text, for the names of the Teian envoys
  are contained within two engraved crowns next to each other immediately below the
  first line, each crown with three lines of text.
2 Although King Kotys had fought on the side of Perseus throughout the Third Macedonian War, his son Bithys even having been taken by the Romans as a hostage to Italy,
  he soon won great favor in Rome.
3 Abdera in Thrace was a colony of Teos.
4 Robert has corrected an error of previous editors, showing that 'best' and not 'desired' is
  the correct reading.
5 Robert suggests '[authorities]'.
6 The Latin word is simply transliterated, its earliest appearance in Greek.
7 Restoration by Robert.
8 The text continues on for fifteen more lines, concerned with orders for the publication
  of the decree on a stone stele and its erection in a public place in Abdera and Teos.

27   Romans admitted to the Samothracian Mysteries. Second and first centuries.

Various inscriptions, Samothrace.

A: Fraser, **Samothrace* 28a (Latin), p. 77 (+ photograph). Late second or early first century. Block of white marble inscribed on three faces, Samothrace. **B**: Fraser, **ibid.* 30
(Latin), pp. 82–3 (+ photograph). Early first century. Fragment of blue-gray marble
broken on all sides, Samothrace. **C**: Fraser, **ibid.* 32 (Greek and Latin), p. 85 (+ photograph). 76 BC. Fragment of marble with top molding, Samothrace.

A. Fraser, *Samothrace* **28a**

[--|--] Ides of June. Epopta[1] | [-] Cornelius, son of Lucius, Lent[ulus] |
5 legate with praetorian power.[2] *vv* ‖ *vv* Mustae[3] devout: *vv* | [Lucius C]or-

nelius, freedman of Lucius, Phil[o; | Gaius] Mutius, freedman of Gaius, Erun[-;] (eight more names are listed).

B. Fraser, *ibid.* **30**

[--]tius[4] | [ep]optes devout. | *vacat* | [-]oninus, Gaius Marius[5] | [--] *vv* | [--]

C. Fraser, *ibid.* **32**

(On the molding, in Greek) When the king was [---][6] | (In the field, in Latin) In the consulship of Gnaeus Oc[tavius, son of Marcus,] | and Gaius Scrib[onius, son of Gaius, (Curio) (76 BC),] | on the [--] day
5   before [the -- of --] || Mustae [devout:] Q. Minuc(ius, son of --,] | The[r-mus,] | P. Magnul[nius | --]aberi[us --][7]

1 The Greek 'epoptes' (often spelled 'epopta' in Latin) was the highest level of initiation reached by the worshippers of the Samothracian gods called the Kabeiroi.
2 It is not certain which particular Cornelius Lentulus is meant. The ten Roman citizens whose names follow are all freedmen of different individuals and were presumably part of Lentulus' entourage.
3 A transliteration into Latin of the Greek 'mystai'. They were initiates into the mysteries, of a lower grade than epoptae.
4 The 't' is doubtful on the stone. Despite Fraser's objection, '[Ma]rius' is possible.
5 This is almost certainly the great Marius, who traveled to the east in 99–97 BC. Fraser believes the very doubtful reading on the stone (-onini) is not that of a name but a word such as 'slave'.
6 The Samothracian 'king' was the eponymous magistrate when the island enjoyed independence under Roman protection.
7 Q. Minucius Thermus may be the governor of Asia of the year 51/50 BC: Broughton, *MRR* II 243. A certain M. Magulnius is known about this period at Delos: *I. Délos* 1687. The third individual is either '[F]aberius' or '[L]aberius'. The official position, however, of all these Romans while on Samothrace in 76 BC is unknown. The nearness of the Roman province of Macedonia to Samothrace made the shrine there a popular resort for Roman officials from very early times: Fraser, *Samothrace* pp. 15ff.

28   Decree of the senate concerning the Sarapieion at Delos. About 164 BC.
Stele of white marble with small projections at the top in the form of acroteria, letters of the second century, Delos.

SIG[3] 664; **RDGE* 5.

Laidlaw, *Delos* 178–9; *RDGE* pp. 37–9; S. V. Tracy, *HSCP* 83 (1979) 214.

The strategoi[1] to Charmides the gover|nor of Delos, greetings. There was | lengthy discussion in the Boule[2] | concerning the decree which was

5   brought ‖ from Rome by Demetrios the Rhenai|an concerning events at
the Sarapi|eion. It was decreed not to prevent hi|m from opening and
10   administering | the sanctuary as be‖fore, and to write to you too, | in order
that you might know about these matters. We have, below, atta|ched for
15   you, in addition, | a copy of the decree brought | by him. *vv* ‖ Quintus
Minucius, son of Quintus, | praetor,[3] consulted the senate | in the Co|mi-
tium on the intercalary Ides.[4] | (Witnesses) present at the writing were:
20   ‖ Publius Porcius, (son) of Publius; Ti|berius Claudius, (son) of Tiberius, |
(of the tribe) Crustumina; Manius Fonte|ius, (son) of Gaius. Whereas
25   Demetrios | the Rhenaian said ‖ that on Delos the sanctuary of Sara|pis
was his to administer, | but that he was prevented by the Delians and | by
30   the governor, who from Athens | had come there, fr‖om administering it,
about this | matter it was as follows de|creed: just as formerly he used to
ad|minister it, as far as we are concerned | he is to be permitted to admin-
35   ister it, ‖ so that nothing contrary to the | decree of the senate is to be
done. | Decreed. *vv*

1 These were Athenian 'generals', officials elected annually to administer the government. In 167/6 BC Rome made Delos a free port and placed it under the general supervision of Athens.
2 I.e. the one in Athens. On the Boule see the Glossary.
3 The year of his praetorship is unknown, but the events took place not very long after
167/6 BC. See *RDGE* p.39.
4 The word 'intercalary' is transliterated in this document from Latin into Greek. Since
the Roman calendar in this period was lunar, i.e. based on the phases of the moon, and
thus had only 354 days in its year – eleven days less than a solar year – the months that
were supposed to come in the spring gradually slipped backward into the winter. To
avoid this the Romans at irregular intervals inserted an extra month into their lunar
year. This was called an intercalary month, and the special days that were used to
divide each month into three parts were then called the intercalary Kalends, Nones and
Ides. (See the Appendix on Greek and Roman chronology.) This intercalary month
was inserted in the month of February. Thus, 'the intercalary Ides' mean the thirteenth (or fifteenth) day of this month that was inserted in the calendar. Further
details in A. K. Michels, *The Calendar of the Roman Republic* (Princeton 1967) 9–15 and
160ff.

29   A letter of King Attalus II of Pergamum to the priest in Pes-
sinus. In or soon after 159 BC.

One of a series of documents inscribed on three marble blocks, letters of
the late first century,[1] Pessinus in central Asia Minor.

OGIS 315 C VI; Welles, *RC* 61 (+ photograph).

Welles, *RC* pp. 245–7 and 250–1; Magie, *RRAM* I 25–8; Hopp, *Untersuchungen* 68–70;
Sherwin-White, *JRS* 67 (1977) 64.

[King Attalus (II) to Attis the priest,[2] greetings. If you are well, it would
be] | as I wish. I too am in good health. When we came | to Pergamum and
I brought together not only Athenaios | and Sosandros and Menogenes
5   but also many other ‖ 'relatives',[3] I set before them the matters about
which in Apameia we had | made plans, and I told them what we had
decided about them.[4] There were | exceedingly many speeches, and at
first everyone was inclin|ed toward the same opinion as ours, but Chloros
was most energetic | in putting forward the Roman (view of) things and
10 advising us in no way to do any‖thing without the Romans. At first few
shar|ed this opinion, but afterwards, in our day-after-day consider|ations,
it began to make more of an impression on us, and to come to a hasty deci-
sion with|out them (i.e. the Romans) seemed to hold great danger. For to
us, if success|ful, would accrue envy, a taking away (of success) and hate-
15 ful suspicion, such as ‖ they conceived about my brother, and if unsuc-
cessful, ruin | in plain sight: for (in the latter case) they would not turn
back toward us, but it would give them pleasure to se|e (our disaster),
because we had set such things in motion without them. But as things are
at present, if – may it | never happen – we were unsuccessful in anything,
after having with their | approval done each and every thing, we would
20 receive their help and ‖ might retrieve a defeat, with the goodwill of the
gods. Therefore, I decided | in each instance to send to Rome men who
would immediately re|port (to the Romans) *those things about which we are in
doubt*, and, for ourselves, to make preparations | [carefully, so that, if there
is need, we could help] ourselves [--]

1 It is not clear why this letter, along with the others of the same series, all concerned
    with events of 163–156 BC, was not engraved until more than a century later. Welles
    (p. 247) suggests that 'In a time when independent political activity had come to an end,
    the priests might well wish to recall to visitors that their predecessors had corresponded
    with kings.'
2 The temple of Cybele, the 'Great Mother', an ancient Asianic goddess at Pessinus,
    owned domains of great size, and the priest of the temple was actually the ruler of a
    vast independent principality.
3 The word 'relatives' here does not mean literally members of the royal family. The
    word had become a mere honorary title.
4 At this meeting between Attalus and the priest presumably some great military expedi-
    tion had been agreed upon, perhaps against the Gauls of Galatia who were old enemies
    of Pessinus.

30   Treaty between King Pharnakes I of Pontos and the city of Chersonesos. 155 BC.

Marble stele broken at the top, Chersonesos in the Crimea.

IOSPE I[2] 402. Cf. Polybius 25.2 for background to the treaty.

Magie, *RRAM* I 192–4; II 1090 n. 45; V. F. Gajdukevič, *Das Bosporanische Reich* (Berlin 1971) 312; Walbank, *Commentary* III 20 and 274; S. Burstein, *AJAH* 5 (1980) 1–12.

[-- we will assist in guarding his] *kingdom* | [with all our power, as long as he remains] with *us* [in | friendship and] maintains his friendship [with
5   the Rom]ans | [and does nothing] in opposition to them; || and may it be good for us swearing a true oath and for us swearing a false oa|th the opposite. This oath was ta|ken on the fifteenth of the month of Hera-kleios, | when the king was Apollodoros (son) of Herogei|tes, and when
10 the secretary was Herodotos (son) of Hero||dotos. *vv* The oath which King Pharnakes swore when the envoys Matrios and Herakle[i]os went to him: | I swear by Zeus, Earth, Sun, all the Olympian gods | and goddesses. I will be a friend to the Chersonesitans for all | time, and if the neighboring
15 barbarians should make an expedition || against Chersonesos or the land controlled by the Cherso|nesitans or should commit an act of injustice against Chersonesitans, and if they call up|on me, I will help them just as if mine were the cri|sis, and I will not plot against the Chersonesitans in
20 any | way, nor will I make an expedition against Chersonesos, nor || will I stockpile weapons against Chersonesitans, nor will I do | anything with respect to Chersonesitans which would tend to harm | the People of the Chersonesitans, but I will as|sist in guarding democracy with all | my
25 power, as long as they remain in friendship with m||e and have sworn the same oath | and maintain their friendship with the Romans | and do nothing contrary to them. | May it be good for me swearing a true oath
30 and for me swearing a false oath the oppo|site. This oath was taken in || the one hundred and fifty-seventh | year, in the month of Daisios, as King Pharnakes | *vv* reckons (time).[1] *vv*

1 The defensive alliance, as sworn to by both parties here, was previously dated to 180–179 BC, but recently Burstein has shown that the era used in lines 30–31 cannot be one which began with the accession of Mithridates II to the throne of Kios in 337/6 BC, as previously thought, but must be the Seleucid era of 312/11 BC, which produces a date of 155 BC when applied to our document. Thus, a recognized condition of friend-ship had been established between Rome on the one hand and both Pharnakes and the city of Chersonesos on the other sometime prior to 155 BC. That friendship also seems to have been recognized soon after 179 BC, when Rome became reconciled with Phar-nakes at the conclusion of the Pontic War (183–179 BC). See Burstein, *loc cit.*

31   Testament of Ptolemaios VIII Euergetes II, leaving his king-dom of Cyrene to the Romans. 155 BC.

Stele of white marble perfectly preserved, letters of the second century, Cyrene.

G. Oliverio, *Documenti antichi dell'Africa Italiana* I: *Cirenaica* Part 1 (Bergamo 1932) pp. 11ff. (+ photographs); *SEG* IX 7.

Oliverio, *op. cit.* 11–84; M. N. Tod, *Greece and Rome* 2 (1932) 47–51; P. Roussel, *REG* 45 (1932) 286–92; E. Bickermann, *Gnomon* 8 (1932) 424–30; W. Otto, *Abhandlungen der Bayerischen Akademie der Wissenschaften, Phil.-hist. Abteilung*, N.S. 11 (1934) 97–119; Th. Liebmann-Frankfort, *RIDA* 13 (1966) 73–94; B. A. Kouvelas, *Platon* 24 (1972) 300–4.

In the fifteenth year,[1] in the month of Loos. | With good luck. This is the testament of King | Ptolemaios, (son) of King Ptolemaios | and of Queen
5   Cleopatra, gods ‖ manifest, the younger (son).[2] Of this another copy | has been sent to Rome.[3] May it be mine | with the good will of the gods to take vengeance | worthily upon those who have organized against me | the
10   unholy plot and have deliberately chosen ‖ not only of my kingdom but also | of my life to deprive me. But if anything happens to me, | in accordance with human destiny, before successors | are left (by me) for my
15   kingdom, I bequeath | to the Romans the kingdom belonging to me,[4] ‖ for whom from the beginning friendship and | alliance have been preserved by me with all sincerity. | And to the same (Romans) I entrust my possessions | for them to protect, appealing to them by all the gods | and by their
20   own good reputation that, if any persons ‖ attack either my cities or my territory, they may help, | in accordance with the friendship and alliance which {toward} | toward each other we (now) have and (in accordance with) | justice, with all their power. And I make witnesses to these (dis-
25   positions) Jupiter ‖ Capitolinus and the Great Gods | and the Sun and the Founder Apollo,[5] to whose (custody) the text of these (dispositions) is also consecrated. | With good luck.

1   From 170 BC to the summer of 163 BC Ptolemaios VI Philometor and his younger brother Ptolemaios VIII ruled Egypt jointly. The fifteenth year of their reign is 155 BC. Dissensions between them caused Roman intervention and a division of the realm: the older brother retained Egypt and Cyprus, the younger only the Cyrenaica, to which he withdrew in 163 BC. For all details see Will, *Histoire* 262–75 and 302–6.
2   The 'younger (son)' is Ptolemaios VIII Euergetes II, who was nicknamed 'Physkon' ('Pot-belly').
3   No literary sources mention the existence of this will. Its terms were never carried out, since Ptolemaios VIII eventually had children and recovered Egypt, seizing the throne after the death of his brother in 145. He died in 116 BC. Bickermann argues that we have before us not an authentic will at all, but rather an official extract, published in 155 BC, of an earlier will. Roussel accepts Bickermann's main conclusions.
4   He probably considered Cyprus as much a part of his kingdom as Cyrene.
5   Apollo was considered the founder of Cyrene.

32·   Decree of the senate concerning Ariarathes and the city of Priene. About 155–154 BC or soon afterwards.

Two fragments of stone from the wall of the temple of Athena Polias, Priene.

OGIS 351; *I. Priene* 39; *RDGE* 6 B. Cf. Polybius 33.6.

Magie, *RRAM* I 117 and 202; II 969. n. 93; *RDGE* pp. 40–3; Hansen, *Attalids*[2] 130–1; Hopp, *Untersuchungen* 67–8; A. N. Sherwin-White, *JRS* 67 (1977) 63; Walbank, *Commentary* III 547–9.

B. Decree of the senate[1]

[Ariarathes] *having besieged* the city [of Priene[2] | and plundered] *property* and [carried off most of the] live booty[3] [private and] | public [--] and having let go [--|--] which Orophernes [had deposited] in the temple of

5   A[thena, it was decided to ans‖wer] them kindly [-- neither the] | senate nor the People for [--] | concerning these matters [it was decreed as follows: that X[4] should write to] | King Attalus and King Aria[rathes about their] *at|tack* as [might seem] to him [in keeping with the best

10   interest of the Republic ‖ and his own good faith. Decreed.]

1 This decree is preceded on the stone by another document which is either a decree of Priene or a covering letter from some Roman magistrate. It is extremely fragmentary.
2 In 159 BC King Ariarathes of Cappadocia was driven out of his kingdom by his half-brother Orophernes, but two years later the Roman senate ruled that the two should rule jointly. Ariarathes, however, drove out his half-brother with the aid of King Attalus II of Pergamum. When Ariarathes then tried to withdraw 400 talents which Orophernes had deposited in the temple of Athena at Priene, that city refused to comply. Ariarathes and Attalus marched on the city with their armies. Priene appealed to Rhodes, and finally Rome was called in. See Polybius 33.6.
3 The word could mean 'animals' (beasts of burden) or, more commonly, 'slaves'.
4 Here would appear the name of the consul or praetor who presided over the meeting of the senate.

33   Treaty between Rome and Methymna. Perhaps as early as 154 BC.[1]

Marble (not otherwise described), whose letters point to a period before the Mithridatic wars, Methymna on Lesbos.

IG XII 2.510; *IGRR* IV 2; **SIG*[3] 693.

Magie, *RRAM* II 967–8, n. 89; Täubler, *Imperium* 45 and 55ff.

[-- neither with weapons nor with money nor with ships shall they give aid | with public sanction (and)] in *bad* [faith]. The People [of the Romans | to the enemies and] *opponents* of the People of the M[e|thymnaians shall not grant passage through their own] *land* and through (the land) which

5   the People of the R[o‖mans rule,] with public sanction and in [bad] | faith, [with the result that (such enemies)] would wage war upon [the People] of the Methymnaians and those whom | [the People of the Methymnaians] rule, | [and to Methymna's enemies neither with weapons] nor with money nor with *sh|ips* [shall they give aid with

10   public] sanction (and) in bad faith. ‖ [If anyone takes the initiative] in
waging [war] against the People of the Meth[ym|naians, then the
People of the Rom]ans [shall give aid] to the People of the
Methy[m|naians as may seem] appropriate; and if anyone | [takes the
initiative in waging] war [against the] *People* of the Romans, then [the
Peop|le of the Methymnaians] shall give aid to the *People* of the Romans,
15   ‖ [as may seem appropriate in accordance with their] treaty and oaths
to the | [People of the Romans and the] People of the Methymnaians. |
[--] *this* treaty with mutual [con|sent --] with public consent and both |
20   [---] *add* in the treaty ‖ [---]² the treaty.

1 For a discussion of the date see Magie, *loc. cit.*
2 For the nature of the material in lines 17–20 see the treaty with Kibyra (above, no. 25,
   lines 9–11) and with Astypalaia (below, no. 53, lines 45–8).

34   A letter of the praetor Marcus Aemilius and a decree of the senate concerning Magnesia and Priene. Middle of second century or a little earlier.
Marble block, Magnesia.

*SIG*³ 679 IIb; *RDGE 7.

Tod, *Arbitration* 44–5; Magie, *RRAM* I 113–14; *RDGE* pp. 44–7.

[- Decree obtained] *from* the Ro[man] senate [by the envoys who had
35   been sent ‖ concerning the Prienean affair.]¹ Marcus Aemilius, [son] of
Marcus,² [praetor, to the Mylasan | Boule and People, greetings.]
Envoys from Magnesia and [Priene came to me, | that] I might give
[them (an audience with the) senate.] I *gave* them (an audience with the)
senate. [Decree of the senate. On the -- day before | the -- of --]ber in the
Comitium. (Witnesses) present [at the writing] were: [--|-- Fo(?)]n-
teius, (son) of Quintus, (of the tribe) Papiria; Titus Mallius, (of the
40   tribe) Fa[--³‖--] Whereas the Magnesian envoys Pythodoros, Hera-
kl[eitos, --, | fine and good men] from a fine and good People, friends and
allies [of ou|rs,] spoke *in person*, and whereas the Prienean *envoys* [---, | --,]
fine and good men and friends from a fine and [good] People, *fri|ends* and
45   allies of ours, spoke in person about the territory ‖ from which the Magnesians had withdrawn and the possession of which territory they had
ceded | to the People of Priene, in accordance with the decree of the
senate that a special court be appointed for them, concerning [this] |
matter it was decreed as follows: that Marcus Aemilius, son of Marcus,
praetor, shall grant them a *free* | *state* as arbitrator which shall be
mutually acceptable to them. But if one mutually acceptable to them is
not fou|nd, that Marcus Aemilius, son of Marcus, praetor, [shall give]

50 them a free state as arbitrator ‖ for this controversy, as seems to him to be
in keeping with the interest of the Republic | and his own good [faith.]
Decreed. (The free state), which will act as arbitrator between Mag-
nesia and Priene about this | territory, excluding the (land) of the
Prieneans, from which the Magnesians say they have | withdrawn – to
the one of these two Peoples which is found | to have possessed this terri-
tory at the time when it entered into friendship with the Roman People,
55 ‖ to that one it shall award this territory and establish the borders.
Decreed. In like manner whereas the same Pri|enean envoys spoke in
person against the Magnesian envoys | about the wrongs which Mag-
nesia had committed against them, concerning this matter as foll|ows it
was decreed | that Marcus Aemilius, son of Marcus, praetor, shall order
the same state | which was appointed arbitrator concerning the territory
60 to judge also these wrongs. If (wrongs) were *comm‖itted* by the Magnesians,
a penalty shall be imposed as much as appears good and fair, and |
Marcus Aemilius, son of Marcus, praetor, shall send a letter [to] the same
arbitrating state about this ma|tter, on what day each of the two (parties)
shall be present for each of the two *hear|ings*, [and by what] day they shall
decide [--] that [--]

1 This heading serves to separate the present letter and decree from a preceding document. There were four other documents engraved on the other sides of the present
block, and from their remains we learn that Magnesia had engraved an entire file of
the pertinent documents on this and other marble blocks placed on top of each other
and engraved on all four visible sides. Remains of the other documents are in *SIG*³ 679
Ia, IVc and Vd. The first of them is a Magnesian decree honoring the Magnesian public
advocates and ordering the engraving of the whole dossier, also informing us that
Mylasa had been the arbitrating state and that Magnesia had won; the second is
our letter and decree of the Roman senate; the third document is lost; the fourth contains the decision of the Mylasan arbitrators; and the fifth lists the names of the Magnesian advocates who had successfully pleaded their city's case.
2 The omission of his cognomen makes identification difficult. Possible candidates are: M.
Aemilius Lepidus (cos. 158 and praetor in 161 at the latest); M. Aemilius Lepidus
Porcina (cos. 136, praetor in 140 at the latest). The lettering places the document not
long after the Roman war against Antiochus.
3 The tribe is either Falerna or Fabia. This Titus is almost certainly a Manlius. See
Broughton, *MRR* Supplement 38.

35   Destruction of Corinth and new Roman regulations for Greece. 146 BC.
Extract from Pausanias.

Pausanias 7.16.7–10. Cf. Polybius 39.2–6; Dio 21.72; Livy, *Per.* 51–2.

Larsen, *Greece* 306–11; Accame, *Dominio* 1ff.; Larsen, *States* 498–504; Schwertfeger, *Bund*,
passim; Bernhardt, *Historia* 62–73.

(7) Those of the Achaians who had escaped to Corinth after the battle[1] immediately fled from there at night, and the majority of the Corinthians themselves fled. Mummius,[2] although the gates were open, for the moment hesitated to enter Corinth, suspecting that an ambush might be waiting for him within the wall, but on the third day after the battle he took Corinth by force of arms and burned it. (8) Most of the survivors the Romans killed, but the women and children Mummius sold. He also sold the household slaves, all those who had been set free and had fought alongside the Achaians, but had not at once met death in the deeds of the war. Those votive offerings and other ornaments that especially aroused admiration he carried off; the rest, those of less value, Mummius gave to Philopoimen, the general sent by Attalus (III). The Pergamenes still had these Corinthian spoils of war up to my time. (9) As for those cities which had fought against the Romans, Mummius destroyed their walls and took away their weapons even before legates[3] were sent by the Romans. And after those men had arrived who were to advise him, he put an end to the democracies and he established governments on the basis of wealth. Tribute was assessed on Greece[4] and the wealthy were prevented from acquiring property beyond their borders. All confederacies (formed) by groups of Peoples, whether Achaian, Phokian, Boiotian or any other in Greece, were dissolved. (10) But not many years later the Romans were moved to pity for Greece and restored the old confederacies by groups of Peoples to each, also the right to acquire property beyond their borders, and they remitted the fines which Mummius had imposed on them. For he had ordered the Boiotians to pay a hundred talents to the Herakleans and to the Euboians, and the Achaians two hundred to the Lakedaimonians. The Greeks secured remission of these (fines) from the Romans, but a (Roman) governor down to my time was still being sent (to Greece).[5]

1 This was the final battle of the Achaian War in 146 BC.
2 L. Mummius, consul in 146 BC: Broughton, *MRR* I 465–6.
3 These were the ten Commissioners sent out to arrange matters in Greece. Polybius (39.5) says they finished their work in six months. Memorials of their presence have been found in many cities: list and references in Schwertfeger, *Bund* 19–20, n. 4.
4 Pausanias writes as if all Greece had to pay tribute. No such penalties seem to have been imposed on those parts of Greece which had remained loyal to Rome in the war. Many, perhaps all, of the Greek cities which had resisted Rome were forced to pay tribute, but direct evidence is lacking. Schwertfeger, *Bund* 67ff.
5 Pausanias here creates the impression that Greece received a separate governor and was thus a separate province after 146 BC, but that did not happen until 27 BC. Pausanias was writing sometime about the middle of the second century AD. Accame (*Dominio* 2ff.) has demonstrated that in 145 BC those Greek states which had fought against Rome in the Achaian War were placed under the supervision of the Roman governor of Macedonia, while those which had not fought against Rome retained their freedom. Schwertfeger, however, questions this arrangement and elevates the Achaian League to a level of great importance in the administration of the conquered area of Greece. Bernhardt objects and believes the conclusion of Accame to be correct.

36   The builder of the Via Egnatia in Macedonia. About 146–143 BC.

Cylindrical milestone of dull white marble, bilingual inscription with lettering of the second century, found near Thessaloniki by the river Gallikos.

C. Romiopoulou, *BCH* 98 (1974) 814 (+ photograph). Cf. Strabo 7.7.4.

Romiopoulou, *op. cit.* 813–16; P. Collart, *BCH* 100 (1976) 182–3; G. Daux, *Journal des Savants* (1977) 145–63. For the whole route see N. G. L. Hammond, *A History of Macedonia* I (Oxford 1972) 19–58.

(Latin) 260 (miles).[1] | Gnaeus Egnatius, son of Gaius,[2] | proconsul. |
5 (Greek) Gnaeus Egnatius, (son) of Gaius, ‖ proconsul of the Romans. |
260 (miles).

1 The distance is from Dyrrachium to the milestone.
2 He ought to be Cn. Egnatius C.f. of the tribe Stellatina mentioned as a witness to a decree of the senate dated between 175 and 160 BC: *RDGE* 4, lines 16–17.

37   Conclusion of a letter by a Roman magistrate to the Dionysiac Artists. After 146 BC.

Stone broken on all sides, the surface greatly eroded, Thebes.

IG VII 2413; *RDGE* 44, lines 1–9.

Accame, *Dominio* 1ff.; *RDGE* pp. 249–52; Larsen, *States* 498–504; Bernhardt, *Historia* 62–73.

[--- | Macedonia,] the province of the Romans, and (that part?), which they rule, | [? of Greece,[1]] I grant to you for the sake of Dionysos[2] *and* | [of
5 the other] *gods* and of the way of life which you have preferred, ‖ that [you] *in every way* are to be immune from liturgies and from *bille|ting* and *immune* and *exempt* from every war-contribution, | [both yourselves and] your wives and children until [they reach] *adult|hood*, just as you asked. *vv* | *vv* With good luck. *vv*[3]

1 The mutilated phrases in lines 2–3 have led to a controversy on the status of Greece after 146 BC. Accame's solution, accepted by many scholars, divides Greece into two parts: one is subject to the governor of the new province of Macedonia, while the other remains free and independent. See Pausanias on the destruction of Corinth (above, no. 35).
2 The mention of Dionysos suggests that the letter was addressed to a guild of Dionysiac Artists, on whom see the glossary.
3 The next four lines on the stone form the beginning of a new letter by a Roman consul or proconsul to the Ionian and Hellespontine Guild of Dionysiac Artists.

38   Decree of the senate concerning Narthakion and Melitaia. 140 BC or earlier.

Grayish stone slab, letters of the second century carefully engraved on both sides, Narthakion in Thessaly.

IG IX 2.89; *SIG*[3] 674; **RDGE* 9.

Tod, *Arbitration* 23–4; *RDGE* pp. 49-53; Larsen, *States* 281–8; Schwertfeger, *Bund* 24.

When the *strategos*[1] of the Thessalians was Leon | (son) of [Hag]esippos from Larisa, and when in Narthakion | [the tagoi[2] were] Kriton (son) of Ameinias, Polykles | (son) of [Phei]dippos, and Glauketas (son) of
5 Agelaos, ‖ a decree was engraved (and set up), passed by the sen|ate when the strategos of the Thessalians was Thessa|[los (son)] of Thrasymedes of Pherai. *vv* | [Gaius Hos]tilius, son of Aulus, Mancinus, prae|tor,[3] con-
10 sulted the senate on the ‖ [--day] before the *Nones* of July in the Comi-tium. | (Witnesses) present at the *writing* were: Quintus <S>tatilienus, son of Quintus, | (of the tribe) [Cor]nelia; Gnaeus Lutatius, son of Gnaeus, | (of the tribe) [--en]sis;[4] and Aulus Sempronius, son of Aulus, (of the tribe) [Fa]‖lerna. *vv* Whereas the Thessalian *envoys* from Melitaia,
15 Harmo‖[xenos (son) of Ly]sandros, and Lampromachos (son) of Politas, | spoke, being men fi|ne and good, friends from a People fine | *and good*, our friends and allies, | and renewed their goodwill, [friendship and] *alliance*,
20 ‖ (and whereas) [they spoke (?)] *about* their public [land] and about the desert area, in possession of which land into friendship | with the [People] of the Romans *vv* they had entered, and which *la*|*nd* the [Nartha]kieians thereafter unjustly | [had made] their own, about this matter (they
25 asked) that ‖ (the senators) direct their attention[5] to it so that the (former) condi|tion might be restored [in full, just as | previously] in (the court of) Medeios and the Thessalian | [--,] and in (the court of) Pyllos (and) the Mace|[donians[6] a judgment] for them had been made, (asking us) [that]
30 these [judg‖ments] be [legally binding;] about this mat|ter it *pleased* us and the Narthakieians | [that ---] should judge the present [contest] in
35 M[eli|taia (?) --] on this land [--| both] Peoples [entrusting --‖-] there is [--] | LACUNA [--- and whereas the Thessalian | Narthakieians, N]ika-tas (son) of Ta[--, | --,] envoys, *spoke* [in | person in the] senate, [being
40 men fine ‖ and good,] friends from a People *fine* | [and good,] friends [and | allies of ours, | and renewed goodwill,] *friendship* [and] *alliance* [and | dis-cussed the] *situation* [in their country,] | about the land [and] *sanctuaries*
45 and [about the] ‖ (land) *taken from* [the] rule of [Melit]aia, (land) of the Nar|thakieians in [Acha]ia (Phthiotis), (saying) that in possession of *this* | land into *friendship* with the *People* [of the Ro]|mans the Narthakieians had

50 entered, and that concerning | the land and the sanctuaries they had been
in the courts victor‖ious according to the laws of the Thessalians, la|ws
which they use to the present day, laws which Titus | Quinctius (Flamini-
nus), consul (198 BC), after consultation with the Ten Commission|ers
had given them, also in accordance with a decree | of the senate, (adding)
55 about this mat‖ter that it was now the third year since before three *tri|bu-
nals* they had been victorious – (tribunals) of Samians, Kolo[ph]|onians
and Magnesians – and that the decisions had been made in accordance
with the laws, | (and) that they should all be legally binding, just as for
60 others | had been done, about this matter ‖ it was decreed as follows: that
goodwill, friendship and alliance | be renewed, that they be given a
friendly re|ply and that as fine and good men they be add|ressed, and that
whatever decisions had been made in accordance with laws | which Titus
65 Quinctius, consul, had given them, it seemed best that these ‖ ought to be
legally binding, just as had been decided; | that it was not an easy thing
for that, which in accordance with the laws had been deci|ded, to be made
invalid; and that Gai|us Hostilius, praetor, should order the quaestor to
70 give gifts | of 125 sesterces ‖ to each embassy, as might | appear [to him] to
be in keeping with the interest of the Republic | and his own good faith.
Decreed. *vv*

By this period Rome was regularly consulted by Greek states concerning their contro-
versies with each other – cf. the decree of the senate about Magnesia and Priene, above, no.
34, and see Tod, *Arbitration, passim*, and *RDGE* pp. 195–6. After the two parties through
envoys had presented their respective cases before the senate, the final decision was sometimes made by the senate itself, as in the present instance, or sometimes the senate
merely stated the rule to be applied and then handed the whole matter over to some third
(neutral) city to render the decision, as above, no. 34, between Magnesia and Priene.
Sometimes a senatorial commission would be formed to decide the case. In our document
we see that Melitaia and Narthakion were quarreling for a long time over possession of a
piece of land. After their envoys had presented their arguments, the senate decided in
favor of Narthakion, thus upholding the actions taken more than half a century earlier by
the Ten Commissioners and Flamininus in their settlement of conditions in Greece after
the conclusion of the war against Philip.

1 A new feature of the Thessalian League after its reorganization by Flamininus was that
  its head henceforth was to be an annually elected strategos ('general'): Larsen, *States*
  286.
2 Tagoi were the chief magistrates in Thessalian cities.
3 The latest possible date for his praetorship is 140 BC: Broughton, *MRR* I 480; II 643,
  addendum to I 480.
4 '[Arnen]sis' or '[Anien]sis'.
5 One expects here: '(they asked) that ‖ we direct our attention to it' etc.
6 Medeios and Pyllos were the men who headed two previous tribunals concerned with
  this same controversy, each of them having a team of arbitrators working with him.

39 Decree of Pergamum on citizenship after the death of Attalus III. 133 BC.

Stele of white marble with a break running from the top center to the middle of the right side, broken at the bottom, Pergamum.

OGIS 338; *IGRR* IV 289. For the will of Attalus III cf. Livy, *Per.* 58–9; Strabo 13.4.2; Velleius Paterculus 2.4.1; Plutarch, *Tiberius Gracchus* 14; Pliny, *Nat. Hist.* 33.148; Appian, *Mithridatic Wars* 62; Justin 36.45.

Broughton, *Asia* 505–11; Magie, *RRAM* I 147–50 and II 1035, n. 5; F. Carrata Thomes, *La rivolta di Aristonico e le origini della provincia romana d'Asia* (Turin 1968) 35–41; Hansen, *Attalids*[2] 151–9; Hopp, *Untersuchungen* 121–38; C. Delplace, *Athenaeum* N.S. 56 (1978) 21–8.

In the priesthood of Menestra[tos] (son) of Apollodoros | on the nineteenth of the month Eumeneios,[1] it was decreed by the | People on the motion of the strategoi: since King Attalus | Philometor and Euergetes
5 [passed away] from me‖n and left our *city* free, | having included in it the territory which he judged to be *civic territory*,[2] | and (since) his will must be ratified by the Romans, and (since) it is [necessa|ry] for the common safety that the below lis|ted[3] peoples share in the citizenship
10 because of the whole-hearted good‖will that they exhibited toward the People (of Pergamum), – with good luck, let it be decree|d by the People to give citizenship to the *follow|ing*: those registered in the lists of resident | aliens and of the soldiers living in the ci|ty and its territory, and
15 likewise the Macedonians and My[sians] ‖ and those who are registered in the fort and [the] | old [city] as colonists, and the Masdyenoi[4] and [--] | and the police and the other [free | men][5] living or owning property [in
20 the city] | or the territory, and likewise (their) wives and children. ‖ To the (class of) resident aliens (etc.)[6]

When King Attalus III died in 133 BC, naming the Romans as heirs to his kingdom and granting the city of Pergamum the status of a free city – all subject, of course, to confirmation by Rome – a pretender to the throne called Aristonicus began a revolt that lasted three years and was brought to an end by the combined forces of Rome, Greek cities, and the kings of Pontos, Bithynia and Cappadocia. His appeal to classes such as slaves, serfs, some royal soldiers, and non-Greeks was so great that the Pergamenes, in order to forestall further defection to his cause, passed the present decree granting citizenship to large numbers of the inhabitants who had not possessed it, with the hope that the action would win their loyalty to the city.

1 No precise equivalent in the Julian calendar is possible.
2 Greek cities regularly controlled the adjacent countryside with its smaller communities for some distance out from the city limits proper. P. Foucart, *Mémoires de l'Académie des Inscriptions et Belles-Lettres* 37 (1904) 300, has suggested the phrase 'cities and' for 'civic territory', thus: 'having included in it both *cities and* a territory which he determined'.

3 Hansen translates the phrase as 'subordinate classes', and Delplace as 'les peuples soumis'.
4 The Macedonians, Mysians and Masdyenians were colonists or settlers within Pergamene borders. The soldiers previously mentioned were mercenaries of the king.
5 Restoration by L. Robert, *Villes d'Asie Mineure*² (Paris 1962) 55, n. 6. Prott and Kolbe in *Athen. Mitt.* 27 (1902) 109, n. 1, suggest '[auxiliary troops]'.
6 The text continues on for seventeen more lines, listing the classes of individuals who are to be transferred to the class of resident aliens and depriving certain others who had left the city or who may hereafter leave it of their civic rights. The stone breaks off at a point where further provisions are being made about the granting of citizenship.

40   Decree of the senate concerning the death of King Attalus III. Probably 133 BC,[1] late in the year.

White marble broken on all sides, beautifully engraved, Pergamum.

OGIS 435; *IGRR* IV 301; **RDGE* 11.

Magie, *RRAM* I 33 and II 1033–4, n. 1; *RDGE* 59–62; T. Drew-Bear, *Historia* 21 (1972) 75–87; C. Delplace, *Athenaeum* N.S. 56 (1978) 28–33.

[---] | *vv* [Decree of the] senate. *vv* | [G]aius Popillius, son of Gaius, *prae-*
5   *tor,*[2] sought [the sen|ate's] advice [on the --] *day* before the [-- of ‖ --]em-
ber.[3] Whereas [he] spoke [about] affairs [in Perga|m(?)]um, (about) what injunctions [there will be for the] | praetors who go [to A]sia, (in order that) [whatever in Asia] do|wn to the death of Attalus by the [kings (in Asia)] | had been amended (or) given (or) taken away (or whatever)
10   penalties had been imposed, [that these acts should be] ‖ *legally binding*, the senate [passed a decree] about this [as follows: concerning | what G]aius Popillius, son of Gaius, praetor, [said,] | about this matter [it has been decreed as follows:] | whatever King Attalus and the *rest of the* [ki|ngs] had amended (or whatever) penalties they had imposed (or whatever)
15   [they had taken away (or) given,] ‖ whatever of these things were done down to one [day before | Att]alus died, that *these things* [are to be legally binding,] and [the prae|tors] who go to Asia [-|-][4] but should allow these things to remain legally binding, [all of them just as the *sen|vv ate*] has decided. *vv*[5]

When it was learned in Rome that King Attalus III of Pergamum had died and in his will had left his kingdom to Rome, the praetor – in the absence of the consuls – convened the senate and placed before it the matter of the will and various actions of the kings in Asia. The senate discussed the matter and then passed the present decree, in which all the past actions of the kings 'down to one [day before Att]alus died' were to be legally binding. That included, of course, the will itself. Cf. above, no. 39.

1 E. Badian, *JRS* 70 (1980) 202, suggests 132 BC.
2 This senator is otherwise unknown: Broughton, *MRR* I 496, n. 1.

3 The date must fall between August 16 and December 12, excluding the period September 14 through October 15.
4 *RDGE*: '[are not to disturb his tes|tament (?)]'. Dittenberger (in *OGIS*): '[are not to
   disturb anything to no good purpose]'.
5 On the next line is found the heading of a new document: 'Letter of [Pu]blius Ser-
   vil[ius --]'.

41   The cult of the goddess Roma in Miletus. About 130 BC.
Two fragments (A–B) of a marble anta, Miletus.

Milet I 7, no. 203 (+ photograph); Sokolowski, **Lois* no. 49.

Mellor, *Worship* 53–4 and 135; Fayer, C., *Il culto della Roma* (Pescara 1976) 47–8.

(A) With good luck. The man who buys the | priesthood of the People of
5   the Ro|mans and of Roma | shall immediately register a priest with ‖ the
treasurers and kings,[1] a ma|n not younger than twenty years. | The man
who has been registered shall serve as priest for three years | and eight
10   months, beginning with | the month Metageitnion when ‖ Kratinos is
stephanephoros,[2] or another man | he shall present to serve as priest in
pla|ce of himself for the same period of time, after he has been consecrated
to Zeus | Telesiourgos,[3] and he shall receive from the | treasurer, each
15   year in the month ‖ of Taureon on its first day, dra|chmas (to the number
of) sixty, and he shall sacrifice to the Peo|ple of the Romans and to Roma
on the | first day of the month Taureon | a fully grown victim. And on the
20   eleventh day ‖ of the same month there shall be a sacrifice, as they en|ter
into office, by the gymnasi|archs, along with the ephebes, of a full|y grown
victim to the People of the Romans and | to Roma, and likewise, as they
25   leave their office, ‖ the gymnasiarchs shall make a sacrifice, along with
their ephebes who have finished training, of a [fu|lly grown victim,] and
each of these groups (gymnasiarchs and ephebes) shall give to [the |
priest] the prescribed perquisites.

(B) [--] and for the other athletic contests assigning to ea|ch the appro-
priate prizes, also setting up for de|dication (other) prizes, weapons of war
5   no | less than three, having also the inscription ‖ on them of (the name of)
the contest, and displaying the ut|most zeal regarding them, in accor|-
dance with the piety of our People toward the divine | and with our grati-
tude toward the Ro[man]s. | And there shall take part, [together with] the
10   priest, ‖ in organizing these (contests) and administering them, the gym-
nasiarchs of the | young men, in order that the contests might be as splen|-
did as possible; on the eighth day of the third decade | of the same month[4]
he shall put on the contest, in the chil|dren's palaestra, of the torch-race
15   and the oth‖er athletic games, providing a fitting | organization for the

games; co-operating in effort | and taking part, together with him, in orga-
nizing this contest and administering it, | shall be the supervisors of the
children's education. And there shall take place the de|dication of the
20 arms, set up (as prizes) in the || Roman Games,[5] for the present in the
gymnasi|um of the young men, but when is completed the temple | of
Roma, (the dedication shall take place) in the Romaion.[6] And there shall
be a sacrifice by the pr|iest, on the first day of each month, to the Peo|ple of
25 the Romans and to Roma of a victim fu|lly grown, (the priest) having
received from the prytany | treasurer ten drachmas for the sacrifice; | on
the seventh day of the month Thargelion there shall be a sacrif|ice by the
aisymnetes,[7] to the People of the Roma|ns and to Roma, of a fully grown
30 ox || and he shall give to the priest the prescribed perquisi|tes, and he shall
sacrifice in Mctageitnion, | on the twelfth day, in the same way and give
the perquisites. | But if the god buys the office of aisym|netes,[8] there shall
35 be a sacrifice by the prosetairoi[9] || of the god, on each of these two days, of a
fu|lly grown victim, and they shall give the perquisites to the priest | as
prescribed. In the month of Boie|[d]romion on the eighteenth day there
40 shall be a sac|rifice, by the fifty archons,[10] of a [fully || grown] pig, and
they shall give the perquisites [to the | priest --]

The worship of the goddess Roma did not begin in Italy – she was not worshipped in Rome
until the reign of Hadrian – but in the Greek world, the evidence placing the start in
Smyrna in 195 BC. Roma was the personification of the Roman state, but still a goddess
with a cult that included priests, temples, epithets, games, etc. The Greeks of the Hellenistic world, accustomed to use religious forms to express political feelings, saw the cult
of Roma as a political and not a religious observance. As Roman domination spread over
the east in the second century, the cult of Roma spread from city to city, eventually dis-
placing the Hellenistic ruler cult. Through Roma the Greek cities expressed their acceptance of Rome as a political force in their world and formally placed themselves under
Roman protection. For a list and discussion of the evidence for such cities see Mellor,
Worship 27–110.

1 Rehm (in *Milet*) believes that Miletus had a college of treasurers with a 'king' as president.
2 Kratinos seems to have been stephanephoros, i.e. the eponymous magistrate, *c.* 130
BC. Rehm observed that such a date is in agreement with the letter-forms and spellings
of the inscription. After the priesthood had been established about this time, each
priest after the first one would serve a full four years.
3 'Who Brings to Completion'. See K. Latte, *Philologus* 85 (1930) 225–8.
4 It is not known whether the count of the third decade in the Milesian month was
forward or backward: Samuel, *Chronology* 115.
5 For these 'Romaia' see Mellor, *Worship* 165–80.
6 The sacred enclosure which included a temple of Roma.
7 A Milesian post involving religious duties, usually burdensome.
8 Sometimes no citizen bought the post of aisymnetes; it was then bought on behalf of the
god and the expenses paid out of the temple funds.
9 These were tribal representatives.
10 The college of fifty archons was an oligarchic institution introduced by the Romans.

42   Manius Aquillius constructs the first Roman roads in Asia. 129–126 BC.

Milestones.

A: *CIL* III 7183; *ILS* 27; *IGRR* IV 264; *ILLRP 455. Milestone between modern Dikili on the coast and Pergamum. **B**: *CIL* III 14202.4; *ILS* 5814; *IGRR* IV 1659; *ILLRP 456. Milestone at Tire in southern Lydia. **C**: *CIL III 7177; *IGRR* IV 880. Milestone at Tacina on the border of Phrygia and Pisidia.

Magie, *RRAM* I 157–8; II 1048–9, nn. 39–40; D. H. French, *ANRW* 7.2.706–7.

A. *ILLRP* 455

(Latin) Manius Aquillius, son of Manius, | consul (129 BC). | (Mile)
5   131.[1] | (Greek) [Mani]us [A]quill[i]us, (son) of Manius, || consul of the Romans. | *vv* (Mile) 131. *vv*

B. *ILLRP* 456

(Latin) Manius Aquilli[us, son of Manius, consul.] | (Greek) [M]aniu[s] Aquilli[us,] son of [Ma]nius, [consul of the Romans.] | (Latin) [L.] Aquillius, [son of Manius,] Floru[s,[2] quaestor,] | restored (the road). *vv* (Mile)
5   [2]4. || (Greek) [Lu]cius Aqui<ll>ius, son of [M]anius, | grandson of [M]anius, [Flo]rus, quaestor, restored (the road). *vv* (Mile) 24.

C. *CIL* III 7177

(Latin) [Manius Aquillius, son of Manius,] | *vv* consul. *vv* | *vv* (Mile) 223.[3]
vv | (Greek) [Man]ius Aquillius, (son) of Manius, || *consul of the Romans.* | *vv*
(Mile) 223. *vv*

1   The Roman miles were regularly numbered from a provincial capital, which in Asia was the city of Ephesus.
2   Nothing else is known about this senator, except that he appears to be a descendant, perhaps the grandson, of the consul of 129 BC.
3   This is clear evidence of the extent of Asia toward the south-east from the very beginning of the province.

43   The city of Bargylia supplies troops in the war against Aristonicus. 129 BC.

Extract from a handwritten copy of a lost stone, Bargylia in Karia.

Holleaux, *Études II 179–86.

Robert, *Ét. Anat.* 463–5; Magie, *RRAM* II 1039, n. 14; Hansen, *Attalids*[2] 158.

(A, lines 13–21)[1] And when Manius | Aquillius, the commander of the
Romans (consul 129 BC), had marched (on campaign) into (that part of)
15   Mysia ‖ called Ab[b]aitis toward the interior[2] and had left behind | in *our*
territory Gnaeus Domitius, (son) of Gnaeus, with command pro praetore,[3]
and when (Aquillius) had detached some of his *for|ces* and the majority of
the allied troops (and assigned them) to Domitius, and when [he had led |
away the soldiers] who had been sent by our People in accordance with
(the) alliance[4] | [and] had won *many* great successes, and when the fortres-
20   s‖es that seemed to be difficult to capture had [all] been captured by him
by force of arms, [(Poseidonios) rejoiced | at the events][5] and performed
the appropriate sacrifices to the gods [--]

(B, lines 21–42) [-- Quintus Caepio --, having re|ceived] as a successor the
[command entrusted] to [G]naeus (Domitius), demanded [a large
number] | of *soldiers* in order to take this [force] (with him) into the field;
[and when there was an outbreak a|gain (?)] of the war, it happened that
25   [our] city was [heavily] burdened [by our] ‖ having continuously engaged
in military operations in the field [together with the Romans in accord-
ance with] the order of Quintus Caepio,[6] | and even more of [our soldiers]
had been sent off by the People and [enrolled] | for the war, [and difficult
times (?)] *followed* (in our city); [and therefore | the People,] thinking that
Poseidonios was [equal to the task (?),] called upon him to [re|new (?)]
our former requests concerning the soldiers, [in order that there might
30   not] be *im‖plemented* upon the city this [order (for troops)] from Quintus
Caepio [in accor|dance with the policy of Mani]us Aquillius the com-
mander; [when called upon,] (Poseidonios) ea|gerly complied and,
setting out from the city with his [fellow envoys,] me|t with [G]naeus
(Domitius),[7] and, having spoken [appropriately (?)] on behalf of our
35   city, | he brought back the soldiers and relieved [the city of the] ‖ expense
[for them;] in return for these services the People *confirmed* the [previous]
decree [and praised hi|m,] one and all, and performed sacrifices to the
gods and ordered [the stephanephoros (?)] | to summon the envoys to the
temple for the sacrifices; [and in this(?)] | (Poseidonios) was thought
worthy of [great] *fa|vor*[8] by Gnaeus, so that [he was enrolled] among the
friends (of Gnaeus), and | the sons of Gnaeus, writing [on behalf] of him
40   (their father) to [our city, made it clear] that they had en‖rolled Poseidonios also as a paternal [friend of theirs (?); in return for these things the
People] *accepted* [this policy of theirs] | *in a hospitable way* (?) and enrolled on
[the stele of proxenoi and benefactors (?) | both Gnaeus and his sons (?)
---]

1   This document is part of a long decree passed by the city of Bargylia in south-western
    Karia to honor Poseidonios, one of its most prominent citizens. Neither its beginning

nor its ending is known, the extant central portion being concerned with the reasons for honoring Poseidonios. A handwritten copy of the lost stone shows that three fragments of it had been found (A–C). Lines 1–13 of A inform us of Poseidonios' repair of the Town Hall of Bargylia, the regulations he introduced about the appointment of stephane-phoroi and about the honors and sacrifices to be made to Apollo; lines 13–21 of A and 21–42 of B (translated here) are concerned with the Roman military actions against the rebel forces of Aristonicus and the aid given by Poseidonios to his city in those difficult times. The third fragment (C, lines 42–57) informs us that Poseidonios had gone to Rhodes to settle a dispute between the Rhodians and the city of Stratonikeia in Karia. Many of the restorations made in this inscription, especially in B, are highly conjectural, although the general sense has been made reasonably clear. The most speculative of these restorations are queried in the present translation.

2 The reference is to the war against Aristonicus, who began a revolt against the estab-lishment of Roman domination in 133 BC after Rome had accepted the will of Attalus III of Pergamum, bequeathing his possessions to the Roman People (cf. above, nos. 39–40). In 131 BC a Roman army was sent to Asia, but it was not until 129, under Manius Aquillius, that the last of the major rebel forces were subdued in the district of Abbaitis between Mysia and Phrygia. See Magie, *RRAM* I 147–54.

3 Gnaeus Domitius, son of Gnaeus, Ahenobarbus (consul 122) was a legate under Aquillius: Broughton, *MRR* I 505. For the command pro praetore see the Glossary, *s.v.* Promagistrate.

4 Holleaux argues that this ought to mean 'as an auxiliary force' because of the absence of the definite article in the Greek. But idiomatic omission of the article is not unknown, and, thus, 'in accordance with (the) alliance' is possible.

5 For Poseidonios see n. 1.

6 Probably Quintus Servilius, son of Gnaeus, Caepio, the later consul of 106 BC: Broughton, *MRR* I 505.

7 He is no longer in the vicinity of Bargylia, since Caepio had replaced him there, but he is apparently Caepio's superior officer.

8 An alternative for '*favor*' is '*reception*'. Thus: '[a fine] re|*ception*'.

44   Decree of Pergamum to celebrate its friendship and alliance with Rome. Probably about 129 BC.

Marble stele cut in half vertically, broken at top and bottom, damaged on both sides, found *c.* 5 km above the mouth of the Caicus River.

*SIG*³ 694; *IGRR* IV 1692; Sokolowski, *Lois* no. 15, pp. 44–5 (lines 31–61 only).

[--] (son) of Theon (?) [--|--] of this [--|--] | *vv* [It was decreed by the
5 Boule] *and the People,*¹ ‖ [-- (son) of Nik]anor, | [-- (son)] of Dion[y]sios, |
[-- (son) of Ar]chias, | [-- (son) of Me]nandros, | [P]olystr[atos (son) of
10 M]enon, ‖ the strategoi, made the motion: | [since] our *People*, from the
beginning [preserving] | their *goodwill and* friendship [with] the [R]omans,
| have given [many] other [exhibitions] | of their friendly policy in the
15 [most pressing crises,] ‖ and likewise in *the war against* | [Ar]istonikos have
applied themselves with [all] | enthusiasm and have *undergone* great

dangers | both on land and [on] sea, [in consequence of which] | the
20 People [of the Rom]ans came to know the *friendly poli‖cy* of our [People,]
accepted | our goodwill and *have received* our *People* | into *friendship* and *alli-
ance;* | and since there has been dedicated *in* [Rome] in the temple of |
25 Jupiter Capitolinus a bronze plaque [and] ‖ on it has been set out the
decree *passed* | by the [senate] about the alli|ance, and likewise the
[treaty,] and (since) it is proper | that [these] also be engraved *among us* on
30 two plaques | of bronze and *placed* in the temple ‖ of Demeter and *in* [the]
Hall of the Boule | *beside* the statue of [Democ]racy,[2] it is *decreed* | by [the]
Boule and the *People* that the auditors of public accounts | [through] the
proper men *let out a contract* for the | preparation [of the] plaques and for
35 their ‖ *engraving,* [and] likewise for two stelai of mar|ble upon which, when
[the] plaques have been comple|ted, [they] are to be affixed. And there is
to be engraved | [on the] stelai a verbatim copy | [of this] decree, and
40 [when] the erection ‖ of them has been completed, [the] stephanephoros
and | [the] priests and [priestesses] and the magistrates | [on behalf of the]
citizens [are to open] the temples | [of the] *gods,* offer frankincense, and
45 *pray:* | 'For the good luck [and] *safety* of ‖ our People [and of the Rom]ans
and of the Asso|ciation of the *Artists* of Dionysos Our Leader | (we pray
that) for all time there will remain with us the | friendship and *alliance* with
the [Ro]mans.' And there is to be pre|sented a sacrifice, as fine as pos-
50 sible, to ‖ [De]meter and Kor[e, the] presiding | goddesses of our city, and
likewise to | [Rom]a[3] and to all the other [gods] and goddesses. | And the
day is to be *holy,* and there is to be an exemption | for the children from
55 their [studies,] and for the house‖hold slaves from their work. And there is
to be celebrated, after the | *sacrifice,* a parade for the *boys* and young men, |
under the direction of the supervisor of the boys' education | and the
gymnasiarch. The expense incurred | *for* the preparation [of the] plaques
60 and for the other things ‖ is to be paid by Eukles and Di[onysi]os, the trea-
surers, | [from the] *revenues* which they control.

1 Since the stone was found almost midway between Pitane and Elaea, on the right bank
of the Caicus River, and some thirteen miles downstream from Pergamum, the identity
of the city passing the decree was long in doubt, but, as Robert pointed out (*Ét. Anat.* 49
n. 3), the mention of the Dionysiac Artists in line 46 could only indicate Pergamum,
seat of their Association.
2 The representation of Democracy in art in the Greek world dates back at least to the
fourth century BC in Athens (cf. Pausanias 1.3.2). For a relief on a stele showing a seated
Demos being crowned by a standing Demokratia see the inscription published by B. D.
Meritt in *Hesperia* 21 (1952) 355–9, with Pls. LXXXIX–XC, the text now in *SEG* XII
87 (of 337/6 BC). Cf. A. E. Raubitschek, *Akte des IV. Internationalen Kongresses für Griechische
und Lateinische Epigraphik* (Vienna 1964) 332–7 (parallel publication in *Hesperia* 31
(1962) 238–43 with Pl. LXXXVI).
3 See above, nos. 18 and 41.

45   Decree of the senate concerning Pergamene land. Probably 129 BC.

Stone blocks from Adramyttium (copy A) and Smyrna (copy B).[1]

IGRR IV 262 (copy A); A. Passerini, *Athenaeum* 15 (1937) 252ff. (copy B); R. K. Sherk, *GRBS* 7 (1966) 361–9 (B+A, photograph of B); *RDGE* 12 (B+A). Cf. Appian, *Bell. Civ.* 5.4ff.

Passerini, *loc. cit.*; Magie, *RRAM* II 1055–6, n. 25; G. Tibiletti, *JRS* 47 (1957) 136–8; L. R. Taylor, *The Voting Districts of the Roman Republic* (Rome 1960) 170–5; *RDGE* pp. 63–73; H. B. Mattingly, *AJP* 93 (1972) 412–23; Badian, *Publicans* 60 and 132.

(Copy B) [--] and concerning [--|--, concerning this] matter [it was decreed as follows: the Per|gamene envoys as men fine and good] and as friends [from a People fine | and good, our friends and allies,] that they are to be addressed (in that way, and) that goodwill, [friendship and
5   alliance ‖ are to be renewed. Concerning the land which] is *under* controversy and [concerning --, | -- that concerning these] matters, about which they spoke, [-|-- X^2 --] is to determine what are the boundaries of the Pergamenes, [if it seems best to him, | --] (the land within ?) the boundaries exempted and safeguarded [so that it may not be exploited (? by the publicans ?)[3] | And Manius Aquillius and Gaius Sempro]nius,[4] the
10   consuls (129 BC), between themselves [are to see to it that either ‖ they or --,] the urban *praetor*, [to whomever of them it seems best, in regard to the decision which | --, - X -,] may make about these [matters, (they) are to communicate (that decision) to the senate. | Likewise, (it has been decreed that) the] senate wishes and [considers it just and] | believes that [it is in keeping with the best interest of our] *Republic* that, [as it may seem best to --, | -- X --,] about these matters, [our magistrates who on Asia
15   ‖ impose the revenues or][5] *let out the contracts* for the revenues of Asia [are to see to it that, as may | seem best to them and in keeping with the best interest] *of the Republic* and their own good faith, [thus these matters are to be handled (?), | and that Manius Aq]uillius,[6] the consul, *v* if it seems best to him, is to order that Th[--[7] | are to be provided with quarters, furnishings] and gifts according to official procedure, {if it seems best to him},[8] [the quaestor (being ordered) to let out contracts (for these things) | and send them off,] as may seem best to him and in keeping with the best
20   interest of the *Republic* ‖ [and his own good faith.] Decreed. *v* Decision concerning the land. *v* Record Book *v* 2 *v* page[9] [--.] (Copy B+A) [On the | third day before the Kalends] of July (June 28) in the Comitium. With his Advisory Board [-- | -- X --] concerning the land which is under controversy between the *publicans* [and the Per|gamenes gave his decision (?).]

Present [on the] Advisory Board were: Quintus Caecilius, (son) of Quintus, (of the tribe) [Aniensis; Gaius | --ius, (son) of Gaius, (of the tribe) Me]nenia; (etc.)[10]

After the annexation of Asia by Rome in accordance with the bequest of King Attalus III of Pergamum in 133 BC, a controversy arose between Pergamum and the publicans about the location of the boundaries of the Pergamene territory (cf. line 7 of the present document). Pergamum sent envoys to Rome and they explained their side of the argument to the senate. The publicans explained theirs. The senate replied by passing the present decree. The date is crucial, for in the decree one sees that the publicans are already at work collecting the taxes. See nn. 4 and 6.

1   Copy A was found near Adramyttium over 100 years ago and it contains mutilated parts only of the present text, from line 21 to 37. Thus, in that area, both copies can be used to reconstruct the text more fully. Copy B, from Smyrna, first published in 1934, is engraved on a huge building block that may once have been the anta block of a public building in the agora. Its inscribed surface is badly damaged on all sides, but it is the fuller of the two copies. It is the text presented in *RDGE*, with its restorations in lines 21–37 reproducing the extant remains of copy A.
2   The name of a Roman magistrate once stood in this space.
3   The text of this entire line is badly preserved. Passerini felt that the Greek of 'exempted and safeguarded' translated a Roman legal term (*exceptum cavitumve*) and, as a parallel, he cited the *lex Agraria* (*CIL* I 2.585; *FIRA* I 8, line 6).
4   Mattingly does not believe that the consuls whose names once stood in this line were the consuls in office. He restores the names of Gnaeus Domitius Ahenobarbus and Gaius Fannius, the consuls of 122 BC.
5   For this important phrase, restored here, see the decree of the senate concerning Asclepiades (*RDGE* 22, line 23), and *OGIS* 441, line 108. See Passerini, *op. cit.* 261.
6   Mattingly believes that he is the younger Manius Aquillius, the consul of 101 BC and thus, like Magie, dates the document to the year 101 BC.
7   One expects here the names of the Pergamene envoys.
8   Passerini thought that this phrase was engraved in error, the eye of the engraver seeing the same phrase in the previous line.
9   The Greek word translated here as 'page' means literally 'wax'. The records in the Roman archives were originally in the form of wax tablets bound or strung together in series, each tablet evidently being given a number. See *RDGE* pp. 9–10.
10   The list of names continues on to line 47, the total number of names being 55. For the list see *RDGE* pp. 69–70 and the discussion in Taylor, *loc. cit.* Lines 48–53 contain the decision of the Roman magistrate about the controversy. It is hopelessly mutilated.

46   Samos honors Gnaeus Domitius Ahenobarbus. 129–126 BC.

Statue base, letters of the last half of the second or first half of the first century, Samos.

IGRR IV 968; Robert, *Opera* I 559.

The People of Samos (dedicate this statue of) Gnaeus Domitius, | son of the Gnaeus who was given by the | (Roman) senate as patron[1] to our

5   People, | for his (interest) in the temple of ‖ *vv* Artemis *vv* | Tauropolos,
because of his excellence | toward them, to Hera. | Philotechnos (son) of
Heroides made (the statue).

1   The father may have been one of those ten commissioners who had been sent out by
the Roman senate to assist Paullus in organizing Macedonia in 167 BC: Broughton,
MRR I 435. He may have been assigned to speak on behalf of the Samians in some
(legal?) difficulty. His son, the present Gnaeus, served under Manius Aquillius in Asia:
Broughton, *MRR* I 505.

47   Roman negotiatores (businessmen) in the Greek East. Second and first centuries.

A: *OGIS* 135; Durrbach, **Choix* 105; *I. Délos* 1526. Soon after 127 BC. Marble base, Delos.
B: Durrbach, **Choix* 95; *I. Délos* 1645. Soon after 126/5 BC. Pedestal of a statue, Delos.
C: *CIL* I² 845; Ch. Picard, *BCH* 34 (1910) 540 (+ photograph); *I. Délos* 1999; **ILLRP*
343. Base on which rested the statue of a naked man bending down on his knees, letters of
early first century, Delos. (Latin and Greek). **D**: Durrbach, **Choix* 138; *I. Délos* 1725. Early
first century. Rectangular base, Delos. **E**: J. Bingen, **BCH* 78 (1954) 84; *AE* 1954, 31;
ILLRP 370. Limestone plaque, letters and spelling of the first half of the first century,
Aigion in Achaia. (Latin). **F**: *CIL* I² 746; *ILS* 867; **ILLRP* 374. 68 BC (?). Statue base,
Argos. (Latin). **G**: *CIL* III 455 = 7160; *ILS* 891; **ILLRP* 433. 34 BC (?). Statue base,
Mytilene. (Latin). **H**: *OGIS* 354; **IG* II² 3426. Middle of the first century. From a copy of
the original, Athens.

A. Durrbach, *Choix* 105, Delos

The Roman shipowners | and merchants who in the cap|ture of Alexan-
5   dria were treated kindly by King | Ptolemaios Euergetes, god,[1] ‖ (dedicate
this statue of) Lochos (son) of Kallimedes, kinsman[2] of Ki|ng Ptolemaios
and Queen Cleopatra, because of his excellence and | kindness toward
them, | to Apollo.

B. Durrbach, *Choix* 95, Delos

(This statue of) Theophrasto[s (son) of Herak]l[eitos of (the deme)
Achar]nai, past governor of Delos,[3] | who improved the market-square
and with the breakwater enclosed the harbor, | has been dedicated by the
Athenian colonists on Delos and by the merchants and shipowners | of
5   the Romans and the other foreigners residing here, ‖ because of his
excellence and noble qualities and kindness toward them.

C. *ILLRP* 343, Delos

(Latin) [Gaius Marius, son of Gaius (?),][4] *legate* (?), (is honored by) the
Italians who were in Alexandria, | because of his [excellence] and

kindness. | (Greek) Agasias (son) of Menophilos, | of Ephesos,[5] made (the statue).

D. Durrbach, *Choix* 138, Delos

The merchants and those who work (on) the (market?) square[6] | (dedicate this statue of) Maraius Gerillanus, son of Maraius, Roman, | banker at
5 Delos, | because of his *noble conduct* toward them, ‖ to [A]pollo, Artemis (and) Leto. | Agasias (son) of [Menophilos, of Ephes]os, made it.

E. *BCH* 78 (1954) 84, Aigion in Achaia

(Latin) *vv* The Italians *vv* | who do business at Argos | (honor) P. Rutilius, son of Publius, Nudus, | q(uaestor).[7]

F. *ILLRP* 374, Argos

(Latin) (Set up to) Q. Caecilius, son of Gaius, Metellus,[8] | imperator, (by) the Italians | who do business at Argos.

G. *ILLRP* 433, Mytilene

(Latin) The Roman citizens who | do business at Mytilene | (dedicate this statue) to M. Titius, son of Lucius, proconsul, | prefect of the fleet,
5 ‖ consul designate,[9] their patron, to honor him.

H. *IG* II² 3426, Athens

King Ariobarzanes Philopator, son of King | Ariobarzanes Philoromaios and of Queen | Athenais Philostorgos,[10] (is honored by) those who had
5 been commissioned | by him for the construction of the Odeion, ‖ Gaius and Marcus Stallius, sons of Gaius,[11] and | Menalippos, as their benefactor.

Roman and Italian negotiatores had spread rapidly over the Greek East during the second century in the wake of Roman wars and the expanded Roman political activity. They were not small traders, but big businessmen ready and able to invest their capital for profits in banking or other financial enterprises: cf. below, no. 74, on the brothers Cloatii. They came largely from leading southern Italian families and many of them were familiar with Greeks even before coming to the East, because of their activities in southern Italy. In Greek they were called 'Romaioi', whether Romans or Italians, but in Latin they were *Romani* or *Italici*. See Hatzfeld, *Trafiquants, passim*; Broughton, *Asia* 543–54; Rostovtzeff, *SEHHW* II 762–4; 788–90; 817–19; 958–60; Nicolet, *L'ordre* 357ff.

1 Ptolemaios VIII Euergetes II, nicknamed Physkon, after being driven out of Egypt, put down a revolt in Alexandria in 127 BC and regained his throne. See P. M. Fraser, *Ptolemaic Alexandria* (Oxford 1972) I 119–22.

2 This Lochos is known to have been governor (strategos) of the Thebaid in Egypt in 127 BC: Bengtson, *Strategie* III 101 and 227. The word 'kinsman' applied to him was a court title and shows that he enjoyed the highest rank in the court of the king: Fraser, *op. cit.* I 102–3. On the negotiatores in Egypt see Fraser, *op. cit.* I 155ff.

3 Theophrastos was governor of Delos in 126/5 BC: P. Roussel, *Délos, colonie athénienne* (Paris 1916) 105–6. In 167/6 BC the island of Delos was named a free port by Rome and placed under the supervision of Athens. Athenian colonists moved there, and each year a new epimeletes (governor) arrived from Athens. Roussel, *op. cit.* 97–125, discusses these governors and gives a list of them in chronological order. Cf. Laidlaw, *Delos* 176ff.

4 It was T. Mommsen (*Ephemeris Epigraphica* 5 p. 600) who first suggested that the name of Gaius Marius might be restored in this inscription. Picard later (*BCH* 56 (1932) 498–530) took up the suggestion, placed on the base a statue found nearby which represented a wounded warrior and believed it referred to the victory of Marius over the Cimbri. The base and the statue could have been erected when Marius was in the East in 99–97 BC (Plutarch, *Marius* 31.2). For another view, however, and some objections see the discussion by Fraser, *op. cit.* II 271, n. 192.

5 The sculptor Agasias seems to have flourished *c.* 100 BC.

6 The interpretation is controversial. Roussel in *BCH* 34 (1910) 110ff. believes that the phrase 'those who work the square' means 'makers of Herms' because of the squared posts on which they were placed and because several other references apply the phrase to these Herms. See Durrbach, *Choix* 226.

7 Rutilius Nudus, commander of the fleet at Chalcedon in the spring of 73 BC, was put in charge of the Roman land forces on the Bosporos and was defeated by the advancing army of Mithridates. See Magie, *RRAM* I 325 and II 1206, n. 8.

8 Quintus Caecilius Metellus (consul 69 BC) was apparently honored because of his victory over Crete and the pirates while he was proconsul in Crete. For this he was later given the title 'Creticus'.

9 In 39 BC the consuls for the next eight years were designated in advance (Dio 48.35.1). M. Titius was proconsul (governor) of Asia in 34 BC and consul in 31 BC.

10 Ariobarzanes II Philopator became king of Cappadocia after the abdication of his father in 63 or 62 BC and was killed in 52 or 51 BC.

11 These two brothers must have been Roman architects or contractors or bankers. The Odeion was that of Perikles, destroyed by Sulla's soldiers in 86 BC: Vitruvius 5.9.1.

48   Lete honors M. Annius, quaestor. 119 BC.

Stele from Lete in Macedonia.

*SIG³ 700.

F. Papazoglou in *ANRW* 2.7.1 (1979) 312.

Year 29,[1] Panemos 20. *vv* | The politarchai[2] of Lete, after a prelim|inary decree was passed by the members of the Boule, made the motion: Marcus Annius, son of Pub|lius, a noble and good man, having been sent out as
5   quaestor b‖y the People of the Romans to duty in Macedonia, | in the entire earlier period had continued | to put above everything else things

advantageous in common to all Mace|donians and to exhibit the greatest
forethought for | things of importance for our city in particular, of zeal and
10   ar‖dor omitting nothing, and in the present crisis, when the Gal‖lic nation
assembled and made an expedition against the lands to|ward Argos[3] with
a huge army, against which there mar|ched out Sextus Pompeius the
praetor[4] and faced them in battle formation with | his own troops, and
15   (when), as it happened, he died in the fighting, ‖ and for this reason his
troops were disheartened, (against the Gauls) mar|ched Marcus the
quaestor with the men attached to him. He rou|ted the opposing forces,
recovered the fallen (dead)[5] and kill‖ed *many* of the enemy; he seized many
horses and arms, | and with concern for the safety of the guards in the for-
20   ward zones ‖ had them sent to the encampment; and after many | days
even more Gallic horsemen assembled, and | with them came Tipas, chief
of the Maedi,[6] with a *horde* | even *larger*, but (Annius) repulsed the oncom-
ing assault of the barbarians; and oth|er soldiers, to fulfill treaty obliga-
25   tions by the Macedonians, he decided not ‖ to send for, because he did
not wish to afflict the cities with soldiers' pay, | preferring the mass (of the
population) to remain at their work; he went on the attack wi|th the
soldiers he had in the encampment, and, avoiding no danger or *suffer|ing*,
deployed his troops and defeated the enemy in com|bat, with the provi-
30   dence of the gods, and many of them in hand-to-hand fighting ‖ he killed,
but he also took some alive, and many of their horses and arms he sei|zed,
and in such a way he held events under control in good spirits | and has
tried to hand over the province to his successors after keeping safe all | those
in the territory, at peace and in the most splendid | settled condition,
35   doing these things in a way worthy of his country and his ‖ ancestors and
worthy of his own fame and bravery and also of the | position of responsi-
bility with which he had been entrusted. Therefore, it is decreed by the
Boule and *People* of Lete | to praise Marcus Annius, (son) of Publius,
quaestor of the Romans, and to cro|wn him for the sake of his deeds with a
crown of (olive) branch, and to establish for him | an annual equestrian
40   *contest* in the month of Daisios, when for other benefact‖ors the contests
are held; and to choose envoys to tra|vel to him with felicitations from our
city and congratulations | on the health of himself and his army, and to
give him this de|cree and to request him to receive with goodwill our
People's es|teem and to be now and afterwards always the author of some
45   good ‖ for our city; and (it is decreed) to engrave this decree and crown on
a | stone stele, to be placed in the most conspicuous place of the agora,
ca|re to be taken for the engraving of the decree and for the erection of the
ste|le by the politarchai and the treasurer of the city. Confirmed by vote |
in the year 29, Panemos 20. As envoys (the following men) were chosen
50   from among the members of the Boule: ‖ Adaios (son) of Adaios, Lyson
(son) of Philotas, Amyntas (son) of Dies.

1 The twenty-ninth year of the Macedonian era is 120/119 BC, since that era began in
148 BC: M. N. Tod, *BSA* 23 (1918–19) 206–17; *ibid.* 24 (1919–21) 54–67; *Studies
Presented to David Moore Robinson* (St Louis 1953) II 382–97.
2 The politarchai were the executive magistrates of the city.
3 This Argos is in Macedonia, near the Epirote border. The 'Gallic nation' are the bar-
barian Scordisci, for whom see G. Alföldy in *AAntHung* 12 (1964) 107–27, and F.
Papazoglou, *The Central Balkan Tribes in Pre-Roman Times* (Amsterdam 1978) 271–345,
and no. 52 below.
4 Sextus Pompeius may have been praetor in 120 and propraetor in 119: Broughton, *MRR*
I 526 and 527, n. 3.
5 The Greek word means, collectively, all the dead who fell previously under Sextus Pompeius, or, possibly, the corpse of Pompeius himself. In either case Pompeius is included.
6 The Maedi were a Thracian tribe living in the middle Strymon River valley.

49   Decree of the senate concerning Phrygia. Either 119 (?) or 116 BC.
Stone broken on all sides, lettering of the later Roman period,[1] Arızlı
(north-east of Apameia) in Phrygia.

OGIS 436; *IGRR* IV 752; **RDGE* 13, lines 6–10. Cf. Appian, *Mithridatic Wars* 2.11–12;
3.15; 8.56–7.

Magie, *RRAM* I 168–9; *RDGE* pp. 74–7; T. Drew-Bear, *Historia* 21 (1972) 79–87; *idem,
Nouvelles inscriptions de Phrygie* (Zutphen 1978) no. 1, pp. 1–5 (+ photograph); B. C.
McGing, *GRBS* 21 (1980) 35–42.

6   [Concerning the things which Quintus Fabius, son of --, Maximus (?)
   and G]aius Licinius, son of Publius, | [Geta, consuls (?),[2] said,] concern-
   ing this matter | [it was decreed as follows: Whatever King Mithridate]s
   wrote or gave to anybody or (whatever) con|cessions he made, [that these
   things should remain legally binding as] he granted them to his last day,
10 || [and concerning the rest of the matters, that they should be decided by
   the (ten?)] legates after they have crossed over to Asia[3] | [---]

Among the territorial possessions of Mithridates V, king of Pontus, was Greater Phrygia.
When he was assassinated in 120 BC, the Roman senate, apparently after some delay,
declared that Phrygia was to be annexed and made a part of the province of Asia. Since the
present decree of the senate was found within the district of Phrygia and since its provisions partly resemble those found in the decree of the senate concerning the death of King
Attalus III of Pergamum (see above, no. 40), it has been assumed that it concerned the
dispositions made by the senate about Phrygia after the death of Mithridates V. Hence, his
name has been restored in line 8.

1 The letters appear to belong to the Roman imperial period, long after the events mentioned in the decree had taken place. This indicates that the inscription had been re-
engraved at the later age for some reason unknown to us.
2 Gaius Licinius Geta may not have been consul when he spoke in support of the
motion before the senate. If he was consul at the time, the date would be 116 BC and
the name of his colleague, Q. Fabius Maximus, would also have appeared in line 6.
But if Licinius Geta presided over the meeting when he was praetor (not later than

119 BC), then the name of Q. Fabius Maximus must be removed from line 6 and the
word 'praetor' must replace 'consuls (?)'.

3 It was the custom of the Roman senate to send out a group of commissioners, usually
ten in number from among the members of the senate, to settle affairs at the conclusion
of a war (cf. above, no. 5, line 69) or to lay down regulations and make arrangements for
the annexation of new provincial land (cf. the commissioners sent to Greece after the
destruction of Corinth, no. 35).

50   Letter of Q. Fabius Maximus to the city of Dyme. 115 BC?

Marble slab broken in four pieces, a small molding at the top, very carefully inscribed letters, Dyme in Achaia.

SIG[3] 684; *RDGE* 43.

RDGE pp. 246–8; Larsen, *States* 499; Schwertfeger, *Bund* 66ff.; Bernhardt, *Historia* 62ff.

v In the priesthood of Leon, when the sec|*v*retary of the Synedrion[1] was
Stratokles. | Quintus Fabius, (son) of Quintus, Maximus, proconsul of the
Romans[2] to the Dymai|an magistrates and synedroi and city, greetings.
5   When the ‖ synedroi in company with Kyllanios explained to me about the
com|mission of crimes among you, I mean about the burn|ing and dest-
ruction of the archives and the public records, | the leader of the whole
breach of the peace having been Sosos (son) of Tauromenes, who | also
10   wrote up laws contrary to the constitution given to the ‖ [A]chaians by the
Romans,[3] concerning these matters point by point we had a discuss|ion in
[P]atrai in the *presence* of my Advisory Board. Now since the perpe|trators
of these actions appeared to me for the worst *conditions* | and turmoil to
have laid a [foundation for all Greeks,] not on|ly (a foundation) for *lack of*
15   *good relations* with each other and for a *cancellation of* [private] *debts*, ‖ but
also (a foundation) alien to the freedom given in common to the Greeks |
and alien to our policy, and when there was a pre|sentation by his accusers
of true proof that So|sos had been the leader of the actions and had writ-
20   t|en the laws for the destruction of the constitution given (to Dyme), ‖ I
judged him to be guilty and sentenced him to death, and likewise | [Phor]-
miskos (son) of Echesthenes, one of the demiourgoi[4] who collaborated
with | [those who] burned the archives and the public records, since he
also | [himself] confessed. But Timotheos (son) of Nikias, who along with
Sosos | [had been] the writer of the laws, since he appeared to have been
25   less guilty of crime, [I or‖dered] to go to Rome, after making him swear
that he would be there on the first day of the nin|th [month,] and I
informed the peregrine prae|tor [of my decision] that *there should be no return*
home for him, unless he [---]

1 The 'Council' of Dyme is meant, its members being called the 'synedroi'. See Accame, *Dominio* 142–3.
2 It is generally believed (thus, e.g., Broughton, *MRR* II 644) that this proconsul (of Macedonia) was probably Q. Fabius Maximus (Eburnus), the consul of 116 BC. However, there are other candidates: see *RDGE* pp. 247–8.
3 This is a reference to the arrangement made by the Romans after the destruction of Corinth in 146 BC: see the extract from Pausanias, above, no. 35. Cf. also no. 37.
4 These were the magistrates at Dyme.

51   Epidauros honors one of its prominent citizens. 112/111 BC.

Limestone base, carefully inscribed letters of the second century, in the Asklepieion of Epidauros.

IG IV^2 1.63.

Schwertfeger, *Bund* 50–1.

Since Archelochos (son) of Aristophantes, being a man noble (and) good, | has led his way of life and has held public office in a good and worthy manner | and, having been appointed envoy to Rom[e] regarding
5   friendship and alli|ance, exercised all enthusiasm and care devot‖edly, and (as a result) friendship and alliance with the Romans were concluded for the cit|y of Epidauros, and (since) of the decree passed and hand|ed over to the (Roman) treasury and of the alliance put up | on a bronze plaque on the Capitolium – of (both) these (documents) copies | have been delivered by him to our public archives – it has been decreed by the
10 synedroi[1] and the People ‖ to praise Archelochos (son) of Aristophantes for his noble quality and for | the documents contributed by him, and to reward him | with a bronze statue and to erect his statue in the most conspicuous | place of the temple of Asklepios. The treasurer appointed |
15 for the thirty-fourth year[2] shall pay the cost of the s‖tatue and its base, and the epimeletes[3] shall let out the contract (for their construction). He (Archelochos) and his | descendants shall have immunity[4] and exemption from taxation, and they shall be summoned *v* | to front-row seats at the [festivals which] the city celebrates. And the engraving | of this decree on the base (of the statue) shall be seen to by [the secretary]. *v*

1 The members of the Council at Epidauros: Accame, *Dominio* 142–3. Cf. above, no. 50, lines 1–5 with n. 1.
2 The thirty-fourth year of the Achaian era is 112/11 BC. It was formerly believed that the era used in Epidauros was the Macedonian, but that has been disproved by W. B. Dinsmoor, *The Archons of Athens in the Hellenistic Age* (Cambridge, Mass. 1931) 234ff.
3 The title given to a magistrate at Epidauros. His full duties are otherwise unknown.
4 The extent of this 'immunity' is confined to the city government of Epidauros and probably refers to special local taxes.

52   M. Minucius Rufus honored by Delphi. Between 110 and 106 BC.

Base of an equestrian statue, Delphi. The inscription is in Latin and Greek, the Latin version being the one translated here.

CIL I² 692; *ILS* 8887; **SIG*³ 710C; *ILLRP* 337. Cf. Livy, *Per.* 65; Velleius Paterculus 2.8.3.

H. Last in *CAH* 9.109; F. Papazoglou in *ANRW* 2.7.1 (1979) 314.

(This statue of) Marcus Minucius, son of Quintus, Rufus, | imperator,[1] after the Gauls, | Scordisti, and Bessi | [and the remaining Thracians
5 || were defeated (by him), because of his] merits, [to Apollo] | was *dedicated* by the People of Delphi.[2]

In the second half of the second and early decades of the first century the Gallic people called the Scordisti posed a serious threat to Macedonian stability. From their home at the confluence of the Save and Danube rivers they constantly attacked and harassed the Roman province. For a particularly violent invasion in 119 BC see above, no. 48. In 114 BC the army of C. Porcius Cato, consul of that year with a command in Macedonia, suffered an ignominious defeat. M. Livius Drusus (consul 112 BC) as governor in Macedonia (112–111 BC) campaigned successfully against them. His successor was M. Minucius Rufus (consul 110 BC), whose victories mentioned in the present document did not bring the northern danger to an end. For all known details of these and later incursions by the Scordisti see Papazoglou, *op. cit.* 312ff.

1 Rufus took up the command in Macedonia while still consul in 110 BC and continued to hold it as a promagistrate until 106: Broughton, *MRR* I 543ff.
2 The Greek version (*SIG*³ 710A), although also damaged and worded slightly differently, assures the restoration of the Latin.

53   Decree of the senate and a treaty with Astypalaia. 105 BC.

From an old hand-written copy, the stone having been destroyed in a fire in 1797, Astypalaia.

IG XII 3.173; *IGRR* IV 1028; *RDGE 16 A–B.

Accame, *Dominio* 80–90; *RDGE* pp. 94–9; Mellor, *Worship* 68–9.

A. Decree of the senate

[--] concerning this matter it was decreed as follows: [With | the People of Astypalaia peace, friendship (and) alli|ance] should be renewed; as a fine and good man [from a Peo|ple] fine and good and friendly (the envoy)
5 *should be addressed* || [and] a friendly response should be given [him]. Decreed. And [that Publi|us] Rutilius, consul (105 BC), should see to it that a bronze plaque of [this] alliance [on | the] Capitolium is nailed up *a*|*s*

seems to him to be in keeping with the interest of the Republic | [and]
10   his own [good faith.] Decreed. [And] that [Publius Ruti‖li]us, consul,
should order the quaestor according to official procedure [to give (the
envoy) gifts] | and [that he (the envoy) be allowed] to make a sacrifice
on the Capitolium, if he wishes, [and that according to] | the Rubrian
and Acilian Law(s)[1] [a copy (of this alliance) may be set up in] | a public
[and conspicuous] place (and) exposed [where the majority | of citi-
15   zens] walk by, and that each year [in the (Astypalaian) Assem‖bly] it
may be read aloud. Decreed. In the consulship of Publ[ius Rutili]us,]
son of Publius, and [Gn]aeus Mallius, son of Gnaeus (105 BC), when
the [praetor i|n the] city was Lucius [--]onius, son of Lucius, and [the
peregrine praetor | was --,] son of Publius, [and in Astypalaian] | (time)
reckoning when [Phile]ta<i>ros (son) of [-- was the --, it was decreed
20   ‖ that a plaque of the alliance should be set up, while Rhodokles (son)
of Antimachos[2] was the envoy, | and that a plaque] of this alliance
should be given to the People [of Astypalaia] | according to (the) decree
of the senate. *vv* |

B. The treaty

25   [--- (three lines missing) --|-- between the People | of the Romans and]
the People of Astypalaia there shall be peace and [friendship | and alli-
ance] both on land and on sea [for a|ll time.] There shall be no war. The
30   People [of Astypalaia shall not grant pass‖age to the] enemies and oppo-
nents [of the People of the Romans | through their own land and the land
which the People of Astypalaia control, with pub|lic] sanction, so that
upon the People of the Romans and those under Roman | rule they may
wage war. And in regard to (Rome's) *enemies*, neither [with weapons] | nor
with money nor with ships shall (the Astypalaians) aid them with public
35   sanction (and) in [bad] *faith.* ‖ The People of the Romans, in regard to the
enemies and opponents [--|--] of the People of Astypalaia, [shall not]
through their own land and the land which | [the People of the Romans
control grant them passage] with public sanction (and) in [bad] faith, |
[so that upon the People of] Astypalaia and those under their | rule they
may wage war. And [in regard to (Astypalaia's) enemies,] neither with
40   weapons nor with money nor ‖ with ships shall (the Romans) aid them in
bad faith. And if anyone [takes the initiative] in waging [war] upon the
People of | Astypalaia, the People of the Romans [shall aid the People of
Astypalaia (?). And if | anyone] takes the initiative in waging war upon
[the People of the Romans, the People of Astypalaia shall aid (the
Romans) in accordance with| the] treaty and oaths [made -- between] |
45   the People of the Romans and the People of Astypalaia. ‖ And if anything
they wish with common consent to add to this treaty or | subtract from it
with public sanction, [whoever (?)] so wishes shall have permission.

Whatever they may add | in the treaty or [whatever] they may subtract from the treaty, these things shall be recorded [on] the | treaty outside (the main text).[3] [And they shall set up] one votive offering of the Romans in the Capitoline temple of | Jupiter, and one of the Astypalaians in the temple
50   of Athena and of Asklepios and near ‖ the altar [--] of Roma.[4]

1   For this, whether one law or two, see G. Tibiletti, *Athenaeum* 31 (1953) 7–16.
2   The name of the envoy is known from a third document engraved on the same stone: *RDGE* 16 C.
3   The hand-written copy, full of small errors throughout, is somewhat confused in lines 47–8. What is meant is that amendments must be recorded, but without erasing the original text. Somewhat different is the statement in the treaty with Kibyra (above, no. 25, lines 9–15).
4   On the worship of the goddess Roma see above, no. 18.

54   Marcus Antonius transports his fleet across the Isthmus of Corinth. Poem in elegiac couplets (Latin). Each line contains one verse. 102 or 101 BC.

Limestone block badly damaged at the bottom, letters and spelling of the early first century, Corinth.

A. B. West, *Corinth* VIII 2 (Cambridge, Mass. 1931) pp. 1–4 (+ photograph); *CIL* I² 2662; S. Dow, *HSCP* 60 (1951) 81–91; *ILLRP* 342. Cf. Cicero, *De orat.* 1.38.82; Livy, *Per.* 68.

Magie, *RRAM* II 1161, n. 12; A. N. Sherwin-White, *JRS* 66 (1976) 4–5; J. Wiseman in *ANRW* 2.7, pp. 495–6.

What nobody has attempted or [--,] | learn of this feat, so that we might extol the man's exploits by wide report. | Under the auspices of [[Marcus Antonius]][1] the proconsul a fleet | was transported across the Isthmus and
5   sent over the sea.[2] ‖ He himself set out to go to Side,[3] while Hirrus at Athens, | (with command) pro praetore, halted his fleet because of the time of the year. | These things were done within a few days with a minimum of confusion, | a great deal of planning and [good (?)] safety. | He who is honest praises him. He who is hostile [looks spitefully at his exploit
10   (?)]. ‖ Let men envy him, so long as [they see ---]

1   The grandfather of the triumvir, his name chiseled out (as also on the Capitoline Fasti) apparently when Antony's name was removed from the Fasti and his name condemned in 30 BC. The grandfather (praetor 102, consul 99 BC) received a command against the pirates in Cilicia and continued to hold it as proconsul until 100 BC, when he celebrated a triumph for his successes: Broughton, *MRR* I 568.
2   For similar portage see Thucydides 8.7 and Polybius 4.19.7–10.
3   On the coast of Pamphylia in southern Asia Minor, not far from Cilicia.

55   Piracy law(s)[1] from Delphi and Knidos. 101 or 100 BC.

A: *Fouilles de Delphes* III 4.37 (+ photographs); *FIRA* I[2] 9; M. Hassall, M. Crawford,
J. Reynolds (= H-C-R), **JRS* 64 (1974) 201–7. Three marble blocks (here numbered
A, B, C from top to bottom) once part of the monument honoring L. Aemilius Paullus
(above, no. 25); small letters, often difficult to decipher, Delphi.[2] Cf. G. Colin, *BCH* 48
(1924) 58–96; H. Stuart Jones, *JRS* 16 (1926) 155–73; Magie, *RRAM* I 283–4; F. T.
Hinrichs, *Hermes* 98 (1970) 471–502; H-C-R, *op. cit.* 195–220; J.-L. Ferrary, *Mélanges de
l'École Française de Rome* 89 (1977) 619–60.

B: H-C-R, **op. cit.* 201–7. Three limestone blocks placed side by side, with the inscription
in five columns (here numbered I–V from left to right); letters comparable to those of the
second century, Knidos.[2] Cf. H-C-R, *op. cit.* 195–220; A. W. Lintott, *ZPE* 20 (1976) 65–82;
A. N. Sherwin-White, *JRS* 66 (1976) 5–8; J.-L. Ferrary, *op. cit.* 619–60; G. V. Sumner,
GRBS 19 (1978) 211–25; E. Badian and T. R. Martin, *ZPE* 35 (1979) 153–67.

A. (Delphi B)[3]

[-- or] for the sake of *public* [business[4] -|-- for whom alliance and] friend-
ship exist with the [People of the Romans --|-- in this] law nothing [has
been proposed.[5] In regard to the praetor | or proconsul who over the Asian
province holds control,] that he should any the less hold control also over
5   the [province of L]ykaonia just as [before the ratification of this law || was
the case, (as regards this matter) within this law nothing has been proposed.[6] Letters] by the consul who was (elected) first (?)[7] to the Peoples
[and states, to whom | it might seem best to him, shall be sent out
(announcing) that the People of the Romans have acted energetically
(?)] in order that the citizens of the Romans and the Latin allies from Italy
and whoever [of the nations outside | (Italy) are in the friendship of the
People of the Romans] with safety might be able to sail the seas. And (he
shall write) that Cilicia for these reasons [according to this law | has been
made (by the Romans) a praetorian (?)[8] province; and likewise (he shall
write)] to the king who rules[9] on [the] island of Cyprus, and to the king
[who in Alex]|andria and Egy[pt rules, and to the king who in Cy]rene
10   rules, and to the kings who in Syria rule, [with all of whom || there exist]
friendship and alliance [with the People of the Romans, (to all of whom)
having written, he shall make it clear] also that [it is] just that they see to
it that neither from their kingdom [nor] from their | territory or borders
[any] pirate [sets out, and that no magistrate or commanders whom] they
will appoint should receive [the] pirates under their protection, and that
they should see to it, as much as is [in] *their* power, | that the People of the
Romans [have them as enthusiastic fellow workers for the safety of every-
body.] The letters being sent [to] the kings according to this law to the |
[Rho]dian envoys [--- he shall give. The consul] who is in charge of these
matters shall see to [the] safety [of the|m in accordance with the laws and
with] justice. And if [---][10] shall be established and, if there shall be a

15   need, as they may prefer, before the senate [in that same ‖ manner] he
      shall bring up the matter, and the senate, [just as it may seem best to it
      in accordance with the interest of the Republic] and its own good faith,
      shall deliberate. And whatever concerning this matter the *sen|ate* may
      decree, [every (?)] magistrate or *promagistrate* [shall take thought and see
      to it, in accordance with what seems to be best to him,] that (the decree)
      is implemented. The consul, upon whom it may (devolve?), and who may
      a|sk that he [grant an audience (?)]^{11} to the embassies, [to the envoys
      from the] *People* of Rhodes, whoever of them may be in Rome, he shall
      grant (an audience before the) senate outside [the] | regular order, and
      these [envoys --]^{12} he shall introduce into the senate [outside] the regular
      order, and that a [senate] | decree be passed shall be his concern [at the
      time when they according to this law, whether] it is a [law] or a plebiscite,
20   have been introduced by him. And this, *without penalty* [to himself,] ‖ he
      shall be permitted to do. The *praetor*, [propraetor or proconsul (?), to
      whomever] Asia [has fallen] as his province^{13} [during the consulship] of
      Gaius Marius and Lucius Valerius (Flaccus) (100 BC), | [shall send]
      letters to the Peoples [and states immediately and to] the kings men-
      tioned above, and likewise [to those whom] also the consul according to |
      this law [will ask him] to write, as [may seem to be best to him (?). And
      of this] law he shall send a copy to the cities [and] *states* to which according
      to | this law [it is incumbent upon] him to send [letters, taking care, as far
      as may be] in his power, that whatever letters according to this *law* he
      sends to the addressees | are delivered (to them) according to *this* law;
      [and, following the practices] of each of them to whom according to this
25   law *letters* have been sent, upon a *tablet* of bro‖nze the letters shall be
      engraved, [or, failing that, upon a marble stele or] else upon a whitened
      board, so that in the cities *they may be exposed* visibly [in a temple] or agora,
      (in a place) where, | standing [level with the ground, people who wish to
      do so] will be able to read them. [And in no other way] than this shall he
      (i.e. the governor) write, in order that, [on an equal basis, the kings and
      Peoples] over whom they rule shall do these things. | Whoever according
      to this [law holds the province,] they shall see to it [that things are done in
      this way.] The *praetor*, [propraetor or] *proconsul*, whoever according to this
      | law – whether it is a plebiscite [or a law – or according to a decree of the
      senate] will hold the province [in Ma]cedonia, he shall proceed imme-
      diately [to the Kaine]ik [Chersonese]^{14} which Titus Didius during his
      command | conquered. And the province's [---] shall be (?), and in regard
30   to this province [--] he shall act (?) as may seem to him ‖ to be best, in
      order that they^{15} may collect the public *revenues* [which] are [in that pro-
      vince, --] who will leave the task (of doing so); and he, each ye|ar, no less
      than *sixty* days [-- areas] before the [---, as far as he can,] that they | [with]
      whom to the People [of the Romans --- this] prae|tor [---]

A. (Delphi C)

[--|--] to contribute (?) [-|-- until to R]ome he returns. [The quaes|tor or
proq]uaestor, to whom the Asian or Macedo[nian quaestorship has fal-
5   len, ---] shall care for the public ‖ *monies* and shall levy fines, [---] when he
was in office; and he shall not be *account|able* until [he returns] to Rome
[---. Whatever] *according* to this law it is necessary for him [to d|o,] he shall
do, and no magistrate [or promagistrate shall obstruct him (in such a
way) – in regard to] those matters upon which according to this law | he
must act – that what has been [prescribed does] not [take place.] The
praetor [or proconsul who] has the province of either Asia or Macedonia, |
within the next ten days after he *learns* that [this] law [has been ratified by
10   the People] in the Assembly, shall swear an oath that whatever ‖ (the
People) order him to do in this law, these things he will do and nothing
contrary [to these things] in bad faith. Whatever magistrates | are *now* (in
office), with the exceptions of tribunes and governors,[16] within the [next]
five days [after] the People ratify this law, (and) whoever there|after will
hold a magistracy, with the exception of governors,[16] these within the next
five days after they enter office [shall swear an oath,] whoever of them
are in Rom[e.] | They shall swear by Jupiter and the ancestral gods to do
whatever has been placed on record in this law – {to do} everything – and
to see to it that (everything) is *im|plemented,* and to do nothing contrary to
this law, and to do nothing by reason of which someone else might so act,
15   and not to do anything other than is in this law to make it hap‖pen.[17] No
one shall do anything contrary to this law in bad faith. Whatever any persons must do according to this law they shall do; no one shall act in such a
way that th|is law is invalidated by deception in bad faith; no one shall
act or issue an edict to prevent the implementation of what must be done
according to this law; and | those who must act, who must swear an oath,
shall act and shall swear so that nothing[18] is done less than or otherwise
{otherwise} than has been written in this law; whoever con|trary to this
law commits an act or issues an edict, whatever he fails to do according to
this law or (if he) does not swear the oath according to this law, that he |
should go unpunished shall not be permitted, nor any the less shall it be
possible (for anyone who) wishes to bring him to trial.[19] If anyone does
anything contrary to this law, and if (anyone of) those, who must accord-
20   ing to ‖ this law do <or swear> anything, does not do it or does not swear,
and if anyone acts so that what is in this law is not done (?),[20] or in any
other way acts contrary to what in this *la|w* has been written, acting or
issuing an edict or breaking the law in bad faith, he <shall be fined>
200,000 sesterces on each count which is ille|gal; and if anyone does not
act – contrary to what has been written in this law – and if anyone does act
other than what has been recorded in this law,[21] to the People this | is the

amount he shall be obligated to give. And this money anyone who is free-born in this state, against (any of) those from whom according to this la|w it is permitted to claim the money and whom it is permitted to bring into court, shall institute proceedings and bring (him) into court and enter his name (for trial) before (the magistrate) in charge of such matters. No
25   magistrate or ‖ promagistrate shall act (in such a way) that he is not brought into court, nor shall he prevent this money from being made the object of legal proceedings and being sued for, nor the court from being set up, nor | the money from being handed over. Whoever does anything contrary to these (actions) or obstructs them or issues an edict (against them), he shall be fined on each count just as if | he had acted contrary to this law, or as if he was required to do something according to this law and did not do it; and he shall be fined in the same way a|s has been described in the other instances. Whatever money according to this law is sued for, if this money, when it has been sued for, whoever has been sued for it, is not [paid,] the *sa|me* praetor to whom the action about this matter was brought at the beginning shall assign a [judge or a] court (with instruc-tions) that as much (money) as [seems right to him,] by whoever was
30   sued for it [according to th‖is] law, [shall be paid without evasion (?)] to the People (of the Romans). And he [---]

B. (Knidos, col. II)[22]

5   [--] *People* of the Roma|[ns --|--|--] outside, ‖ gave back [--|--] to act with-out bad faith, [and the] ci|tizens of the Ro[m]ans and [the] *allies* of the Lat[in] na|me and [likewise] of the nations those | which are in the friend-
10   ship of the People of the Romans ‖ in order that with *safety* they may be able to sail | and obtain justice. *v* |

The consuls[23] in office, in regard to soldiers who by | law or vote (of the
15   plebs) to the prae|tor [or] propraetor or proconsul ‖ in control of the pro-vince of M[ace]donia | are to be returned to this (governor) and | handed over, (these consuls) who are under an obligation to do this (or) to see to this, or | will be under such an obligation, these consuls in regard to these |
20   soldiers, to the Macedonian ‖ province they shall not send (them) back, | and for their dispatch and handing over | they shall not provide, and for them, without | (legal) personal liability, it shall be lawful to do this.
25   Where|as also the same (?) consuls before the sen‖ate by the law or vote (of the plebs) | are or will be obligated to introduce a motion for these | sol-diers who are in Macedonia | to be given as much grain as the senate | con-
30   siders just that a contract be let for, in order that a con‖tract may be let for this (purpose), the consuls before the senate | shall not introduce such a motion, nor for such a contract (col. III) [shall they provide (?) -- -- (*c.* 60 lines are lost) --|-- concerning a] state (?), a king and nations a decree[24] | [--] and to each according to the decision [-|-] and nobody in regard to

5   these things con|trary to what is in the law which Marcus *Porcius* || Cato,
     praetor,[25] passed on the third day before | the *Feralia* (?)[26], outside the
     province shall dra|w up (soldiers) in battle formation, nor shall he [--,]
     nor shall he mar|ch from the province for the purpose of giving assistance
     (?) knowingly in bad | faith; and no magistrate or promagistrate [shall --]
10 || outside the province in which province he a|ccording to this law is obli-
     gated to be or will be so obligated; | and, except as a result of a decree of
     the senate, he shall not g|o on march and shall not march forth (his troops)
     except for the sake of through passage | or public business, and the men of
15   hi||s (entourage) he shall prevent, <without>[27] bad faith, (from doing
     these things). |
         Whatever[23] peoples and nations, when this la|w is ratified by the People
     (of the Romans), to a king or kings or Peo|ples – with whom friendship
     and alliance with the Peo|ple of the Romans exist – contribute taxes or
20   revenues || or troops, (as regards them) within this | law nothing has been
     proposed.[28] *v* |
         In regard to the praetor[23] or proconsul who over the Asian pro|vince
     holds control, that he should any the less also over Ly|kaonia hold control,
25   and that any the less his || province (should also be) Lykaonia just as
     before the | ratification of this law was the case, (as regards this matter)
     within | this law nothing has been proposed.[29] *v* |
         Letters by the consul[23] who was (elected) first (?)[30] | to the Peoples and
30   states, to whom || it might seem best to him, shall be sent out (announcing)
     that the Peo|ple of the Romans [have acted energetically (?)][31] <in order
     that> the | citizens of the Romans and the La|tin allies and whoever of the
     nations outside (Italy) are in | the friendship of the People of the Romans
35   with sa||fety might be able to sail the seas. *v* (And he shall write) that Cili|cia
     for this reason according to this la|w has been made by them a praetorian
     (?)[8] province; | and likewise (he shall write) to the king who in Cypr[us]
40   ho|lds control,[32] and to the king who in Alexandri||a and in Egypt rules,
     and to the kin|g who over Cyrene rules and to the kin||[g--] *vv*
         (Col. IV) (*c.* 60 lines lost) | [---|---|--] according to his law [--|--] they
5   may hold, in order that this law may thus be im||plemented [--] they shall
     see to it.[33] *vv* | The praetor, *propraetor* (or)[34] proconsul who | according to
     [this] law or plebiscite or (according to a) senate *de*|*cree* holds [Macedo-
     ni]a as his province or will ho|ld it, [immediately to the] Kaineik Cher-
10   sonese, which Ti||tu[s Didius] captured by force of arms, he shall *pro*|*ceed*.
     And he who shall have as his province[35] (the) Kai|n[eik] Chersonese, |
     this province together | with Macedonia he shall govern and bring it
15   about, | as may seem best to him, th||at the public revenues in that | terri-
     tory according to law[36] are collec|ted by whoever, in regard to these public
     reve|nues, shall have the task of collecting them; and he each | year shall
20   be in those areas for no less a period || – before another (governor) succeeds

him – than sixty days; | and he shall see to it, as far as he may be ab|le
to do so, that those, who with the People | of the Romans have friendship
and alliance, that | they are not driven out of their borders and that no-
25   body to them may be an im‖pediment and that they may not be unjustly
treated. And {in order that} this praetor or proconsul, who over the
Macedo|nian province holds control, before leaving the pro|vince, accord-
ing to the decree of the senate | passed during his (magistracy ?),[37] shall
30   set[38] the boundaries of the Kaine[i]k Chersonese, ‖ just as seems to him
be|st, as quickly as possible. *vv* |
   If[23] this praetor to whom the Asian (or) Macedonian | province has
fallen resigns from his magistracy or resigns[39] | by order of [--,] he shall
35   have power in all re‖spects, to attend to (**wrongdoing, i.e.**) **to punish, to**
administer justice, | to make decisions, to assign arbitrators (or) foreign
judges;[40] over sureties, proper|ties, [-,] (and) manumissions in the same
way | he shall (have) jurisdiction[41] as in his magistracy it was permitt|ed
40   this proconsul until he ‖ returns to [R]ome. *v* |
   If[23] the quaestor or proquaestor, to whom the Asian (or) Maced[o]|nian
quaestorship falls, resigns from his magistracy | or resigns (?), equally for the
monies which are *pu|blic* [--]
   (Col. V)[42]

1   After the defeat of Antiochus III at Magnesia (189 BC) and the removal of his control
    over Asia Minor west of the Taurus Mountains, much of Cilicia, especially Cilicia
    Tracheia, became a base for pirates. Protected by the mountains of the interior from
    a northern assault, they operated almost freely in the eastern Mediterranean. The
    Roman government did nothing to oppose them. Toward the end of the second cen-
    tury there was a general expansion of this piracy and the Romans finally took action.
    The first indication of this action in our sources is found in the mission of Marcus
    Antonius (above, no. 54). But the pirate menace continued. The present law(s),
    translated here, illustrate the seriousness of the menace, but despite their far-ranging
    provisions it was not until the campaigns of Pompey in 67 BC that the pirates were
    effectively brought under control. See Ormerod, *Piracy* 186–247; Magie, *RRAM* I
    281ff.; Sherwin-White, *op. cit.* 2ff.
2   When the new text from Knidos was discovered, it was thought by H-C-R that it was
    'in date and content closely related to (perhaps identical with) the text found at
    Delphi'. Therefore, they published the Delphi text, with revision, along with the new
    Knidian text. The two texts exhibit remarkable similarities in many ways, and the
    differences between them were explained by H-C-R and others by assuming that
    two separate translations from Latin to Greek had been made (perhaps at different
    times, as suggested by Sumner), each independently of the other. The precise
    relationship, however, of the one to the other is still a matter of controversy. A new
    and better reading of the Knidian text by Joyce Reynolds is expected, but mean-
    while she has kindly communicated to me some of these new readings, for which I am
    most grateful. Where these have been used in the present translation a reference is
    added in the notes to 'J.R.'.
3   Delphi A has been omitted, since only a few connected words are extant, such as:
    '[K]oinon', 'of the People [a decision (?)]', '[P]amphylia and Ly[kaonia?]'. '[K]oinon'

also has the more general meaning 'common', but if it has the meaning here of 'League', then all of Block A may be a letter of introduction to the Piracy Law.'

4 Alternative meaning: 'for the sake of the *Republic*'.

5 From this point in the Delphian text to line 9 restorations may be made by comparison with the Knidian text, col. III 21–41.

6 I.e. the governor of Asia was to retain Lycaonia as part of his province, as before.

7 For a discussion of this phrase see the collection of evidence by Ferrary, *op. cit.* 648ff., and cf. below no. 102, line 138 with n. 16. Colin translates: 'the consul who opened the year', while H-C-R have 'the senior Consul'.

8 Or: 'a general's sphere of command'. The status of Cilicia at this period is still controversial. Was it a regularly organized and administered province, or merely a field command?

9 In the Knidian text (col. III, line 39) the verb is different: 'to the king who in Cyprus holds control'.

10 H-C-R do not claim to understand this sentence and they give a translation of what they think is the sense: '[? If ambassadors about this matter] are presented and it is necessary (to?) as they ?choose he is to [?bring the matter before the senate likewise] and the senate is to deliberate [as it thinks best in the public interest and according to] its conscience.'

11 The intent of this section is not clear. H-C-R translate with hesitation: 'The consul to whom (the relatio) falls, whoever [?asks] that [?he reply] to the embassies', etc. Colin, *op. cit.* p. 86, with a different restoration, has: 'Que le consul à qui incombera le soin de (communiquer) aux ambassades (étrangères) [les décisions du Sénat].'

12 Colin: '[envoys, offering no excuse for delay,]'.

13 Provinces were assigned to qualified senators by lot at a meeting of the senate.

14 For the people called Caeni see Pliny, *Nat.Hist.* 4.40 and 47; Ptolemy, *Geography* 3.11.6; Livy 38.40.7. They lived in Thrace, and the Caenian Peninsula seems to be the one leading down to the Bosporos. T.Didius, consul in 98 BC, was praetor in an unknown year, but the latest possible date would be 101 BC: Broughton, *MRR* I 571. See parallel Knidian text, col. IV, 4ff.

15 Cf. the Knidian text, col. IV, lines 6ff.

16 The Greek eparchoi means 'governors' or 'prefects'. In line 12 the reference is to future governors (or prefects).

17 The sense intended appears to be that the magistrates shall not act in any way other than to make happen what the law intends.

18 The text here is very disturbed, but again the intent is clear enough: to make sure that no circumvention of the law shall be allowed.

19 The text is again very disturbed at this point.

20 H-C-R translate: 'if anyone diminishes the effect of this law'. The Greek expresses the idea in a very clumsy fashion.

21 I.e., anyone failing to act is just as liable to a fine as one who acts contrary to this law.

22 Col. I is here omitted, since its lower half may not have been inscribed, and only a few letters of the upper half can be made out.

23 The engraver has started this word in the margin to the left of the rest of the text, to indicate a new paragraph.

24 For lines 1–10 I have used the new readings by J.R.

25 Sumner, *op. cit.* 220, is convinced he is the son of M. Porcius Cato, the consul of 118 BC (cf. Broughton, *MRR* I 527), but H-C-R merely list the possibilities of identification, p. 210.

26 The original reading by H-C-R was 'three days before the Nones of February', i.e. February 3. *Feralia*, the new reading by Reynolds communicated to Badian by letter, was a festival of the dead that took place on February 21.

27 The Greek translator here has committed an error. Literally his phrase would mean
   'knowingly without bad faith'. Other errors connected with the translation of the
   Latin terms are to be seen in Delphi C 10 and 15–16. See Badian, *op. cit.* 161–7.
28 Thus, the rights of friends and allies of Rome over their own subjects were not affected
   by this law.
29 Cf. Delphi B 4–5 with n. 6.
30 Cf. Delphi B 5 with n. 7.
31 The text here is difficult. I follow Martin, *op. cit.* 160.
32 See Delphi B 8 (with n. 9), where the verb 'rules' is used in place of 'holds control'.
33 New reading by J.R.
34 The stone has 'and'.
35 Here it appears to be a case of instructions to future governors. Cf. lines 18–19; the
   phrase 'each year' is significant.
36 Since the word 'this' is omitted before 'law', the possibility exists that the reference is to
   some other law which spelled out regulations about the collection of public revenues.
   Another possibility is that the reference is to the future regulations to be made about
   the revenues.
37 As suggested by Martin, 157–8.
38 As suggested by Martin, 153–6. J.R. is now inclined to think it is right.
39 The Greek translator has repeated the verb 'resigns', the second time in the middle
   voice to indicate an action upon the subject, i.e. upon 'him'. The translator apparently
   made a very literal translation of the Latin first and then repeated the verb in the
   middle voice for the sake of his Greek readers. See Ferrary, *op. cit.* 634–5.
40 This is the meaning of the Greek phrase, but the original Latin for 'foreign judges' at
   this point is unknown.
41 H-C-R suggest that the phrase 'not accountable' should appear here, basing it on the
   appearance of that phrase in Delphi C 5–6. The proconsul, thus, would not be held
   accountable until he returns to Rome.
42 The first nineteen lines of col. V are so badly obscured on the stone that no connected
   sense can be obtained, and about one third of the right side of the column's remaining
   twenty-seven lines are missing. The subject matter is the trial procedure to be followed
   in cases concerned with violation of the law, i.e. with empaneling of a jury by the magistrate from a list of 300 names, and the guidelines to be followed in the hearing of the
   case.

56   The rise of Mithridates and his war against the Romans. About 100–87 BC.

Extract from Memnon.

Memnon (*FGrHist* 434 F 22.1–10). Cf. Appian, *Mithridatic Wars* 10–30.

Magie, *RRAM* I 199–220; E. Badian, *AJAH* 1 (1976) 105–28; W. V. Harris, *War and Imperialism in Republican Rome* (Oxford 1979) 273; E. Olshausen in *ANRW* 1.1.806–15.

Afterwards, the grievous war of Mithridates, king of Pontus, against the
Romans broke out, its apparent cause being the seizure of Cappadocia.
By means of deception and oaths that led to agreement Mithridates
gained control of this (land), after arresting his nephew Arathes[1] and kill-

ing him with his own hand. Arathes was the son born to Ariarathes by the sister of Mithridates. (2) Mithridates was most murderous right from childhood. Not long after coming to the throne as a thirteen-year-old he put his mother, who had been left by his father as joint ruler of the kingdom with him, in prison and destroyed her by the use of force and the passage of time; and he (also) killed his brother. (3) He also subjugated by war the kings around the Phasis as far as the regions beyond the Caucasus, increased his kingdom and became puffed up with great arrogance. (4) For these reasons the Romans became all the more suspicious of his intent and decreed that he should restore to the Scythian kings their ancestral rule. He obeyed their orders only to a certain extent, but associated himself in an alliance with the Parthians and Medes and the Armenian Tigranes and the Scythian[2] kings and the Iberian (king). (5) He added (to these activities) other causes for war. For when the senate in Rome set up Nikomedes, son of Nikomedes and Nysa, as king of Bithynia, Mithridates set up [Sokrates][3] surnamed The Good in opposition to Nikomedes. However, the decision of the Romans prevailed despite Mithridates. (6) Later, when Sulla and Marius were firing up civil discord over the Roman government, Mithridates gave his general Archelaos forty thousand infantry and ten thousand cavalry and ordered him to campaign against the Bithynians. Archelaos engaged the enemy and was victorious in battle, and Nikomedes fled with a few men. When Mithridates learned this and when his allies had joined him, he set out from the plain at Amaseia and marched through Paphlagonia at the head of an army of one hundred and fifty thousand. (7) Manius (Aquillius), when the allies of Nikomedes had scattered at the mere mention of Mithridates, with a few Romans took up a position against Menophanes,[4] the general of Mithridates. Manius was routed, took to flight and lost all his troops. (8) Mithridates with impunity broke into Bithynia and seized the cities and the countryside without a fight. Some of the other cities throughout Asia were captured, others came over to the side of the king, and a complete reversal of everything took place, the Rhodians alone showing regard for their friendship with the Romans. For this reason Mithridates both on land and sea made war upon them, and the Rhodians had such an advantage that Mithridates himself came close to being captured in a naval battle. (9) After this, when Mithridates learned that the Romans, who were scattered among the cities, stood in the way of his plans, he wrote to all (the cities) to murder the Romans among them on a single day. Many obeyed and brought about such a massacre that eighty thousand on one and the same day met death by the sword. (10) When Eretria and Chalkis and all Euboia joined the forces of Mithridates, and other cities came over to his side, and the Lakedaimonians were defeated, the Romans sent out Sulla with a considerable army.

1 The manuscripts have 'Arathes', but it must be a corruption of 'Ariarathes', if Justin 38.1 is right.
2 The manuscripts have 'Scythian', which might be right. Modern editors have changed it to 'Phrygian' on the basis of Appian, *Mithridatic Wars* 13. But the same passage in Appian shows that Mithridates had Scythians as his allies.
3 The manuscripts here have 'Nikomedes', but Appian, *Mithridatic Wars* 10, records that Mithridates had sent 'Sokrates surnamed The Good' against Nikomedes, adding that Sokrates was the brother of Nikomedes.
4 Jacoby (in *FGrHist*) thinks the name 'Menophanes' is a mistake or a corruption, but there is a general of that name who conducted a campaign for Mithridates. See Magie, *RRAM* II 1101, n. 27.

57   Letter of Q. Mucius Scaevola to Ephesus. 98/97 or 94/93 BC.
Fragments of bluish-white marble, Pergamum.

OGIS 437, lines 25–55; *IGRR* IV 297, lines 32–61; **RDGE* 47, lines 26–57.

Magie, *RRAM* II 1064; *RDGE* pp. 256–9.

Quintus Mu[cius,] *son* [of Publius,] Scaevo[la,] | proconsul of the Romans,[1] to the [Ephesi]an Boule [and] | People, greetings. Since, *having been judged* (to be in a state of) friendship[2] (with the Romans), | the Peoples and [Tribes[3] have decreed] the establishment of thea‖trical *and* [gymnas-
30   tic] *games* coming every *four*|*th*[4] year [and have planned --] concerning the |
35   [--|--] | LACUNA [--‖-- Sardia]ns, a *disturbance* (?) [-|--] hatred and dis-agreement [--] | more conspicuous and more glorious, [in order that those] | Peoples who have *withdrawn* from them[5] might *with* [all good | will]
40   come together to a meeting, *we have sent* [-‖--]sos (son) of Phylotimos, an Athenian, [--] | a *fine* and good man and [wor|thy of our greatest] trust, to [yo|ur] People and to the (People of the) Sardians, to call up|on them to
45   give us their hands (as pledges) toward [an agreement.] ‖ Since [both] Peoples have reached agreement | in regard to their demands and have sent their en|voys, yours being Hikesion (son) of Artemidoros, [Posei]|donios (son) of Poseidonios (grandson) of Dionysios, A[risto]‖geiton (son) of
50   Patron, Artemidoros (son) of Art[emido]‖ros, Menekrates (son) of Mene[kra]t[es] (grandson) of Ar[temi]|doros, Apollod[oros (son) of Her-mo]kr[ates, Hermip]|pos (son) of Menoites, and those of the Sa[rdians being the] *gener*|*als* Menekrat[es (son) of Diodoros, Phoinix (son) of
55   Phoinix,] Archelaos (son) of Theo[philos --‖--] | to act as arbitrator[6] [--] | to collect (?) [---]

Preceding this letter to the Ephesians on the stone is an identical letter, very badly mutila-ted, to the Sardians. At the top of the stone is a heading: '[Treaty between Sardia]ns and [Ephesia]ns'. The present letter to the Ephesians is followed by the text of the treaty itself.

1 The date of his governorship of Asia is disputed, but it is either 98/97 or 94/93 BC. For a
   summary of the controversy see B. A. Marshall, *Athenaeum* N.S. 54 (1976) 117–30.
2 There was an actual register of such friends of the Roman People recorded in Rome
   called the 'formula amicorum (et sociorum)'. See Badian, *FC* 12, who believes that
   both friends and allies were part of a single list.
3 For the full phrase see the next document, no. 58.
4 The Greek ('pentaeteric') means 'every fifth year', i.e. including the first and the fifth in
   the count.
5 The word 'them' seems to refer to the games.
6 Pergamum was the arbitrating state.

58   The Organization of Peoples and Tribes in Asia. Early decades of the first century (?) BC.

Marble block, Poimanenum in the province of Asia.

OGIS 438; *IGRR* IV 188.

J. A. R. Munro, *JHS* 17 (1897) 276–7; Magie, *RRAM* I 173–4, II, 1064–5, n. 48; T. Drew-
Bear, *BCH* 96 (1972) 460ff.

The Peoples and the Tribes in Asia[1] | and those judged individually (to be)
in (a state of) | friendship with the Romans[2] and those others cho|sen to par-
5   ticipate in the Soteria *vv* and || Moukieia[3] *vv* have honored *vv* | Herostratos
(son) of Dorkalion,[4] because he has been a good man | and has excelled in
trust and excellence | and justice and piety and on behalf of their common |
10   advantage has applied the greatest || zeal and has achieved many great
things | for the assembly's common affai|rs of matters involving fame and
eternal memory, | [because of] his excellence and goodwill | *toward* them-
selves. *vv*

1 This phrase is found in several other documents of the first century, showing that some
   sort of an organization of Greeks in Asia had arisen as early as Scaevola's letter to the
   Sardians and Ephesians (above, no. 57). It speaks here with one voice to honor a man
   who had served it well. This early organization seems to have developed into the larger
   League or Commonalty later called the Koinon of Greeks in Asia. Cf. below, no. 65.
2 See the preceding document, no. 57, n. 2.
3 Pseudo-Asconius (on Cicero, *II Verr.* 2.21.51): 'He (Mucius Scaevola) governed Asia
   so well that a festival was established by the Greeks in his honor, called the Mucia.' For
   other such cults of Roman magistrates in the East see Bowersock, *Augustus*, 150–1. In the
   present inscription the joining of 'Soteria and Moukieia' seems to indicate that the new
   festival was simply added to the older Soteria, which were usually elaborate city or
   national festivals celebrated at regular intervals to commemorate events of great
   importance.
4 Munro suggested that the Herostratos of this text was identical with the Herostratos
   mentioned by Plutarch, *Brutus* 24, who was sent by Brutus after the death of Caesar into
   Macedonia to win support for him. His suggestion was rejected by Dittenberger (in
   OGIS) who dated the present inscription to the period between Scaevola's governorship
   of Asia (see above, no. 57) and the beginning of the First Mithridatic War.

59   Exemption of sacred territory from the revenue contracts of the publicans. 89–87 BC.
Round stone base, Ilium.

OGIS 440; *IGRR* IV 194; *ILS* 8770; **I. Ilion* 71.

I. Ilion pp. 172–3.

The People | (dedicate this statue of) Lucius Iulius, | son of Lucius, Caesar, | who became censor (89 BC),[1] || restored the sacred | territory to Athena | Ilias and removed | it from the revenue contract.[2]

1 L. Iulius Caesar belonged to the same clan (*gens*) as the later dictator, but no close relationship existed. The reason for interest in Ilium by the Iulii was the connection between that city and the legendary origin of their ancestors from Aeneas. See above, no. 5, n. 3.
2 For a similar case of encroachment by the publicans on sacred territory see below, no. 70.

59a   Plarasa-Aphrodisias[1] decides to aid the Romans against Mithridates. 88 BC.
Two blocks (A–B), both damaged, from a Doric entablature with architrave and frieze, originally part of the theater, with inscription[2] on one metope and the frieze, Aphrodisias.

Reynolds, **Aphrodisias*, Document 2 (photograph Pl. II 1–2). Cf. Livy, *Per.* 78; Appian, *Mithridatic Wars* 17 and 20.

Reynolds 11–16; Magie, *RRAM* I 211–14.

A. (In a metope) Decreed by the Bou|le and the People, | [<moved by the magistrates (?)>] | and by Pereitas | [(son) of <--,>] |[3] (grandson) of
5 Antiochos, sec||retary of the People, | and by Attalos (son) of Me|nandros the | territory's gen|v eral v.

B. (On the frieze below Col. 1) Since Quintus Oppius, son of Quintus, proconsul of the Ro[mans][4] has sent (a letter) that a siege is being conducted against Laodikeia and | himself, and the People have decided to help him in full strength and also to have their paroikoi[5] and slaves march out with them, and they have chosen in | the ekklesia also a man to lead them; *v* and (since) it is necessary to send out envoys as well to explain to the pro|consul the policy which our People have toward the Romans, who are saviors and benefactors, and, in case the governor
5 gives any other or||der to our city, to arrange that the order is made clear and carried out – it has been decreed by the People to choose as envoys

men from among those who have been honor|ed (by our city)[6] and who
hold our trust and who are favorably inclined toward the Romans, men
who will go to Quintus Oppius the pro|consul and explain to him the
policy which our People has toward him and toward all Romans, and
who will show that not | *vv* only in full strength have we decided to fight
on his side but also that as the man in charge of the force to engage in this
fighting we have chosen *v* | (Col. 2) Artemidoros the stephanephoros, a

10   man from among those who have been honored (by our city) ‖ and who
hold our trust, a man who is of outstanding bravery in armed combat; |
and they will explain to him that our entire People, with our wives | and
children and our entire means of livelihood, are ready to take our
chances on behalf of | Quintus and the Roman cause, and that without
the | *v* Roman leadership we do not even choose to live.

1 Plarasa was a neighboring city whose political life had merged with that of Aphrodisias by a process called *sympoliteia*.
2 The text which we have is a re-engraving of the second century AD.
3 Two lines appear to have been accidentally omitted by the engraver: one line after line 2
and another after line 3.
4 Q. Oppius (praetor in 89 BC (?)) was proconsul in 88 BC when he took the field against
Mithridates and was besieged in the city of Laodikeia, where he was captured: Broughton, *MRR* II 42.
5 The 'paroikoi' may have been resident aliens or (more likely) the native peoples without
citizenship who farmed the city's land.
6 The phrase 'men who have been honored' means those men who had held public office
in the city.

59b   Letter of Q. Oppius to Plarasa-Aphrodisias after the war against Mithridates. Very late in 85 or early in 84 BC.

A damaged pilaster and its capital with an inscription (A–B),[1] originally
terminating the south wall of the north parodos of the theater, Aphrodisias.

Reynolds, *Aphrodisias*, Document 3 (photograph, Pl. I 2–3).

Reynolds 16–20.

A. (On the molding of one face of the pilaster's capital) Quintus Oppius,
Quintus' | son, proconsul of the Romans, | praetor (?),[2] to Plarasa-
5 | Aphrodisias' magistrates, ‖ Boule and People, greetings. |
B. (On the pilaster) [-- | --] Antipat[ros | (son) of -]stos, Pereitas (son) of
10   Apollo|[nio]s, Artemidoros (son) of Myon, ‖ Dionysios (son) of Menis,
Teimou|kles (son) of Zenon, envoys | of yours, men fine and | good, met
15   me in | Kos and congratulated me and ‖ gave me the decree in which it
was made cle|ar that you rejoice great|ly at my presence,[3] | and this

20   (rejoicing), in view of your | good wishes to me and our Repub‖lic, I
     firm|ly believe (is sincere); for at the critical tim|e when from Laodikeia
25   to *v* yo|u I sent a letter that | you should send soldiers to me,[4] ‖ you were
     among the first to se|nd them, and you did this a|s is the duty of all|ies who
30   are good friends of the Peo|ple of the Romans to do, ‖ and as to your men
     sent | to me as envoys, | I made use of their fine and complete service.[5] | *v*
35   For these reasons *v* | I (will) take care [both in pu‖blic (?)] and in private
     [life,] | while keeping | my good fai|th, to do for you whatever I ca|n and for
40   your pub‖lic affairs | to be of service, | and always of some good | to be the
45   author (for you); | and (I will take care) that to the senate ‖ and the People
     those things which you | have done | I will, when I return to Rome, | make
50   clear; | the same envoys beg‖ged me that it might be possible | for you also
     to enjoy my patronage, | and those men I | accepted, and (undertook)
55   because of my rega|rd for you‖r city | to be your People's pa|tron.[6] *v*

1   The text which we have is a re-engraving of the second century AD.
2   There is an error here in the engraving. Apparently the phrase (in Greek) 'strategos
    anthypatos' stood in the previous line, as in the previous document (no. 59a), but the
    engraver separated those two words and placed 'strategos' in this line. Oppius was not
    a praetor at this time.
3   Oppius, captured by Mithridates, was released after the peace of Dardanus (85 BC)
    between Sulla and Mithridates.
4   See above, no. 59a.
5   The envoys mentioned in this context must be those described in the decree of
    Plarasa-Aphrodisias, above, no. 59a.
6   Cf. nos. 26.23; 46.3; 47 G5; 73.8; 75 E2; 79 B–C; 98 D2. But this is the earliest epi-
    graphic account of a Roman's acceptance of a client from the Greek world.

60   Chaeremon of Nysa, friend of the Romans, enemy of Mithridates. 88/87 BC.
Stele of Amygdaloid rock, originally from Nysa on the Maeander.

A: *SIG[3] 741 I; *RDGE* 48 (letter of the governor of Asia to Nysa). **B**: *SIG*[3] 741 III; (Welles, *RC 73 (letter of Mithridates). **C**: *SIG*[3] 741 IV; Welles, *RC 74 (letter of Mithridates).

Welles, *RC* pp. 294–9; Rostovtzeff. *SEHHW* II 819–21; *RDGE* pp. 260–2.

A. *SIG*[3] 741 I

[The] *People* [of Nysa and the Boule have honored] | Ch[aer]em[on] (son)
of Pythodoros. | Gaius Cassiu[s][1] *sends greetings* to the magistrates of
5   [N]ysa. | [Ch]aeremon *son* of Py[thodor]os, *your* citizen, ‖ *came* to me in
     Apameia and asked [that] | I give him permission to attend my council. |
     I gave him this permission, when | he *promised* [the] council that out of
     respect for the *sen|ate* and *People* of the Romans he would give (us) in our

10 army camp ‖ a *gift* of sixty thousand modii[2] of *wheaten flour*. | Concerning
this matter, I answered | that he had *acted* well and that I, in turn, *would see*
| to it that he would learn that this *was* pleasing to us, | and *we* [will report
(?) this] to the senate and the People of the [Roman]s. *vv* ‖

B. Welles, *RC* 73

King [Mithrid]ates to Leonippos, satrap, | *sends greetings. vv* | Since
Cha[er]emon (son) of [Py]thodoros *is* most hateful | and warlike in his
5 dispo‖sition *toward* our cause and from the beginning with our most hated
enemies has [associa|ted,] and now, having learned of my presence, has
sent away his *so|ns* Pythodoros and Pythion and has himself | fled, make
this announcement: if anyone cap|tures alive Chaeremon or Pythodoros
10 or Pythion, his reward will be forty talen‖ts, and if anyone brings in the
head of any [of these,] | his reward will be twenty talents. *vv*

C. Welles, *RC* 74

King Mithridates to Leonippos sends greetings. | Chaeremon (son) of
Pythodoros, in the past when some of the Romans had escaped, | removed
them together with his sons to the city of Rhod[es,] | and now, having
5 learned of my presence, ‖ *he has fled* into the temple of Ephesian Artemis, |
and from there is sending letters to the common | *enemies* (of all), the
Romans.[3] His freedom from punishment for the crimes | he has committed
10 is an incen|tive to operations against us. *See to* ‖ *it* that if at all possible you
bring him in to [us,] | or that (at least) he be kept under guard and in
prison until I may be free from the | enemy. *vv*

Sometime, probably soon, after Sulla had concluded the terms of peace with Mithridates
in 85 BC, the city of Nysa had this stele erected, containing the testimonials to Chaeremon's services. Chaeremon seems to have perished in Ephesus, but his sons escaped.

1 Proconsul of Asia in 88 BC: Broughton, *MRR* II 42.
2 The Roman modius was a dry measure, about a fourth of a bushel.
3 The engraver made a mistake in the word 'Romans', putting it in the Genitive instead
   of the Accusative case, which makes it mean 'common enemy of the Romans'.

61 Ephesus declares war against Mithridates. End of 86 or beginning of 85 BC.

Plaque of white marble broken at top and bottom, Ephesus.

SIG[3] 742. Cf. Appian, *Mithridatic Wars* 48.

Rostovtzeff, *SEHHW* II 943; Magie, *RRAM* I 224–5; Bernhardt, *Historia* 69ff.

[-- with the People | keeping] toward the Romans, the *common* [saviors (of mankind), their ol|d] *goodwill* and to all their orders [being enthusiastically | agreeable.] *v* Mithridates, [king] of Cappadocia,[1] [having trans-
5 ||gressed the] treaty with the Romans and assembled [his forces, | attempted] to become master of our [land,] which did not *belong* to him, | and, having first seized the cities located before us, he also tre|acherously gained control of our city after terrifying us | [by the] size of his forces and
10 the unexpectedness of his attack.[2] || Our People, from the beginning having kept their goodwill toward the Roma|ns and having (now) seized the opportunity to aid our common inter|ests, have decided to declare war on Mithridates on behalf | of the leadership of the Romans and of our common freedom, *v* | all our citizens unanimously having dedicated them-
15 selves to the || struggles for these things. *v* Therefore, it is decreed by the People, since it is a matter con|cerning the war and the protection and security and | safety of the temple of Artemis and the city and the terri|tory, *v* that the strategoi and the secretary of the Boule and the | proedroi should introduce a decree immediately, also (a decree) concerning con-
20 cessions,[3] || as the People have determined is beneficial concerning this matter. *vv*

1 Cappadocia was a part of the Pontic kingdom of Mithridates.
2 The city of Ephesus here has played with the truth. Back in 88 BC it welcomed Mithridates, its citizens overthrowing the statues of the Romans. From his headquarters at Ephesus Mithridates issued his infamous order for the massacre of Romans in Asia. See Appian, *Mithridatic Wars* 21 and 23.
3 Lines 21–64 of the present inscription contain much of a very long decree of Ephesus outlining these concessions. They were intended to unite the people at this critical moment and included such measures as extension of the citizenship, abolition of debts, etc. On this portion of the inscription see Broughton, *Asia* 559–60, and J. H. Oliver, *AJP* 60 (1939) 468–70.

62   Two letters of Sulla concerning the Dionysiac Artists. About 84 and 81 BC.

Upper part of a stele of white marble inscribed on both sides (A and B), with a small projecting cornice on the front face, the letters carelessly engraved, Cos.

RDGE 49.

RDGE pp. 263–6.

(A. 81 BC) *vv* With Good Luck. *vv* | [L]ucius Cornelius, son of Lucius, Sulla Epa|phroditos dictator to the magistrates, Boule | (and) People of
5 Cos, greetings. To Alexandros of Laodikeia, ci||tharist, a good and fine

man, ou|r friend, envoy from the United Association of Dio|nysiac
Artists in Ionia and Hellespont | [and] of the Artists of Dionysos the
Leader,[1] I have *given per|mission* to *erect* a [stele] among you in the most
10   conspicuous place, ‖ [on which] will be engraved the privileges given by
me | [to the Artists.] Since [he now] came as an envoy | [to Rome,] and
the senate [passed] a decree *about* | [these matters,] accordingly I wish
you to see to it that [there be de|signated among you] *a most conspicuous*
15   [place] in which will be erec‖ted [the stele about the Artists.] I have
appended | [copies of the letter from me and of the decree] of the sen|ate
[---] LACUNA
(B. *c.* 84 BC) [---] and the *goodwill* which you have toward *us,* | accord-
ingly I wish (you) to learn that I, in accordance with my advisory |
board's vote, have reached a decision: those privi|leges and honours and
5   immunities from the liturgies[2] which to you out of res‖pect for Dionysos
and the Muses and favor toward *your corporate* | *body* our senate, magis-
trates and pro|magistrates have *given* [(and) gran]|ted, these you shall
10   keep, and, [just as formerly, | you shall be] *immune* from every liturgy ‖ and
military service, and you shall not pay any [tax or public expen|ses,] and
you shall not [be disturbed by anyone] | for supplies [and billeting, and
you shall not | be forced] to receive any [lodger,] | and in order that [---]

1 Originally these were two guilds which united about the middle of the second century to
   form a single association. See the works cited in the Glossary *s.v.* 'Dionysiac Artists'.
2 On the liturgies see the Glossary.

**63   A letter of Sulla to Stratonikeia, followed by a second letter
introducing a decree of the senate concerning that city. 81 BC.**
Building blocks, now in many fragments, once part of the wall of the
temple of Hekate at Lagina in Karia.[1]

OGIS 441; **RDGE* 18.

Magie, *RRAM* I 234–5; *RDGE* pp. 105–11.

(Col. 1: the first letter) [Lucius Cornelius, son of L]ucius, Sulla Epaphro-
ditos, | [dictator,] to the magistrates, Boule and People of [Stratoni]keia,
greetings. | [We are not unaware that] from the time of your ancestors
5   most justly | [you] have acted [toward our] leadership and at ‖ [every
opportunity] have conscientiously preserved your loyalty [to] *us,* | and
that [in the] war [against Mithrida]tes you were the first of those in |
[Asia to oppose him] and for those reasons (there were) many dangers, | of
different kinds, which you on behalf of our Re|public most readily took
10   upon yourselves, ‖ [-- (dangers)] both [public] and private, | *because of*

[your friendship] toward us, your goodwill | [and kindness,] and that [in the] crisis [of the war] | *you sent envoys* to [the other cities of Asia] and to | [those of Greece --] ‖ LACUNA

15   (Col. 2: the second letter) Lucius Cor[nelius Sulla Epaphroditos, dic-t]ator, | [to the magistrates, Boule and People of] Strato[nikeia, greetings. | I have given] this decree, [passed by the senate,] to your envoys. | (The decree) Lucius Corneli[us, son of Lucius, Sulla Epaphroditos, dic]-

20   tator, | *consulted* the senate [on the sixth day before the] *Kalends* ‖ of April (March 27) in the [Comitium. (Witnesses) present at the writing were: G]aius | Fannius, [son of] Gaius; [---; G]aius | Fundanius, [son of] Gai[us; ---. Whereas the envoys] from Chrysaorian[2] | [Stratonikei]a,

25   Paionios, son of Hier[okles; | ---;] ‖ Hekataios, son of Pa[---; ---;] | and Dionysios, son of E[---,] spoke | *in harmonious* [agreement with the decree of Stratonikeia, | asking for a share in our joy over the fact that] the public

30   *affairs* of the People | [of Rome] are [now in better] *condition*: ‖ [that they be permitted to dedicate a golden crown | of] two hundred [talents from their] own city to the senate, | [that] they be permitted to perform a [sacri-fice on the Capitol] (to celebrate) the *victory* | [and leadership of the People] of Rome, | [and that hereafter Lucius Cornelius,] son of [L]ucius,

35   Sulla Epaphroditos, ‖ [dictator, think it best (?) to] treat the People [of Stratonikeia] kindly; | [and since the People (of Stratonikeia) in the period of peace] preserved their | [goodwill, loyalty and friendship] toward the People of Rome, | [and were the first of those in Asia, when Mith-r]idates | [was a most fearsome tyrant] there, [to prefer] to oppose him,

40   ‖ [and since the king marched against their city,] captured and took | [---] | LACUNA [--- to Lucius Cornelius, son of Lucius, Sulla,] | dictator, [---] | and since the People (of Stratonikeia) [have always preserved their exist-

45   ing] ‖ goodwill and *loyalty* and alliance [toward the People of Rome, | con-ducting] *their own* affairs [in keeping with] the policy [of the latter, and upon Mithridates] | made war, and, displaying their [spirit most zea-lously in their opposition] | to the violence and power of the king, [---] | LACUNA (asking) that they might enjoy *their own* [jurisdiction] and *their*

50   *own* laws and customs [as they had ‖ previously,] and that whatever [dec-rees they passed] | because of [this] war which [they declared] against King [Mithridates] | (all) those should be legally binding; | [and that Pedasos (?),] Themessos, Keramos and the places, [villages, harbors and the re|venues of the] cities which Lucius Corn[elius Sulla, imperator,]

55   ‖ *for the sake of* their courage and honor [added and assign|ed to them, that] they should be *permitted* to possess (all of these); | [the temple] of Hekate, most famous [and most great goddess, that (her) long] revered (temple)

60   [--- | and its sacred precinct should be] inviolate; ‖ [and concerning their] *losses* [in the war, that] | (Col. 3) the *senate* should issue instructions to the magistrate going to Asia | *to see to* and to turn his attention to (this), | that

he should see to the restoration of things proved to be theirs, and that their
men captured in war | should be restored to them, and that they receive
65   just treatment in the other matters; ‖ and that to envoys coming from
Stratonikeia to Rome | the (Roman) magistrates should give (audience
before) the senate outside the regular procedure – | about this matter a
decree was passed as follows: that the envoys | of Stratonikeia be given in
person in the senate a friend|ly response; that goodwill, friendship and
70   alliance be renewed ‖ and that the envoys be **addressed as fine and good**
men, friends | and allies of ours from a fine and good People, | friends and
allies of ours. Decreed. | Whereas these [envoys] spoke and *whereas* |
75   Lucius Corneli[us Sulla] Epaphroditos, dictator, *spoke* ‖ (to the effect) that
[it was known to the Ro]mans [by letters sent | from those who have held]
Asia and Greece [and from those | who have been] legates [in these] pro-
vinces | that friendship and [loyalty and goodwill toward the] | People of
Rome (are things which) the Stratonikeians continuously [in times of
80   peace and war] ‖ have always preserved, and that *with soldiers* [and grain
and huge | expenditures of money] the Republic [of the People of Rome] |
has been most zealously protected (by them) [---,] | and that because of
[their own] highmindedness [they joined with (the Romans) in fight|ing]
85   against King [Mithridates' commanders] ‖ and *forces*, and most cour-
ageously on *behalf* of [the cities of Asia and] | Greece they opposed (those
commanders and forces), *v* | [about these matters a decree has been passed
as follows: it pleases the sen|ate to *remember* good and] just [men and to
90   pro|vide that Luci]us Cornelius Sulla Epaphrodit[os, ‖ dictator, shall
order the] *proquaestor* [to give] them gifts according to official procedure, |
and that their own laws and customs [which] they formerly | [enjoyed,]
these they shall enjoy; *v* | [and that whatever laws] and decrees [they them-
selves] have passed [because of] this [war] | against Mithridates, [all
95   these ‖ are to be legally binding] *upon them*; and whatever (things) [for the
sake of] their courage [and hon|or,] *according to* the vote of his advisory
board, Lucius Sul[la, im|perator,] added and assigned to them, (con-
sisting of) [communi|ties (?), revenues,] *lands*, villages and harbors, [these
100 | they are to be permitted to keep;] *the* People of Rome [---‖---] in a man-
ner *befitting* and worthy of them [---|---] the Stratonikeians [---|---] *shall
be* acceptable; and *that* Lucius Corneli[us Sul]la Epaphroditos, dictator,
105   [if to him] | it seems best, shall review whatever *communities*, ‖ villages,
lands and harbors which he as imperator had added to Stratonikeia (and)
shall establish [how much] | revenue [each] of them should pay to Strato-
nikeia; | and that, *when* he has established it, he shall send letters to those
communities (?) which | he has added to Str[atonikeia] that such an
110   amount of *revenue* | is to be paid (by them) to Stratonikeia; *v* ‖ and that those
who, at any time, are in charge of the [provinces] of Asia and Greece | shall
take thought and see to it that [these things] | *v* are done in this way; (Col. 4)

that the temple of Hekate *shall be* [inviolate;] | whatever proconsul at
115   any time is in charge of the *province* of Asia, ‖ shall investigate what things
are *missing,* | who stole them, and who (now) possess|es them, so that he
may see to it that they are recovered from them | and restored, and that
their prisoners of war | they shall be able to recover, and in regard to the
120   other matters ‖ shall obtain justice, as may | seem to him to be in keep-
ing with the interests of the Republic and | his own good faith. Decreed.
v | As for the crown sent from the people (of Stratonikeia) [to the
125   senate,] | wherever Lucius [Cornel]ius ‖ Sulla Epaphroditos, dictator, |
may think it [good, (there) they shall be permitted to set it up; | and as
for a sacrifice on the Capitol, if they wi|sh, they shall be permitted to
130   perform it. | As for the envoys coming from Stratonikeia to ‖ Rome, it
has been decreed that (audience before) the] senate | *be granted* [to them
by the magistrates outside the regular procedure. Decreed.]

At the conclusion of the war against Mithridates (85 BC) a general reorganization of the
cities in Asia was made by Sulla. Cities loyal to Rome were rewarded, while those which
had sided with Mithridates were punished. Stratonikeia had remained loyal and was
accordingly rewarded by Sulla. After Sulla returned to Rome, the city sent envoys to
the senate to obtain confirmation of all the benefits and privileges it had been given.

1 It was estimated by Diehl and Cousin in *BCH* 9 (1885) 437–74 that these documents
   had been engraved on the wall of the temple of Hekate in five parallel columns. Following the senatorial decree on the wall there is a decree of the city of Stratonikeia which
   authorizes the engraving of the list of those cities which had recognized the inviolability
   of the temple. It is found in the last half of col. 4 and in col. 5.
2 According to Pausanias 5.21.10 the territory and the city of Stratonikeia had been called
   Chrysaoris in early times. See Magie, *RRAM* II 1031, n. 77, and J. Crampa, *Labraunda,*
   Swedish Excavations and Researches III: *The Greek Inscriptions* Part 1 (Lund 1969) 33ff.

64   A letter of Cn. Cornelius Dolabella to Thasos. 80 BC.
Fragment of a marble building block, Thasos.

Dunant-Pouilloux, *Recherches* no. 175, pp. 45–6 (+ photograph); **RDGE* 21.

Dunant-Pouilloux, *Recherches* pp. 47–55; *RDGE* pp. 121–3.

[Gnae]us Cornelius, [son] of Publius, [Dolabella, proconsul,][1] sends
greetings to the magistrates, Boule and People of Thas|os. Mikas son of
Mikas, Sa[-- son] of Eurymenides [by adoption] but of Lyetes by nature,
envoys | of yours, *fine* [and good] men, [friends from a] *fine* and good
[People,] friends and allies of ou|rs, [met me] in Thessalo[nike and infor-
5   med me] that the senate of the Roman People ‖ (passed) [a decree] in favor
of your [city on account of] your respect for (our) Republic. | This decree

10   [--] | I learned [--] | had [--] | in the war [--] ‖ fell into hard times [--] |
      imperatores[2] and [--] | goodwill, [friendship and alliance to renew --] |
      which, having *learned* that you [--] to the envoys from Abdera in the man-
      ner in which Lu{c}|cius Cornelius Sul[la --] *decided* and the senate deter-
15   mined as just and the Peo‖ple of the Romans *ordered* [--] were to be sub|ject
      to you, and [whatever ---][3] revenues the senate [of the Ro]|mans has
      conceded in order that [you might] *enjoy* [--] these [--] were to be [--,]
      simi|larly to the Peparethians and [Skiathians] I have sent letters that
      they are to be subject to you in the manner in which our | senate wished.
20   *vv* ‖ And if concerning the land which, bordering on Ismaros (?)[4] [--] land
      I have determined | is to be reserved for you, to return any (land) reserved
      [for you --] to whom [--] lett|ers I have sent, in order that concerning this
      land [--] they should | withdraw and return the land reserved for you, just
      as [--] | and if Rhoimetalkas or Ablouporis or Tuta[5] [--] occupy any of
25   your [property,] ‖ they are to return that which is reserved for you; and
      likewise [--] | to take care that these [-- of] yours be restored [--] about
      those matters concerning y|ou publicly or privately that to me [--] | And
      concerning the remainder, if (it comes) to a dispute [--] | let envoys come
      to me [about] the matter [--] | whatever (cities or peoples?) have remained
      in the friendship of the People of Rome [--] |[6]

In the autumn of 88 BC, after his conquests in Asia, Mithridates sent two armies to
invade Europe: one by land through Thrace and Macedonia, and another across the
Aegean. After almost all Greece had come under the king's control, Sulla arrived early
in 87 with an army, bottled up the enemy forces in Athens, besieged and captured
Athens in 86 and then defeated the Mithridatic army in Boiotia. In the winter of 86/5
Sulla marched northward toward Macedonia. In the spring he sent part of his army
on a punitive expedition against native tribes of the north which had been plundering
Roman territory. In autumn of 85 BC Mithridates accepted the peace terms offered by
Sulla. The letter of Cn. Cornelius Dolabella, translated here, is part of a series of docu-
ments that originally had been engraved on some part of an official building in the agora
of Thasos. They are concerned with the difficulties faced by Thasos at home and espe-
cially on the Thracian coast opposite the island. The documents include a letter of Sulla to
Thasos with a decree of the senate, dated to 80 BC, both badly mutilated (*RDGE* 20).
The decree shows that Thasos had resisted enemy forces – probably Thracians in the
anarchy following the advance of the Mithridatic army – and had remained loyal to
Rome. For those reasons the senate had decreed to renew friendship and alliance with
Thasos and to grant the city certain privileges. When the senatorial decree was brought
back to Thasos, it was brought to the attention of the governor of Macedonia, Cn.
Cornelius Dolabella, who sent the present letter to the city.

1 Consul in 81 BC, he was governor of Macedonia 80–77 BC. For his family see E. Badian,
   PBSR 33 (1965) 48–51.
2 The Latin word is here simply transliterated into Greek.
3 Dunant-Pouilloux: '[communities, places,] *harbors*, [villages and] revenues'.
4 The stone has, apparently, EMARON, but no such place is known, while Ismaros is in
   Thrace, north of Maroneia.

5 All three are Thracians, apparently the chiefs of Thracian tribes who had been plundering Thasian territory on the mainland coast. Thrace remained independent of Rome
   throughout the whole Republican period and did not become a Roman province until
   the reign of Claudius.
6 A second letter of Dolabella follows on the stone in a very mutilated form, but it appears
   to contain instructions of some kind about Peparethos and Skiathos.

65   Decree of the Koinon of Asia. Between 80 and 48 BC.

Stone block broken at the top and left side, Aphrodisias in Karia.

T. Drew-Bear, *BCH* 96 (1972) 444; photograph in *PBSR* 37 (1969) Pl. X–XI; Reynolds,
Aphrodisias, Document 5.

Drew-Bear, *op. cit.* 443–71; Reynolds, *Aphrodisias* pp. 26–32.

[-- on the motion of] the proedroi and the secretary: *vv* since the cities |
[and the tribes, being oppressed] by the publicans and the [--|--] and
[having come (?)] to the final stage of despair through certain (indi-
5 viduals), | [the Koinon] of the Greeks met and unanimously decided ‖ [--]
in the city of Ephesus to send envoys to | [the senate and] the (Roman)
leaders, (envoys drawn) from the most prominent and most honor|ed
[men, to discuss with] *them* about the aforementioned matters and the
other things | [of interest to the Greeks,] and to ask them to take the pro-
vince in hand and | [to --] it; and when the envoys were chosen, among
10 whom (were) *vv* ‖ [Dionysios and Hier]okles, (sons) of Iason (the son) of
Skymnos,[1] being Aphrodisians and also *cit*|*izens* in Tralles but not in
residence, the proedroi sent | [a man (?) to convey] to the People of
Aphrodisias a *letter* that they had been chosen | [--] because of the com-
mon interest of the Greeks (well) known being | their reputation [among
15 the Greeks] for excellence and honor, just as in detail (?) ‖ [concerning
each particular] is revealed [in] the letter sent about them | [--] they were
called upon by the People after an Assembly had been convoked | [and
they undertook] to perform the embassy; and because of this embassy
many | [great] dangers were they subjected to; and they gave our decrees |
20 [to the senate] and the (Roman) leaders, and they besieged at *ev*‖*ery*
[opportunity] those leaders; they took upon themselves many great
(judicial) contests | [on behalf of the] Koinon of the Greeks and were
present at all those contests; and *con*|*ducting* [the] embassy in a fine and
successful manner worthy of the Koinon of the Greeks | [and of their own
personal] reputations, they successfully accomplished matters of the
greatest importance and interest to the | Peoples and Tribes [who are in
25 the whole of (?)] Asia – (therefore) it is decreed by the Koinon in Asi‖a [of
the Greeks] to praise the aforementioned men and to crown with a gold |
[crown] *each* of them for the courage and zeal which they demonstrated

vv | [and to erect] bronze statues of them among whatever People or Tribe they wish, | the *inscription* (on the statues) *being v* The Peoples and Tribes in Asia have honored Dionysios and Hierokles, | [the (sons) of Iason] (son) of Skymnos, for their most successful accomplishments, on account of their excellence.

1 Iason son of Skymnos was one of the most prominent men in Aphrodisias, having been a local magistrate connected with the mint of the city. His name appears on a number of coins of Aphrodisias: Drew-Bear, *op. cit.* 467 ff.

66   Decree of the senate concerning three Greek naval captains. 78 BC.

Bilingual inscription on a bronze tablet,[1] Rome.

IGRR I 118; *CIL* I^2 588; *FIRA* I 35; *ILLRP* 513; **RDGE* 22; Moretti, *IGUR* I 1; photograph in Degrassi, *Imagines* no. 393. Cf. the letters of Octavian concerning Seleukos of Rhosos, below, no. 86.

RDGE pp. 124–32; A. J. Marshall, *AJP* 89 (1968) 39–55.

In the consulship of Quintus Lutatius, son of Quintus, Catulus and Marcus Aem[ilius, son of Quintus,] | grandson of Marcus, L[e]p[i]dus (78 BC), when the urban and peregrine praetor[2] was Lucius Cornelius, [son of --,] | Sisenna, month of May. Quintus Lutatius, son of Quintus, Catulus the consul consulted the senate | on the eleventh day before the Kalends of June (May 22) in the Comitium. (Witnesses) present at the writing were Lucius Faberius, son of Lucius, (of the tribe) Sergia; Gaiu[s

5   --,] son of [Lu]||cius, (of the tribe) Poplilia; Quintus Petillius, son of Titus, (of the tribe) Sergia. Whereas Quintus Lutatius, son of Quintus, Catulus the consul said that A[sklepiades] | son of Philinos the Klazomenian, Polystratos son of Polyarkos the Karystian, and Men[i]skos son (by adoption) of Eirenaios (and by nature son) of Thargelios the Mile[sian --] | had been present with their ships at the beginning of the Italian War,[3] had given valiant and faithful service to our Republic, | and that he wishes to send them back to their countries in accordance with a decree of the senate, if it pleases (the senate), that for their fine accomplishments [and brave] | deeds for our Republic they might receive respect, concerning this matter it has been decreed as follows: that Asklepiades son of Philinos the

10   Klaz[omenian,] || Polystratos son of Polyarkos the Karystian, and Meniskos the Milesian son (by adoption) of Eirenaios and by descent (son) of Thargelios[4] *vv* are to be *addressed* as fine and good men, (our) *friends.* | The senate and the People of the Romans consider the deeds of these men have been good and brave and loyal to our Republic, | and for this reason the

senate decides that they, their children, and their descendants are to be
immune in their own cities from all liturgies and financial contributions;
if any taxes | have been levied on their properties since these men left in the
service of our Republic, these (taxes) are to be given back (and) returned
to them; if any | of their fields, houses or properties have been sold since
these men left their homeland in the service of our Republic, all of these

15   are to be returned to them in their entirety;[5] ‖ if any fixed day (for payment of debts) has passed since they left their homeland in the service of
our Republic, this is not to be detrimental to them, | and no debt owed to
them is for this reason to be less (valid), nor is it to be any less lawful for
them to sue (or) exact payment (of such debts); and whatever inheritances
have come to them or their children, | these they are to hold, possess and
enjoy; whatever lawsuits they, their children, their descendants, and their
wives may bring against another person, and if other persons | bring law-
suits against them, their children, their descendants, and their wives,
these men and their children <and their descendants> and their wives
<are> to have the right and the choice | of having the case decided in
their own cities by their own laws, if they wish, or before our magistrates

20   by Italian judges, or in a free city, one which has remained constantly ‖ in
the friendship of the People of the Romans, – wherever they may prefer,
there the trial about these matters is to be held; if any judgments | have
been made about them in their absence since they left their homeland,
these are to be returned to their former condition and a new trial accord-
ing to | the decree of the senate is to take place; if their cities owe any public
debts, they are not to be obligated to contribute toward (payment of) these
debts; | our magistrates, any (of them) who may at any time farm out (the
contracts for) Asia and Euboia or may impose taxes on Asia and Euboia,
are to take care that these men are not obligated to give anything; | Quin-
tus Lutatius and Marcus Aemilius the consuls, one of them or both, if it
seems good to them, are to see to it that these men be entered on the roll of

25   friends, ‖ that they be permitted to set up on the Capitolium a bronze
tablet of friendship and to perform a sacrifice there, and that gifts to
them, according to official proce|dure, and lodging and board be con-
tracted for and sent by the urban quaestor, (the consuls) are to order; and
if concerning their own affairs | they desire to send envoys to the senate or
to come themselves, permission is to be granted to them, their children,
and their descendants | to come as envoys or to send them; Quintus
Lutatius and Marcus Aemilius the consuls, one of them or both, | if it
seems good to them, are to send letters to our magistrates, who are in

30   charge of the provinces of Asia and Macedonia, ‖ and to their (city)
magistrates, that the senate wishes and considers it just that these things
be done in this fashion, | as may appear to them to be in keeping with the
interest of the Republic and their own good faith. *vv* Decreed. *vv* Askle-

piades (son) of Philinos the Klazomenian, Polystratos (son) of Polyarkos the Karystian, and Meniskos (son) of Eirena[ios the M]ilesian.[6]

1 The Latin original text occupies the upper half of the tablet, but only parts of it are extant. The Greek translation, which is translated here, is complete.
2 See the Glossary *s.v.* Praetor.
3 Probably the war of 90–89 BC is meant, although the Sullan war of 83–82 cannot be discounted.
4 Here is stated somewhat differently exactly what is said above in line 6.
5 On this technical expression in Roman law see L. Gallet in *Revue historique de droit français et étranger*[4] 16 (1937) 407–25.
6 The three Greeks added their names at the end, when they had the tablet nailed up – holes are in the lower two corners and in the middle – somewhere on the Capitolium.

67   P. Servilius Vatia in Cilicia and Isauria. 78–75 BC.

A: Eutropius 6.3. **B**: A. Hall, *Akten des VI. Internationalen Kongresses für Griechische und Lateinische Epigraphik*, Vestigia 17 (Munich 1973) 570 (Latin) with photograph. Rectangular building block of mottled red and gray limestone, slightly damaged at top right corner, Isaura Vetus in Isauria in Asia Minor. Cf. Strabo 12.6.2; Sallust, *Hist.* 2.82–7 (Maurenbrecher); Florus 1.41.5; Orosius, *Adversum Paganos* 5.23.21. Livy, *Per.* 93.

H. A. Ormerod, *JRS* 12 (1922) 35ff.; Magie, *RRAM* I 287–90; Hall, *op. cit.* 568–71.

A. Eutropius 6.3

The ex-consul, P. Servilius,[1] a vigorous man, was sent to Cilicia and Pamphylia. He subdued Cilicia, besieged and captured the most famous cities of Lycia, including Phaselis, Olympus, Corycus in Cilicia. He also attacked the Isaurians, reduced them to (Roman) rule, and within a three-year period brought an end to the war. He was the first of all the Romans to make a march in the Taurus (Mountains). Upon his return he received a triumph and earned the name of Isauricus.

B. Hall, *op. cit.* 570

Servilius, son of Gaius, imperator, | defeated the enemy, captured Isaura
5 Vetus | and sold the captives. | Whether it is a god or goddess who ‖ protected Vetus | Isaura, *vv* he fulfilled his vow.[2]

1 He was consul in 79 BC and then received the command in Cilicia for 78, his authority subsequently extended each year to 75.
2 Hall believes that a ceremony similar to *evocatio* was performed during the siege of Isaura Vetus. *Evocatio* was a ceremony to hasten the fall of a city by inducing its god(s) to leave it, thus making the city easier to capture. This would mean that the Romans would have to accept the god or gods in Rome. For the ceremony and formula see Macrobius, *Sat.* 3.9.7ff. But here in Isaura Vetus it may have been only some propitiatory and expiatory ceremony.

68   Murder of publicans in Herakleia in Pontos. 74 BC.
Extract from Memnon.

Memnon, *FGrHist* 434 F 27.5–6. Cf. Plutarch, *Lucullus* 7.5.

Magie, *RRAM* I 324–5.

(5) The fleet of Mithridates sailing along by Herakleia was not received by the city, but it did obtain market (privileges) after requesting them. As was to be expected, when the men mingled with each other, Archelaos the fleet admiral arrested Silenos and Satyros, notable men of Herakleia, and did not release them until he persuaded (the city) to grant him five triremes as allies in the war against the Romans. In consequence of this, a thing which Archelaos also contrived, the people of Herakleia incurred the hatred of the Romans. And when the Romans set up the leasing of the taxes in the other cities, they subjected Herakleia to them as well, for the reason mentioned above.[1] (6) The publicans came to the city in contempt of the customs of its government and demanded money, antagonizing the citizens who considered this to be, so to speak, a beginning of slavery. Although they ought to have sent an embassy to the senate to be relieved of the leasing of the taxes, they were misled by a very headstrong person of those in the city and caused the disappearance of the publicans, so that their very death was not known.

1 Herakleia had been on friendly terms with Rome since the time of the Scipiones in 190 BC: Memnon, *FGrHist* 434 F 18.

69   C. Salluvius Naso honored for his actions against Mithridates. 74–73 BC.
Inscription in Latin and Greek[1] on a marble column from the temple of Diana Nemorensis, Nemi.

CIL I² 743; *IGRR* I 401; *OGIS* 445; *ILS* 37; **ILLRP* 372.

Magie, *RRAM* I 327; II 1208, n. 15.

(Dedicated to) G[ai]us Salluvius, son of Gaius, Naso, | legate pro praetore,[2] (by) the Mysian | Abbaiitai and Epikteteis, because he preserved
5   them | in the war against Mithridates, ‖ on account of his bravery.

1 The Latin copy appears first, followed by the Greek, which is translated here.
2 He served under Lucullus: Broughton, *MRR* II 105 and 113. For the command ‘pro praetore’ see the Glossary *s.v.* Promagistrate.

70   Oropos and the publicans. 73 BC.

Stele of white marble from the Amphiaraion in Oropos in Boiotia.

*SIG*³ 747; *FIRA* I 36; *RDGE 23. Cf. Cicero, *De Nat. Deorum* 3.49.

Rostovtzeff, *SEHHW* II 748–9; Nicolet, *L'ordre* I 351–2; *RDGE* pp. 133–8; Badian, *Publicans* 95–6.

M[arc]us Terentius, son of Marcus, Varro Lucullus and Gaius Cas-
<s>ius, son of Luci[us, Lon]|ginus, consuls (73 BC), *vv* to the magis-
trates, Boule and People of Oropos, greetings. If you are well, it is good.¹
We wish you to know that we, in accordance with the decree of the senate
passed *in* the consulship of [Luci]|us Licinius (Lucullus) and Marcus
Aurelius (Cotta) (74 BC), have reached a decision concerning the dis-
5   putes *between* ‖ the god Amphiaraos and the publicans {reached a deci-
sion}. *vv* On the day before the I[des] | of October (October 14) in the
Basilica Porcia.² On our Advisory Board *vv* were Marcus Claudius, son of
Marc[us,] | (of the tribe) Arnensis, Marcellus; *vv* Gaius Claudius, son of
Gaius, (of the tribe) Arnensis, Glaber; | Marcus Cas<s>ius, son of
Marcus, (of the tribe) Pomptina; *vv* Gaius Licinius, son of Gaius, | {(of the
tribe) Pomptina, *vv* Gaius Licinius, son of Gaius,}³ (of the tribe) Stel-
10   latina, Sacerdos; ‖ Lucius Voluscius,⁴ son of Lucius, (of the tribe) Arnen-
sis (?); *vv* Lucius Lartius, son of Lucius, | (of the tribe) P<a>piria; *vv*
Gaius Annaeus, son of Gaius, (of the tribe) Clu<s>tumina; Marcus
Tullius, son of Marcus, | (of the tribe) Cornelia, Cicero;⁵ *v* Quintus Axius,
son of Marcus, (of the tribe) Quirina; *vv* Quintus Pompeius, son of
Quin|tus, (of the tribe) Ar[nen]sis, Rufus; Aulus Cascellius, son of {son
of} Aulus, (of the tribe) Romilia; | Quintus Minucius, son of Quintus, (of
15   the tribe) Teretina, Thermus; *v* Marcus Publicius, ‖ son of Marcus, (of the
tribe) Horatia, Scaeva; *vv* Titus Maenius, son of Titus, *vv* (of the tribe)
Lemonia; *v* Lucius | Claudius, son of Lucius, (of the tribe) Lemonia. *vv*
Whereas Hermodoros, son of Olympichos, priest | of Amphiaraos, who
has previously been called ally by the senate,⁶ | and Alexidemos son of
Theodoros, and Demainetos son of Theoteles, en|voys of Oropos, said: *vv*
20   since in the law of the (state) contract⁷ those ‖ lands have been exempted
which Lucius Sulla for the protection of the immortal gods (and) of their
sacred precincts | has granted (to a god) {have been exempted}, *vv* (and
since) these reve|nues, which this dispute concerns, have been assigned
by Lucius Sulla to the god Amphiaraos, | that they should not⁸ pay the tax
on these lands to the publican; | and whereas Lucius Domitius Aheno-
25   barbus⁹ *vv* said on behalf of the publicans that, ‖ since in the law of the
(state) contract those lands have been exempted | which Lucius Sulla for
the protection of the sacred precincts of the immortal gods | has granted

(to a god), *vv* and (since) Amphiaraos, to whom these lands are said to
have been granted, | is not a god, the publicans should have permission to
collect the taxes from these lands;[10] *vv* according to the decision of our
30   Advisory Board we have made our dec‖ision, which decision we will
bring before the senate, *vv* and we have entered it also | into the book of
our minutes: *vv* Concerning the land | of Oropos, about which there was
a dispute with the publicans, according to the | law of the (state) contract
this land is exempted, so that the publican | may not collect its taxes; we
35   have made our decision in accordance with the decree of the senate; ‖ in
*the law of the (state) contract the exemption appears to run as follows: |
'except for those (lands)[11] or any (land) which a decree of the senate or a
general or generals | of ours out of respect for the immortal gods and for
the protection of their sacred precincts | have given or left to them to enjoy,
v and except for those (lands) which Lucius | Cornelius Sulla imperator,
40   according to the decision of his Advisory Board, ‖ for the protection of the
immortal gods and of their sacred precincts, has given to them to enjoy, |
and which (gift) has also been ratified by the senate and which has not
afterwards by decree | of the senate been made invalid'. *v* Lucius Cornelius
Sulla according to | the decision of his Advisory Board appears to have
made his decision (as follows): *vv* 'For the sake of fulfilling a vow | I grant
to the temple of Amphiaraos land everywhere in all directions for one
45   thousand feet, ‖ in order that this land too may be inviolate.' Likewise to
the god Amphiaraos | he appears to have consecrated of the city and the
land and harbors of Oropos | all the revenues for the games and sacrifices
which the Oropians | perform for the god Amphiaraos, as well as those
also which afterwards | they might perform for the victory and leadership
50   of the People of the Romans, ‖ except for the fields of Hermodoros son of
Olympichos, priest of Amphiaraos, who | has constantly remained in the
friendship of the People of the Romans. Concerning th|is matter a decree
of the senate *v* when Lucius Sulla Epaphroditos | (and) Quintus Metellus
Pius were consuls (80 BC) *v* appears to have been sanctioned, which the
senate decreed {and} in the following words: 'Whatever to the god
55   ‖ Amphiaraos and to his temple *v* Lucius Cornelius Sulla according to the
decision of his Advisory Board | assigned and granted, these same (pro-
perties) the senate has deemed | to have been given and granted to the
god.' On (Sulla's) Advisory Board were present | the same men (named)
in Book One of (Senatorial) Proceedings, | page fourteen.[12] *v* This is the
60   decree of the senate that was passed: ‖ On the seventeenth day before the
Kalends of November (October 16) in the Comitium: (Witnesses) present
at the writing were *v* Titus Maenius, son of Titus, (of the tribe) Lemonia; |
Quintus Rancius, son of Quintus, (of the tribe) Claudia; Gaius V<i>sel-
lius, son of Gaius, | (of the tribe) Quirina, Varro.[13] *vv* Whereas Marcus
Lucullus and Gaius Cas<s>ius, the consuls (73 BC), have decided and

65   reported that concerning the land of Oropos and the ‖ publicans they have
     made their decision, that also the Oropian | land appears to have been
     exempted in accordance with the law of the (state) contract | and that it
     appears the publicans may not collect the taxes on these lands – | just as
     appeared to them to be in accordance with the best interest of the
     Republic and | their own good faith, so it has been decreed. *vv*

1   This stereotyped formula begins in Greek letters of the Hellenistic period and then
    makes its appearance in official Roman letters. See *RDGE* p. 190.
2   Thus, ten months or more were required to reach a decision.
3   This entry is in part a repetition of the material in the preceding line.
4   Unknown elsewhere, but his name may be ‘Volscius’, since the Greeks spelled it
    ‘Voluscius’. For examples see W. Schulze, *Zur Geschichte Lateinischer Eigennamen* (Berlin
    1933) 523.
5   This Cicero is the famous orator, statesman and author.
6   The special treatment accorded him – see lines 50–1 – shows that he was still so con-
    sidered by the senate. He may have acquired his status through loyalty to Rome in the
    war against Mithridates.
7   Contracts at Rome for public works and services were let out by the censors to private
    companies or groups for such things as army supplies and the collection of taxes in the
    provinces. See Badian, *Publicans* Chapter 1.
8   There is a mistake in the printing of the Greek text in *RDGE* at this point. The word for
    ‘not’ (*me*) was omitted inadvertently.
9   He is the consul of 54 BC, a bitter enemy of the dictator Caesar. He fell at Pharsalus in
    48 BC.
10 The central point in the argument of the publicans is that Amphiaraos is not a god
    but, presumably, a hero and thus his precincts do not belong to the ‘precincts of the
    immortal gods’, making them taxable.
11 This seems to refer to lands previously listed as exempt.
12 This might refer to material on deposit in the state archives in Rome. However, as
    Badian suggests (*per litteras*), the reference to ‘Book One’ makes it difficult to ascribe
    the notation to the state archives. It may be a case of a reference to the minutes of
    meetings of Sulla’s Advisory Board.
13 He was the cousin of the famous Cicero mentioned in lines 11–12, about the same age.
    For his career see H. Gundel in *RE s.v.* Visellius (no. 3), cols. 355–8.

71   Roman naval actions during the Third Mithridatic War. 72– 69 BC.

Extracts from Memnon, and other sources.

A: Memnon (*FGrHist* 434 F 29.5). 72 BC. C. Valerius Triarius ordered to blockade the
Hellespont. **B**: Memnon (*ibid.* F 33.1–2). 72 BC. Triarius defeats Mithridatic fleet off
Tenedos. **C**: Phlegon of Tralles (*FGrHist* 257 F 12.13). 69 BC. Triarius builds a wall on
Delos. **D**: *OGIS* 447; Durrbach, *Choix* 160; *ILS* 8774; *I. Délos* 1855. 69 BC. Base of white
marble; at Delos Milesian combat crew makes a dedication to Triarius. **E**: Durrbach,
Choix 159; *I. Délos* 1856; F. G. Maier, *Griechische Mauerbauinschriften* I, Vestigia I (Heidel-
berg 1959) no. 41, p. 167. Base of white marble, dedication of a wall to Triarius. Delos.
F: *I. Délos* 1857; Maier, *op. cit.* no. 42, p. 168. 69 BC. Doric architrave of white marble;
Smyrnaean combat crew makes a dedication to Triarius. Delos.

T. Reinach, *Mithridate Eupator roi de Pont* (Paris 1890) 318–76; Magie, *RRAM* I 321–50.

A. Memnon, *FGrHist* 434 F 29.5

Lucullus, Cotta, and Triarius,[1] the Roman generals in command, united their forces at Nikomedeia and prepared to invade Pontos. When the capture of Herakleia was announced to them, its betrayal was unknown and it was thought that the revolt was (the fault) of the whole city.[2] It was decided that Lucullus with the majority of the military forces should advance into Cappadocia through the interior of the country against Mithridates and his entire kingdom, Cotta should advance against Herakleia, and Triarius should take the naval forces and wait in ambush around the Hellespont and the Propontis for the return of the ships of Mithridates which had been sent off to Crete and Spain.[3]

B. Memnon, *ibid.* F 33.1–2

Shortly before, Triarius with the Roman fleet set out from Nikomedeia against the Pontic triremes which, as reported above, had been sent out to the waters around Crete and Spain. He learned that the remaining ships – for many of them had been sunk and lost in a storm and in a number of small naval battles – had returned to Pontus. He overtook these (ships that had returned to Pontus) and brought them to battle around Tenedos, having seventy triremes himself, while the Pontic forces were a little short of eighty. (2) When the battle began, the king's ships at first resisted, but later their rout was quite clear and the Romans won an overwhelming victory. Thus the whole naval force of Mithridates, which had sailed off on his side against Asia, was ruined.[4]

C. Phlegon of Tralles, *FGrHist* 257 F 12.13

The pirate Athenodoros enslaved the Delians and defaced the statues of their gods, but Gaius Triarius repaired the damage to the city and fortified Delos with a wall.[5]

D. *I. Délos* 1855. Delos

To Gaius Valerius, son of Gaius, | Triarius, lega|te, the Milesians who
5   campaign|ed with him on board ‖ the bireme bearing the name | Parthenos (Virgin Goddess) made (this dedication).

E. Maier, *op. cit.* no. 41. Delos

To Gaius Valeri|us, son of Gaius, | Triarius, le|gate, the ‖ Milesians who campaign|ed with him | on board the bireme | bearing the name

Athe|[n]a, the First Offic|er[6] and the one in char|ge being Publi|us Iunius, Publ|ius' son, (dedicate this wall).

F. Maier, *op. cit.* no. 42. Delos

To Gaius Valerius, son of Gaius, Triarius, legate, the Smyrnaeans who campaigne|d with him on board the bireme bearing the name | Athena, the Ship-Captain being Nikomachos (son) of Artemidoros, (dedicate) this tower.

1 After the death of Sulla in 78 BC Mithridates of Pontos began making preparations for another invasion of Asia Minor. At Rome Marcus Aurelius Cotta, the consul in 74 BC, was made governor of the new province of Bithynia, and his colleague in the consulship, Lucius Licinius Lucullus, received the command in Cilicia. Lucullus was later given orders to take command against Mithridates. Gaius Valerius Triarius was a legate of Lucullus. Late in 74 or early in 73 BC they arrived in Asia Minor, and in the spring of 73 Mithridates advanced into Bithynia, a huge fleet sailing along the Pontic coast in support.
2 See above, no. 68. Plutarch, *Lucullus* 11.5, gives a different name to the admiral of Mithridates: see Magie, *RRAM* I 325, and II 1206, n. 9.
3 Mithridates had sent ships to Spain to negotiate with the rebel Sertorius, promising him money and ships: see Cicero, *De imperio Cn. Pomp.* 9; *Pro Murena* 32; Plutarch, *Sertorius* 23ff.; Appian, *Mithridatic Wars* 68 and 112. Cf. Magie, *RRAM* I 322–3. Before the ships could reach Spain, Sertorius was killed in 73 or 72 BC. The ships turned around and sailed back to the Hellespont.
4 Triarius was fighting under the auspices of Lucullus, however, and Lucullus was given credit for the victory.
5 Remains of this wall have been uncovered by the French excavations: P. Roussel, *Délos colonie athénienne* (Paris 1916) 331–2, with a plan at the end of the volume. Cf. Laidlaw, *Delos* 267, and Maier, *op. cit.* pp. 166–70. There is a copy of the plan in Rostovtzeff, *SEHHW* II 779, fig. 8. The pirates of the whole area had been actively supported and organized by Mithridates as part of his campaign in Asia Minor.
6 The Greek term (*epiplous*) is here taken to mean the officer who often takes command of a ship in place of the regular captain called the trierarch. See Maier, *op. cit.* p. 170 with references.

72   Antonian law concerning Termessus Maior in Pisidia. 72 or 68 BC.

Bronze tablet[1] with nail holes, Rome.

*CIL I[2] 589; *ILS* 38; C. G. Bruns, *Fontes Iuris Romani Antiqui*[7] (Tübingen 1909) no. 14; *FIRA* I 11; photograph in Degrassi, *Imagines* no. 388.

E. G. Hardy, *Six Roman Laws* (Oxford 1911) 94–101 (with a translation); Magie, *RRAM* I 295; II 1176–7, n. 34; A. N. Sherwin-White, *JRS* 66 (1976) 11–14; R. Syme, *Roman Papers* (Oxford 1979) II 557–65.

(Tablet) I. On Termessus Maior in Pisidia.² *vv* | (Heading) Gaius Antonius, son of Marcus, Gnaeus Corne[lius --, Quintus Marcius --, Lucius Hostilius --, Gaius Popilius --, Marcus Valerius --, Gaius Antius --, Quintus Caecilius --, Lucius V---,]³ | Gaius Fundanius, son of Gaius, tribunes of the plebs, in accordance with the decision of the senate, [---] the plebs; [--] | was the first man to vote.⁴ *vv* |

(Col. I) Those who were citizens of Termessus Maior in Pisidia and those who | by the laws of Termessus Maior in Pisidia | before the Kalends of April, which occurred when Lucius Gellius and Gnaeus Lentulus were consuls (April 1, 72 BC), | were made citizens of Termessus Maior in

5   Pisidia and all those who ‖ were (or) will be born of them, all | these and their descendants, citizens of Termessus Maior in Pisidia, | shall be free, friends, and allies of the Roman People, | and they shall enjoy their own laws to this extent, and they | all shall to this extent be permitted to enjoy

10   their own laws as citizens of Termessus Maior ‖ in Pisidia in such manner as shall not be contrary to this law. | *vv* | Whatever lands, whatever places (and) buildings, public or private, | of Termessus Maior in Pisidia are within their borders | or were (within them) when Lucius Marcius

15   (Philippus) and Sextius Iulius (Caesar) were consuls (91 BC), ‖ and whatever islands are theirs or were (theirs) when they | who were mentioned above were consuls, and whatever | of these possessions under these consuls they held, | occupied, *used*, [and enjoyed,] – those of these pos-

20   sessions which | have not been leased out [---;]⁵ and whatever ‖ of these possessions [---] by this (law?) shall not | be leased out [---,] which has been passed | *in accordance with* [a? the? law? ---,] all these possessions | the citizens of Ter[messus Maior in Pisidia shall hold] and occupy. | And these same [possessions, places, fields, and buildings they shall use and]

25   *enjoy*, ‖ just as *before* that [war against Mithridates which] came first | they held, [occupied, used,] and [enjoyed] them.⁶ |

In regard to the citizens of Termessus Maior in Pisidia, | whatever places, fields, and buildings, public or private, except for those leased out, are theirs | or were theirs before the war against Mithridates which came first,

30   ‖ and whatever of these possessions they | held, occupied, used, and enjoyed before that time, | whatever of (all) this they themselves by their own free will did not alienate from themselves, | all of these shall belong to the citizens of Termessus Maior in Pisidia just as they belong | or did belong to them, and in the same way (as now or at that time) all these pos-

35   sessions ‖ they shall be permitted to hold, occupy, use, and enjoy. *vv* ‖

Whatever free men or slaves the citizens of Termessus Maior in Pisidia | (Col. II) lost in the Mithridatic War, the magistrate or pro|magistrate, whose jurisdiction includes this matter and to whose | court the parties will go about this matter, shall in such a manner pronounce the law about

 5 this matter | and shall set up trials and procedures for recovery as ‖ to enable them to recover them. *vv* |

No magistrate or promagistrate (or) legate or | anyone else shall introduce soldiers into the town of Termessus Maior | in Pisidia or into the land of
10 Termessus Maior | in Pisidia for the sake of wintering over, nor ‖ shall he bring it about that anyone should introduce soldiers there or | that soldiers should winter over there, unless the senate decrees with mention of the (town's) name that | soldiers may be brought into winter quarters in Termessus | Maior in Pisidia; no magistrate | or promagistrate (or) legate or
15 anyone else shall bring it about, ‖ or give any order, that (the citizens) should give or provide any more | or that more should be taken from them than what in accordance with the Porcian Law[7] | is or will be required of *them* to give or provide. *vv* | Whatever laws, whatever right, whatever custom existed, when Lucius Marcius | and Sextius Iulius were consuls
20 (91 BC), between citizens of Rome and citizens of Termessus ‖ Maior in Pisidia, the same laws and the same right | and the same custom shall exist between citizens of Rome and | citizens of Termessus Maior in Pisidia; and whatever | right over any possessions, places, lands, buildings, and towns | belonged to the citizens of Termessus Maior in Pisidia, when those
25 men were consuls ‖ who were named above, whatever of all this, except | for those leased out, (in the way of) places, fields, and buildings they themselves of their own free will have not | alienated from themselves, this same right over the same possessions, places, lands, | buildings, and towns shall belong to the citizens of Termessus Maior in Pisidia; | and (no provision)
30 that these matters written in this chapter ‖ may be, or may be made, any less (applicable), is enacted (anywhere else) in this law. | Whatever law for customs duties on (trade by) land and sea | the citizens of Termessus Maior in Pisidia have established to be collected within their own | borders, that shall be the law for collecting those customs duties, | provided
35 that no duty is collected from those who for the public ‖ revenues of the Roman People will hold the contracts. Whatever | out of this revenue[8] the publicans will transport through their (the Termessians') borders | [---]

---

 1 The original document consisted of several bronze tablets put up side by side, and the heading, in very large letters, went across all the tablets. Only the first tablet has survived. There are three lines to the heading. The first line begins with 'Gaius Antonius, son of Marcus, Gnaeus Corne' and there it breaks off, because the rest of that line would have appeared at the beginning of the next tablet nailed up to its right side. Similarly, the second line of the heading begins with 'Gaius Fundanius' and ends with 'plebs', while the rest of the line originally continued in the second line of the next tablet. Beneath this heading runs the text of the law itself, arranged in columns, two of them to each tablet. In order to hold the names of ten tribunes (see n. 3, below), at least three or four tablets would have been necessary. See the photograph in Degrassi, *loc. cit.*
 2 This notice is not part of the heading. It stands on its own line in small letters just above 'Gaius Antonius'.

3 The restored names are those of the seven other tribunes of the plebs known from another inscription (*CIL* I² 744) to have been in office with Antonius, Cornelius, and Fundanius.

4 Mommsen (in *CIL* and Bruns) restores: '[lawfully proposed to the] plebs [and the plebs lawfully voted in the -- on the -- day before --; the -- tribe was first (to vote); --] was the first man [in that tribe] to vote'. On the first man to vote see E. S. Staveley, *Greek and Roman Voting and Elections* (Ithaca N.Y. 1972) 165–9, and C. Nicolet, *The World of the Citizen in Republican Rome* (translated by P. S. Falla, London 1980) 283–5.

5 Mommsen (in Bruns): '[they shall hold and occupy as before;]'.

6 The entire central portion of the text (lines 19–26) is damaged and illegible. All restorations in this section are conjectural.

7 Mentioned only here.

8 Apparently revenue in kind is meant: wheat, oil, etc.

73   Greek city of Mesambria in Thrace placed under a Roman officer. 71 BC.

Marble stele broken at the bottom and the left side, inscribed on both sides,[1] Mesambria.

IG Bulg. I² 314a. Cf. Livy, *Per.* 97; Appian, *Illyrian Wars* 30; Sallust, *Histories* 4.18 (Maurenbrecher).

G. Tibiletti, *Rendiconti dell'Istituto Lombardo, Classe di Lettere e Scienze morali e storiche* 86 (1953) 69–74 and 98 ff.; Chr. Danov in *ANRW* 2.7.1, 115–16.

Decreed by the Boule and the People. Heraion (son) of Pasio|[n] made the motion: Since Gaius Cornelius, son of Gaius, | the Roman, appointed over
5 our city as | [---]² by Marcus Terentius, *son* of Marcus, ‖ [Lu]cullus imperator,³ has brought many *gr*|*eat* benefits to our *People* and | with (our) *embassies sent* to the imperator | has co-operated in every way, and, as
10 patron⁴ | of our *city*, when our en‖voys *testified* to him about the assign|ment of winter quarters (for Roman troops) [to our city (?),] he exercised every | [---] zeal as (he?) foresaw [---|---]

1 The inscription on the reverse side is older than the present decree, its contents of an entirely different nature.

2 D. Dečev, in the original publication (*Izvestija na Bâlgarskija arheologičeski institut* 17 (1950) 59ff.) suggested '*strategos*', i.e. '*general*', seeing only the last two letters of the word. Tibiletti preferred '*eparchos*', the usual equivalent of the Roman *praefectus*. Mihailov now, in *IG Bulg.* I² (1970), after further study of the stone, believes that the traces of letters are not compatible with either suggestion, although he believes the sense requires *praefectus civitatis*, i.e. a Roman prefect in charge of a city or state.

3 He was proconsul in Macedonia in 72 and 71 BC: Broughton, *MRR* II 118–19.

4 'Patron' is simply transliterated from the Latin and made into a Greek participle.

74   Roman businessmen, Roman officials and the debts of a Greek city. 71 BC.

Marble stele with gable, Gytheion in Laconia.

IG V 1.1146; *SIG³ 748.

Hatzfeld, *Trafiquants* 80–2; Larsen, *Greece* 372–3, 428, 430; Rostovtzeff, *SEHHW* II 951–5; Accame, *Dominio* 131–2.

Since Numerius and Marcus Cloatius, sons of Numerius, Romans, |
proxenoi and benefactors of our city, from the very beginning have con|-
tinued to act justly both toward our city and, privately, | toward those of
the citizens who approached them (with a request), omitting nothing of
5   zeal and ar‖dor, because of which at appropriate tim|es the city gratefully
made public mention and voted *suit|able* honors for them, in the year of
Lachares' | magistracy[1] when they were negotiating our release from the
obligations of the first loan; | and in the year of Phleinos' magistracy, when
10   concerning the second lo‖an of 3965 drachmas, | which the city had
borrowed in the year of Damarmenos' | magistracy, they accepted the
People of Athens as arbitrator in the time of Marcilius[2] | and (then) after
being implored by the citizens, they permitted the | payment of what the
15   citizens persuaded them;[3] and in the ‖ year of Biadas' magistracy, when,
asking for (it as) a personal favor from | Publius Autronius (Paetus) and
Lucius Marcilius, who were their | guests[4] whom they had put up at their
own expense, | they successfully pleaded for (the city) to be spared the
soldiers and other considerable burdens im|posed by them (the legates),
20   through which actions they brought relief to the city, ‖ the aforemen-
tioned (legates) having done this entirely as a favor to them; | and they
have often brought into goodwill and sup|port for the city many of the
(Roman) leaders, the legate Gaius Iul[i]‖us (Caesar)[5] and the legate
Publius Autronius (Paetus) and the legate Fulv|[i]us, doing all these
25   things out of their goodwill toward the ci‖ty and its citizens; and when
there had been imposed on our city | an order for grain by Gaius Gallius[6]
and for clothing by Quintus Ancharius[7] according to (the requisition)
allot|ted to our city, they used all their zeal and ardor | and went to inter-
cede with them in order that our city might not have to contribute, but
might be exempt|ed; and in this they succeeded, and we did not have to
30   contribute; whoever of our citizens ‖ has approached them with a private
request, or has had any need, they | have done everything for everybody,
making themselves available without evasion | in every critical situation;
and in the year of Timokrates' magistracy, | *when* Antonius had come
here[8] and our city had need of ca|sh and nobody else was willing to enter
35   into a contract with us, they l‖oaned us 4200 drachmas under contra|ct at

interest of four drachmas (per mina per month),[9] and, being approa|ched
by the People in the year of Nikaretidas' magistracy with a request (to
accept) simple inter|est, they granted us (instead) *interest* of two drachmas
(per mina per month) and relieved | the city of payment of over 1500
40   drachmas from the ‖ money owed; *in consideration of* all the aforementioned
it was decreed | by the People in a *full* meeting of our Assembly to praise
Nume|rius and Marcus Cloatius, sons of Numerius, Romans, for | all the
aforementioned things that they have done for the city and for those
pri|vate individuals who have appealed to them, and for the goodwill
45   which they have contin‖ued to exercise toward our city; they shall have all
the ho|nors and privileges that belong to the other proxenoi | and bene-
factors of our city; and whatever ephors[10] happen | to be in office at the
time shall invite them and their offspring to front-row seats | in all the
50   games which our city might celebrate, ‖ and they shall be permitted to sit
with the ephors in the front | seats, so that it may be clear to all that our
city honors wor|thy men. The ephors in Nikar|etidas' magistracy shall
engrave the decree concerning these *privileges* on a stone stele | and erect it
55   in the temple of Apollo in whatever lo‖cation the priests may grant *them*,
and the expenses | shall be borne by the city.

1 Lachares, Phleinos (line 9), Damarmenos (11), Biadas (15), Timokrates (32), and
   Nikaretidas (37 and 52–3) were eponymous magistrates, probably of the League of the
   Eleutherolakones (Free Laconians), to which Gytheion belonged, and holding the
   title of strategoi ('generals'). For the relationship of that league to the Lacedaemonian
   League see Accame, *Dominio* 124ff., and K. M. T. Chrimes, *Ancient Sparta* (Manchester
   1949) 435ff.
2 He ought to be the Lucius Marcilius of line 16, probably a legate under M. Antonius
   Creticus: Broughton, *MRR* II 105.
3 Apparently the citizens first went to arbitration. When they lost the case, they begged
   the Cloatii to let them off lightly, and the Cloatii acquiesced.
4 Even though the Cloatii would have been exempted from the burden of housing the
   two Romans, they seem to have gone to the expense in spite of that. That the two were
   actually legates appears highly probable. They may have been on the staff of M.
   Antonius Creticus and engaged in obtaining supplies for the projected campaign
   against Crete: Broughton, *MRR* II 112–13.
5 The future dictator also seems to have been on the staff of Antonius Creticus: Broughton, *MRR* II 115–16, n. 6; M. Gelzer, *Caesar* (Oxford 1968) 24–5. The legate Publius
   Autronius (Paetus) became consul designate in 65 BC but was convicted of bribery.
6 Probably the senator mentioned by Cicero, *Verr.* 3.65.152.
7 Despite Broughton (*MRR* II 112), Quintus Ancharius was probably the proquaestor
   of Macedonia mentioned in *I. Olympia* 328. See Schwertfeger, *Bund* 68 and 73–4.
8 The reference is to Marcus Antonius Creticus, father of the triumvir. For his command and campaign against the pirates see Magie, *RRAM* I 292–3, and, for the
   sources, Broughton, *MRR* II 101ff.
9 This is 4% interest per month, i.e. 48% per year, compounded monthly.
10 The ephors were the most important officials in Dorian cities, especially in Sparta. In

the Hellenistic period they were elected by the assembly of the People and were thus a democratic institution. Details of their organization outside of Sparta are not well known.

75   The Greek East honors Pompey the Great. Between 67 and 62 BC.

Inscribed bases.

A: *IG* XII 2.202; **SIG*³ 751; *IGRR* IV 54; *ILS* 8776. Mytilene. **B**: *SIG*³ 749 A; Durrbach, *Choix 162; *I. Délos* 1641. Delos. **C**: *ILS 9459. Miletopolis in Asia Minor. **D**: *SEG XVII 525. Magnesia near Mt Sipylus. **E**: *Milet I 7.253. Miletus.

A. *SIG*³ 751, Mytilene

The People | (honor) their savior and founder¹ | Gnaeus Pompeius, son
5 of Gnaeus, | the Great, imperator for the third time, who des‖troyed those who had seized | the inhabited world by his wars on both | land and sea. | *vacat* | *vv* Dorotheos, (son) of Hegesandros, | of Olynthos made (the statue).²

B. Durrbach, *Choix* 162, Delos

The People of Athe[ns and the Society] | of Worshippers of Pompeius³ [in Delos (dedicate this statue of) Gnaeus] | Pompeius, [son of] Gna[eus, the Great,] imperator, [to Apollo.]

C. *ILS* 9459, Miletopolis in Asia Minor

The People | (honor) [G]naeus Pompeius, *son of Gnaeus*, | the Great, impe-
5 rator | for the third time, savior and bene‖factor of the People and | of all Asia, guar|dian of land and sea, | because of his excellence and | *goodwill* toward them.

D. *SEG* XVII 525, Magnesia near Mt Sipylus

(Of) Gnaeus Pompeius, the Great, | imperator, the People *dedi|cate* (this statue).

E. *Milet* I 7.253, Miletus

The People (honor) Gnaeus Pompeius, son of Gnaeus, the Great, impera-tor | for the third time, patron and benefactor.

For other dedications similar to those translated here see *I. Ilion* 74; *IG* IX 2.1134 (Demet-rias in Greece); *IGRR* III 869 (Pompeiopolis in Cilicia).

1 The term was purely honorary. However, Pompey had restored the city's freedom, which it had lost because of its acceptance of Mithridates in 88 BC.

2 The name of the sculptor Dorotheos seems to have been engraved in letters of the third
   century BC, so that one might suppose an older base had been used. However, occasionally sculptors had their own way of signing their names.
3 This was a cult society with social aspects: see M. N. Tod, *Sidelights on Greek History*
   (Oxford 1932) 71–93; Laidlaw, *Delos* 202–8.

76   Envoys from Tragurion in Dalmatia meet Julius Caesar in Aquileia. March 3, 56 BC.

Fragments of a limestone slab, letters of the first century, Salonae.

D. Rendić-Miočević, *Studi Aquileiesi offerti a Giovanni Brusin* (Aquileia 1953) 67–76
(+ photographs); **RDGE* 24 A. Cf. Caesar, *Bell. Gall.* 3.7 and 9.

RDGE pp. 139–42.

In the consulship of Gn[ae]us Lentulus M[ar]|cellinus and L[u]cius
Marcius Phi[lip]|pus (56 BC), on the *fifth day* before the Nones of Mar|ch
5 (March 3), [and in Issa] when the hieromnemon ‖ was Zopy[ros] son of
[--]on, of the month Ar[te]|mitios on the [-- (day) from its] *beginning*, the
en|voys from Traguri[on,] Pamphilos son of P[am]|philos, and Kleëm-
10 [por]os son of Tima[sio|n,] and Philoxenos [son] of Dionysios ‖ were in
Aquileia in the presence of Gaius Iuli[us] Cae[sar,] | imperator.[1] Gaius
Gaveni[us, son of --] | (of the tribe) Fabia spoke [about the] |*freedom* of
the Issaians [and the friendship | of the Romans] and Issaians [---]

Issa, oldest and strongest of the Greek colonies on the island of the same name off the
Dalmatian coast (modern Vis), had itself established colonies in the area, including Tragurion, west of Salonae on the mainland. After terms of peace had been agreed upon with
the Illyrians in 228 BC (if not before), Issa came under the protection of Rome. In 167 BC
Rome granted her freedom and immunity.

1 In the autumn of 57 BC Caesar, thinking that the pacification of Gaul was complete
   (*Bell. Gall.* 2.35), left for Illyricum to learn more about that part of his huge provincial
   command. In March of 56 he was at Aquileia and the next month he was at Luca in
   conference with Pompey and Crassus. Trouble in Gaul then caused him to hurry back to
   his troops in the north.

77   Letter of a Roman official to the conventus (judiciary centers) of the province of Asia. 51/50 BC (?) or c. 29 BC (?).

Fragmentary copies of the same letter found on building blocks in Priene
and Miletus.

*RDGE 52, lines 37–60 (Miletus copy).[1]

Magie, *RRAM* II 1059–61, nn. 41–2; *RDGE* pp. 274–6; G. W. Bowersock, *AJP* 91 (1970)
226–7; Chr. Habicht, *JRS* 65 (1975) 68–9 and 71; G. P. Burton, *JRS* 65 (1975) 92–3.

[--] of Quin[t]us T[---|--] for the cancellation of debts which *he (it?) had contracted*, [and,] meeting [Mar|cus] Cicer[o]² he expressed his thanks

40 ‖ and carefuly preserved the [arrangements made] by *me* [---] | Thus, how you have endured the shame|lessness of certain persons in [these mat-ters] amazes me. For these [reasons] | I have written to the Koinon of the

45 Greeks,³ to | you,⁴ to Ephesus, Tralles, Alabanda, M[y‖l]asa, Smyrna, Pergamum, Sardis, | Adramyttium in order that (each of) you to the | cities in your own judiciary district⁵ might dispatch (copies of this letter) and see to it that in the most conspic|uous place on a pilaster on | white

50 stone there is engraved th‖is letter, so that in common for all the province | justice might be established for all time,⁶ and that all the oth|er cities and peoples might do the same thing among themselves, | and that they might deposit (a copy of this letter) in the archives of the Nomophyla|kia and

55 the Chrematisteria.⁷ The reason for which I wrote in Gre‖ek, do not ask, since it was my intention | that nothing contrary to the (correct) interpre-tation of my let|ter could possibly be in your mind. This letter [I have given] | to [Ti]mokles (son) of Anaxagoras and to Sosikrates (son) of

60 Py[thion,] | envoys from Magnesia on the [Maean‖der.] *vv* Farewell. *vv*

Since both the author of this letter and the exact nature of the information it communica-ted to the Koinon of Asia and the various cities in Asia are unknown to us because of the fragmentary condition of the stones, the problem of interpretation is very difficult. That it was an important matter is obvious from the provisions made for the distribution of the letter to all areas of the province and from the wording of lines 50–4.

1 The first 36 lines are too badly mutilated to extract much more than a few words with syntactical connections: *'in* Ephesus', 'the laws', 'I was forced by', 'I wish you to know'.

2 If this is the famous orator M. Tullius Cicero, the date of the letter is likely to be 51–50 BC, when he was the governor of Cilicia and active in the affairs of the whole area. In that case the author of the letter might be Q. Minucius Thermus, the governor of Asia at that time. But Bowersock wants to date the letter to *c.* 29 BC, make Octavian the author, and identify 'Cicero' as the orator's son. The son was consul in 30 BC and then became governor of Asia.

3 See above, no. 58, n. 1.

4 The cities listed after this word were the centers of the Asian conventus (judiciary districts). Since Miletus is missing from the list and since this copy of the letter was found in Miletus, 'you' must be the Milesians.

5 The province of Asia, like others, was divided geographically into these districts, and each of them had a principal city in which the Roman governor held court once each year. See the works of Habicht and Burton.

6 The copy from Priene begins with this phrase and continues to the end, although in a far more fragmentary state than the present copy from Miletus.

7 A Nomophylakion (plural: Nomophylakia) was a building in which a Nomophylax ('Guardian of the Laws') had his office. Here the laws (and decrees) of a Greek city were preserved. Similar is the case with the Chrematisteria, although the precise nature of a Chrematistes in a Greek city in Asia in the Hellenistic and Roman periods is contro-

versial. For the officials in charge of such archives see G. Busolt, *Griechische Staats-kunde*[3] Part 1 (Munich 1920) 489ff.

78   The city of Dionysopolis, King Burebista, and the Romans. 49 or 48 BC.

Marble slab broken at the top, on the right, and on the left, Dionysopolis in Thrace (modern Balčik in Bulgaria).

SIG[3] 762; **IGBulg.* I[2] 13 (+ photographs, Pls. VI–VIII). Cf. Livy, *Per.* 103; Dio 38.10.2; Strabo 7.3.11.

A. Alföldi in *CAH* 11.81–3; E. Condurachi, *AAnt Hung* 26 (1978) 7–14; Chr. M. Danov in *ANRW* 2.7.1, 116–19.

[--|--] he took up [--|--] Theodoros and Epi[--|--] at their own expense
5   [-‖--] fellow travelers *he departed* [-|--] to Argedauon[1] to [his (?)] father[2] |
[--] *having arrived* and met with (him) at once [--|--] from him he won
(him) over completely [and] | *released* his People from the (?) [--;] and
having become priest ‖ [- of the] *Great* [God[3]] the processions and sacri-
10   fices he [per|formed magnificently] and with the citizens he shared [the |
meat (of the sacrifices),] and having been chosen priest of [Sar]apis by lot,
in like manner at his own *expen|se* [he conducted himself] well and as one
who loves goodness, and when the eponymous (god) | [of the city, Dion]y-
15   sos, did not have a priest for many years, ‖ [he was called upon] by the citi-
zens and he devoted himself (to the priesthood), *and* [through|out the]
wintering-over of [Gaius] Antonius[4] he assumed | [the (priest's) crown]
of the god and the processions and sacrifices [he per|formed well] and
sumptuously and with the citizens [he sha|red the] *meat* lavishly, and, in
20   regard to the gods in Samothrace, ‖ having assumed for life their (priest's)
[crown,] their processions [and | sacrifices] he performed on behalf of the
mystai[5] and the *ci|ty*; and when recently King Burebista had *become* first and
[great|est] of the kings in Thrace and over all | [the (land)] *across* the river
25   (Danube) and the (land) on the near side had gained possessio‖n, also to
him he became first and *great|est* friend and procured the greatest advan-
tages for our city by spe|eches and advice of the best kind; and the goodwill
of the *ki|ng* with respect to the safety of his city he urge|d, and in all other
30   ways of himself unsparingly ‖ did he give; the city's embassies with their
dangers he under|took without hesitation to win in all respects | the
advantage for his native city, and to Gnaeus Pompeius, Gnaeus' so|n,
Roman imperator,[6] he was sent by King Burabe[i|s]ta as an envoy, and
35   meeting with him in the area of Macedonia ‖ *around* [Her]aklea-in-Lynkos
not only the negotiations on behalf of the *ki|ng* did he conduct, bringing

about the goodwill of the Romans | for the king, but also concerning his
native city most fruitful | negotiations did he conduct; and in general
throughout every situation of cri|sis he applied himself body and soul,
40   expenses ‖ being paid from his own means of livelihood; and, some of the
material things of the city[7] subsi|dizing by himself, he has exhibited the
greatest zeal for the | safety of his native city: in order therefore that the
People also might be seen honoring | fine and good men and those who
benefit them (i.e. the People), *it is de|creed* by [the] Boule and the People for
45   these services to praise Akornion ‖ (son) of Dion[y]sios and to present to
him at the Games of Dionysos a gold | crown and a bronze statue, and to
crown him also in the *fu|ture* each year at the Games of Dionysos with a
gold *cro|wn*, and for the erection of the statue to *give* him a pla|ce, the most
conspicuous, in the agora. *vv*

1 A variant for Argedava which is mentioned by Ptolemaeus (3.8.4) in the form
   'Argidaua' among the towns of Dacia. See Condurachi, *op. cit.* p. 7, for all details.
2 Not his own father, but the father of the person to whom 'he' has gone as an envoy.
3 A chthonic deity of the Thracians called Darzalas or Derzelas.
4 C. Antonius M.f. Hibrida, consul in 63 BC with Cicero and then proconsul of Macedonia the following year: Broughton, *MRR* II 175–6. His campaign against the Thracians of the north-east ended in disaster not far from Histria and he was forced into
   flight after abandoning the army standards to the Bastarnae.
5 Initiates in the Samothracian Mysteries. See above, no. 27.
6 Pompey was called imperator after the battle against Caesar at Dyrrachium in 49 BC:
   Caesar, *Bell. Civ.* 3.71.3.
7 Possible alternate translation: 'some of the city's public choruses'.

**79   Statues of Julius Caesar dedicated in the Greek East after
Pharsalus. Fall of 48 BC or soon afterwards.**
Inscribed pedestals.[1]

A: A. E. Raubitschek, **JRS* 44 (1954) 65–6, F (+ photograph); *SEG* XIV 121. Athens.
B: **IGRR* IV 305. Pergamum. **C**: **IGRR* IV 928. Chios. **D**: **SIG*[3] 760. Ephesus. **E**: **IG*
XII 5.557. Karthaia on Keos.

Magie, *RRAM* I 405–15; Raubitschek, *op. cit.* 65–75; S. Weinstock, *Divus Iulius* (Oxford
1971) 296ff.

A. *JRS* 44 (1954) 65–6 F, Athens

[The People] | (dedicate this statue of) Gaius Iulius, [son] of Gaius,
[Caesar, pontifex maximus and] | imperator [and] consul [for the second
time (48 BC), savior] | and *benefactor*.[2]

B. *IGRR* IV 305, Pergamum

The People | (dedicate this statue of) Gaius Iulius, son of Gaius, Caesar, |
imperator and pontifex maximus, consul for the second time, | their pat-
5   ron and benefactor, ‖ savior and benefactor of all the Greeks, | because of
his piety and justice.

C. *IGRR* IV 928, Chios

The Boule and the People | (dedicate this statue of) Gaius Iulius, son of
Gaius, Caesar, | pontifex maximus and imperator | and consul for the
5   second time, ‖ patron of the city, because of his excellence, to the gods.

D. *SIG*[3] 760, Ephesus

The cities in Asia and the [peoples] | and the tribes[3] (dedicate this
statue of) Gaius Iulius, *son* of | Gaius, Caesar, pontifex maximus and
5   imper‖ator and consul for the | second time, (descendant) of Ares and
Aphrodite,[4] | god manifest and common savior | of human life.

E. *IG* XII 5.557, Karthaia on Keos

The People of Karthaia | dedicate (this statue of) the god and imperator |
and savior of the inhabited world, | Gaius Iulius Caesar, son of Gaius,
5   ‖ Caesar.

---

1 Other pedestals with inscriptions similar to those translated here: *I. Délos* 1587 (Delos);
   IG VII 1835 as restored by Raubitschek, *op. cit.* 70–1, S (Thespiai); Raubitschek, *op. cit.*
   66, I (Demetrias in Greece); Raubitschek, *op. cit.* 67, L (Megara); Raubitschek, *op. cit.*
   69, Q (Samos); L. Robert, *Hellenica* 10 (1955) 259 (Alabanda in Asia Minor); *ibid.* 257
   (Phokaia in Asia Minor); Caesar mentions (*Bell. Civ.* 3.105.6) a statue of himself in
   Tralles in Asia Minor.
2 Raubitschek thinks this statue might be connected with the pardon which Caesar granted to Athens immediately after Pharsalus: Appian, *Civil Wars* 2.88.368; Dio 42.14.1–3.
3 Cf. no. 58, above, with n. 1. However, the wording of this phrase is different from the
   others. Whether the difference is significant is not known. T. Drew-Bear in *BCH* 96
   (1972) 460ff. has examined all the evidence for the Koinon of the Greeks and concluded,
   in regard to the terminology, that in honorary inscriptions set up on the authorization of
   the Koinon the Koinon itself is designated by the enumeration of its constituent ele-
   ments (p. 466). But the other known examples are different from the present one.
4 The family of Caesar had long prided itself on its descent from Aphrodite (Venus)
   through Aeneas: cf. no. 59 above and see Weinstock, *op. cit.* 15–18; 81–90. For the connection with Ares (Mars): Weinstock, *op. cit.* 128–32. Both gods together were revered
   as the ancestral gods of the Romans.

80   Julius Caesar makes concessions to Pergamum. After Pharsalus, 48–47 BC.

Various documents.

A: **RDGE* 54. Letter of Julius Caesar to Pergamum. Fragment of a building block from the anta of the structure on which the senatorial decree concerning Pergamene land (above, no. 45) had been engraved, Smyrna. **B**: H. Hepding, *Athen. Mitt.* 34 (1909) 336–7; *IGRR* IV 1677; L. Robert, *Opera* I 614 B; A. E. Raubitschek, **JRS* 44 (1954) 68. Pergamum honors Julius Caesar. Base of white marble, Pergamum. **C**: Hepding, *op. cit.* p. 330; **IGRR* IV 1682; L. Robert, *Opera* I 614 A. Pergamum honors Mithridates, son of Menodotos, of Pergamum. Base of bluish marble in three fragments, damaged on the lower left and right, Pergamum.

Hepding, *op. cit.* 329–40; Magie, *RRAM* I 405–6; II 1258–9, nn. 3–4; *RDGE* pp. 281–4

A. *RDGE* 54, Smyrna

[Gaius Iulius Caesar] imperator, [pontifex maximus and dictator for the second time (October 48–October 47 BC) to the Pergamene magistrates, | Boule and People, greetings.] If you are well, [it is good. I with my army am in good health. | I have dispatched to you a copy] of the decision [made concerning the land marked off for you.] | Concerning what Mith[ridates
5   (son) of Menodotos, your citizen and my friend,[1] ‖ has said,] concerning this [matter I have decided as follows: *vv* | the city of P]ergamum and [whatever of its] *land* [King Attalus (son) of King Eumenes marked off for the city,[2]] | except for the Royal [---][3]

B. Raubitschek, *op. cit.* 68, Pergamum

[The People honored] their savior and benefactor | [Gaius] Iulius, son of Gaius, Caes[a]r, imperator and | *pontifex maximus* and dictator for the *second* time (October 48–October 47 BC), [because of] all his excellence, |
5   and because he has restored to the gods the city ‖ [and the] land that is sacred [and inviolate and autonomous].[4]

C. *IGRR* IV 1682, Pergamum

vv The People honored *vv* | Mithridates (son) of Menodotos, hereditary high priest | and hereditary priest of Dionysos the Leader, | because he has
5   restored to the ancestral gods [the city] ‖ and [the] land and has become after [Pergamos][5] | *vv* and Philetairos[6] his native city's new founder. *vv*

---

1   Mithridates of Pergamum was one of the city's most prominent citizens who won the gratitude of Caesar by coming to his aid with an army when he was besieged in Alexandria (winter of 48–47 BC). Mithridates was rewarded with a principality in the Crimea. Some modern scholars (Hepding, Robert and others) think also that Caesar granted

Pergamum its freedom because of the good offices of Mithridates. But of this there is no solid evidence. See below, no. 81.

2 This appears to be a reference to the land originally left to Pergamum by Attalus III in his will (above, no. 39): see Segre in *Athenaeum* 16 (1938) 122ff.

3 Segre suggests 'Garden' or 'Park' or something similar. The inscription continues on for thirteen lines, each of which contains no more than one or two words, such as: 'People of the Romans', 'son of [King] Eumenes', 'inviolability'.

4 Other fragments seem to be part of a second copy of this text, assuring the restorations given here, except for the conclusion of the fifth line. Raubitschek believes that the fragments belong to the same inscription or that there were two identical copies.

5 The mythical founder of Pergamum: Hansén, *Attalids*[2] 7–8.

6 Founder of the Attalid dynasty: *ibid.* 14–21.

81   P. Servilius Isauricus restores to Pergamum its ancestral laws and its democracy. 46–44 BC.

Base of bluish marble, damaged on the upper left and lower right corners, found in the agora of Pergamum.

IGRR IV 433; *OGIS* 449; **ILS* 8779.

Magie, *RRAM* I 416–17; II 1270–1, n. 42; *RDGE* pp. 283–4.

vv The People honored *vv* | Publius Servilius, son of Publius, Isauri|cus, the proconsul (46–44 BC), for having become savior and | benefactor of
5 the city and having restored to the ‖ city its ancestral laws and its demo-cra|*vv* cy unrestricted.[1] *vv*

1 Magie believes that it was Servilius Isauricus who restored freedom to Pergamum at this time rather than Julius Caesar back in 48–47 BC: see above, no. 80. But cf. *RDGE* pp. 283–4.

82   Envoy from the city of Chersonesos to Julius Caesar and the senate in Rome. 46 BC.

Stele of white marble broken on top, with the remains of a small fluted column on the right edge, Chersonesos in the Crimea.

*IOSPE I[2] 691.

M. Rostovtzeff, *JRS* 7 (1917) 27–44.

[-- nomophylakes[1] -- | Lamachos son of Dem]e[t]rios, Apollonios | [son of Zethos,] and the director of finance Athe|[naios] son of Stratonikos
5 made the motion: Since Ga‖[ius Iu]lius, son of Th[eo]g[e]nes, Satyros had been *made* a citi|zen [in the time] of our fathers and has *exercised his citizenship* | in a manner worthy of this favor, having gone as en|*voy* to

Rome and to the Roman *sen|ate* and to Gaius Iulius Caesar,[2] consul for
10 the third time ‖ and [dictator] for the third time for [--|--] our [--]

1 The city magistrates.
2 Through personal friends and connections Satyros was given a grant of Roman
   citizenship about this time, perhaps even through the recommendation of Caesar himself. His new Roman citizenship is not in conflict with his local citizenship acquired
   long before (lines 5–6), perhaps even by his father.

**83   A letter of Caesar with a copy of a decree of the senate con-
cerning Mytilene. Between April 46 and January/February 45 BC.**
From the great monument in honor of Potamon, only some fragmentary
marble blocks of which now remain, Mytilene.[1]

IG XII 2.35, col. b, lines 6–36; *SIG*[3] 764; *IGRR* IV 33, col. b, lines 6–36; *RDGE 26,
col. b, lines 6–36.

Magie, *RRAM* I 415–16; II 1269–70; *RDGE* pp. 146–55.

vv [Letter] of Caesar, god. *vv* | [Gaius Iulius Caesar] *imperator*, dictator for
the *third* time (April 46 to January/February 45 BC), *desig|nate* [for the
fourth time, to the magistrates,] *Boule* and People [of Mytilene] greetings
and good health. I too [with | my army am well.[2] Wishing] to benefit your
10 city and not *only* ‖ [to safeguard the privileges which you acquired]
through us but also to assist *in increasing* | [them - - -] leadership, | I have
sent to you the *copy of the decree* of friendship [which has been passed by
us.] | (Line 13 erased)[3] | [Whereas] the envoys of the Mytilenaians
Potamon (son) of Lesbonax, Phainias (son) of Phainias and (grandson) of
15 Kalli[p‖pos, T]erpheos (son) of Dies, Herodes (son) of Kleon, Dies, (son)
of Matrokles, Demetrios (son) of Kleonymos, | Krinagoras (son) of
Kallippos, and Zoilos (son) of Epigenes spoke, renewed goodwill, friend-
ship and alli|ance, (and asked) that they be permitted to perform a sacri-
fice on the Capitolium and that whatever (privileges) to them | had
formerly been conceded by the senate, those (privileges), written on a
bronze tablet, | they be permitted to nail up (also on the Capitolium),
20 concerning this matter it was decreed as follows: ‖ to renew goodwill,
friendship and alliance, to address them as good men and (our) friends, |
to permit them to perform a sacrifice on the Capitolium, and whatever
privileges to them for|merly had been conceded by the senate, those (pri-
vileges), | written on a bronze tablet, to give them permission to nail them
up (also on the Capitolium), whenever they wish; and that Gaius | Caesar
imperator, if it seems best to him, should order the quaestor to let out a
25 contract for quarters and supplies for them according ‖ to the custom of
our ancestors, just as may appear to him to be in keeping with the best

interest of the Re|public and his own good faith. Decreed. *Since* | previously you met with me and I wrote to you, once again | [your envoys] *reminded* me that *nobody* ought *to be* immune[4] among you according to |

30   [your laws and the] privileges which you have had from us [for‖merly and those which] have been given to you [by this] decree to enable you [--|-- to enjoy] the revenues of your city and its territory *in peace*. | [Therefore, I wish] to reply that I neither grant nor shall grant to anybody | [the right to be immune among you.] Thus assured, be confident and enjoy [-|---]

35   *unhindered*, since I do this gladly [for ‖ you and will try in] the future always [to be] the author of some good | to you. *vv*

1 The fragments were found on the site of the old acropolis of Mytilene. Potamon son of Lesbonax was an orator of great repute in Mytilene and had benefitted his city in a great many ways in the last half of the century. The grateful city erected a huge monument in his honor, its base containing a record of his activities on behalf of the people and the city. Among the preserved documents from that monument are the following: a letter of Caesar soon after Pharsalus, transmitted to Mytilene through the envoys Potamon and his companions, assuring the city of his good intentions (col. a); the very mutilated conclusion of a letter written by some unknown Roman official, perhaps Caesar again (col. b, lines 1–5); the present letter (col. b, lines 6–36); two decrees of the senate and a treaty with Mytilene (col. b, lines 36–43, and cols. c–d), for which see below, no. 97. Quite apart from these 'Roman' documents the monument also contained copies of the local decrees and honors which were passed by the city to show her appreciation of Potamon's benefactions and accomplishments.

2 The formula 'of health' is more common in Greek private letters and does not appear in official Roman letters until the first half of the first century BC. The addition of the phrase 'with my army' is peculiar to Roman official letters. Cf. above, no. 80A.

3 The stonecutter may have started to engrave the prescript but then, perhaps deciding to omit it, erased the line he had begun. The prescript is missing.

4 'Immunity' included freedom both from paying local taxes and from performing the local liturgies.

84   Greek cities honor Brutus the Tyrannicide. 44–43 BC.

A: A. E. Raubitschek, *Atti del III Congresso Internazionale de Epigrafia Greca e Latina* (Rome 1959) 15–18; *SEG* XVII 75. Fragment of a marble base, Athens. **B**: *IG* VII 383; Raubitschek, *op. cit.* 16; *SEG* XVII 209. White marble, Oropos in Boiotia. **C**: *ILS* 9460; *I. Délos* 1622; Raubitschek, *op. cit.* 17. Inscribed base, part of a large pedestal on which once rested four bases with statues. Cf. Dio 47.20.4; Plutarch, *Brutus* 24–5.

Raubitschek, *op. cit.* 15–21.

A. Raubitschek, *op. cit.* 15–18, Athens

[The People | (erected this statue of) Quintus Servili]us, [son] of Quintus, | [Caepio] Brutus.[1]

B. Raubitschek, *op. cit.* 16, Oropos

[The] *People v* of the Oro[pians] | (dedicated this statue of) Quintus
5 Caepio, son of Quin[tus,] | Brutus, their *v* own | savior and benefactor, ‖ to
Amphiaraos.

C. Raubitschek, *op. cit.* 17, Delos

The People of the Athenians and those who live on the island | (dedicated
this statue of) Quintus Hortensius, son of Quintus,[2] uncle of Caepio
(Brutus), | because of Caepio's own benefactions to the city (of Athens), |
vv to Apollo. *vv*

1 Marcus Iunius Brutus was adopted by his uncle, Q. Servilius Caepio, whose name he
   then took, retaining his own cognomen Brutus.
2 In 44–43 BC he was proconsul of Macedonia: Broughton, *MRR* II 345. In Macedonia
   he rallied to the side of Brutus, and the senate extended his command. His father was
   the famous orator Q. Hortensius Hortalus, who was consul in 69 BC.

85   Letter of Marcus Antonius to the Koinon of Asia concerning the Association of Victorious Athletes. 42–41 or 33–32 BC.
Papyrus in the British Museum, found in Egypt.

F. G. Kenyon, *Classical Review* 7 (1893) 476–8; *RDGE* 57.

Magie, *RRAM* I 428–9; *RDGE* pp. 290–3.

Marcus Antonius imperator, | triumvir for the Republic's | constitu-
5 tion, to the Koinon of the | Greeks from Asia, greetings.[1] ‖ Earlier I was
met in Ephesus | by Marcus Antonius Artemidoros, | my friend and
(physical) trainer,[2] along with the e|ponymous priest of the Associa-
tion of | Worldwide Wreath-Wearing Victors in the Sacred Games,[3]
10 ‖ Charopeinos of Ephesus, | in regard to the former privileges of the Asso-
cia|tion, that they may remain intact, and in regard to the | rest of what
it asked of me in the way of honors | and privileges, (namely) freedom
15 from military service ‖ and immunity from every liturgy and free|dom
from billeting, and during the course of the festi|vals a truce, and invio-
lability, and | (the right of the) purple stripe,[4] (asking) that I consent to
20 write | immediately to you (about them), and I did consent, ‖ wishing
both because of my fri|end Artemidoros and for (the sake of) their epony|-
mous priest to do (them) this favor for the honor of the | Association and
25 for its growth. | And now again ‖ Artemidoros has met me (and asked) that
| they be permitted to dedicate a bron|ze tablet and engrave on it | the
30 aforementioned privileges. | Preferring in no way to fa‖il Artemidoros,

who about these matters | has come to me, I granted the *de|dication* of the tablet as he asked me. | I have written to you about these matters.

1 An inscription on stone originally found at Tralles in Asia and later brought to Smyrna contains the opening lines of this same document, with the addition of 'proedroi' in the salutation, a fact which seems to indicate that the papyrus translated here is an abbreviated version. The papyrus is unusual in that it is written on the *verso* of a medical papyrus (*P. Lond.* 137) originating in Egypt, while the contents of the letter relate to the province of Asia. In addition, the papyrus was apparently written in the second century AD, while the letter relates to events of the first century BC. The reason why the owner of the medical papyrus wished to preserve the old letter is unknown.

2 The Greek term shows that Artemidoros was the trainer in a gymnasium. His new name indicates that he had received Roman citizenship through the auspices of Marcus Antonius.

3 This was a professional organization, worldwide in scope, and the victors mentioned here could have been either athletes or dramatic performers. See C. A. Forbes, *CP* 50 (1955) 239–41.

4 This is not a reference to the purple border of the Roman toga, but to the right to wear purple decorations along with the golden ornaments which certain distinguished persons in Greek cities and organizations were permitted to add to their clothing on formal occasions. See F. Poland in *RE s.v.* Technitai, vol. V A 2, col. 2491.

86   Letters of Octavian concerning Seleukos of Rhosos. Between 42 and 30 BC.

Limestone tinged with blue, surface badly eroded, perhaps originally the left leaf of the double door to a tomb, Rhosos in Syria.

P. Roussel, *Syria* 15 (1934) 34–6; *FIRA* I 55 (text by Arangio-Ruiz); *IGLS* III 1.718; **RDGE* 58. Cf. the decree of the senate concerning Asklepiades, above, no. 66.

Roussel, *op. cit.* 36–74; F. de Visscher, *L'Antiquité Classique* 13 (1944) 11–35; *ibid.* 14 (1946) 29–59; *RDGE* pp. 294–307; Sherwin-White, *Citizenship*[2] 296–9.

(Letter I) Year [--,] the month Apellaios [the -][1] *vv* | *Imperator* Caesar, son of the god Julius, imperator for the fourth time (36–33 BC), *consul* | designate for the second and third time,[2] to the magistrates, Boule (and) People | of Rhosos, holy and inviolate and autonomous (city), greetings. I too
5   with the army || [am in good health.[3]] The documents written below were extracted from a stele from the Capitolium in Rome, | [documents which I ask you] to enter into your public archives. And send a copy | [of them to] the Boule and People of Tarsus, the Boule and People of Antioch, | the Boule and People [of Seleukeia[4]] that they might enter it (into their archives). *vv* Farewell. |
(Letter II) [- Caesar] imperator, triumvir for the constitution of the
10 Repub|||lic, [by virtue of the] Munatian and Aemilian Law conferred (Roman) citizenship and tax-exemption for all | present property on the

following terms: *vv* | [Since Seleu]kos (son) of Theodotos of Rhosos has
campaigned with us in the | [---] toward [---][5] under our command, has
on our behalf suffered many great hard|ships, has faced danger without
15   flinching from any terror in his steadfastness, || has exhibited [complete]
affection and loyalty for the Republic, | has linked [his own] fortune to our
safety, has undergone every suffering on behalf of the | *Republic* of the
People of the [Rom]ans, and in our presence and absence | has been *of
service* [to us,] *vv* |
[to him and his] parents, his children, his descendants,[6] the wife who
20   [here||after] will be his [--] *we give* (Roman) citizenship and tax-exemption
for his present proper|ty in the same way as [those] (Roman) citizens
[who are] tax-exempt by the best law and the best legal right, | and [they
are to have] *immunity* [from military service] and from every public |
liturgy. vv |
Let him (who is) *mentioned above*, [and his parents,] and *descendants* belong
25   to the tribe Cornelia || [and let them cast their vote (?)] *there* [and ---]   And
if they while absent | *wish* [to be enrolled in the census -- and if] they wish
to be [---] of Italy | [---][7] *vv* | [In the same measure as] the *aforementioned*
[and his wife and parents,] *children* and [descendants,] before he became
a [Roman] citizen, | tax-exempt, [had (?) ---,][8] once he had become a
30   [Ro]man *citizen*, tax-exempt, || [---,] if he wishes to [enjoy (?) ---] priest-
hoods[--] honors, privileges | and [property (?), he is permitted to hold and
enjoy them by (?)] legal right [in the same way as anyone who] holds and
[enjoys them by the best] *law* and the best legal | right. *vv* | [-- lines 33–46][9]
| or [--] of the Romans they wish to take [--|-] take [--] to him into the city
or country of the provinces of Asia and Europe | [-- of the Re(?)]public
50   [--] he may import or export for his own use || [from] the *city* or from the
country [---] he may export from his own possessions and his cattle | *for his
own need* [--] no government or | *publican* [shall levy on him] a tax for these
things. *vv* |
[If anyone] wishes to accuse them and to *introduce a complaint* and to set up a
55   trial against them | and to join issue[10] [--,] for all these procedures || [if]
they wish *the case to be tried at* home by their own [laws or in] free [cities] or
before our magistrates or pro|magistrates [--][11] theirs shall be the choice, |
[--] and no one otherwise [than is written] *herein shall act* or shall judge
concerning them or shall declare his *opinion* after having referred | (the
matter to another authority (?)[12]). [And if any trial] *takes place* [about
them] *contrary* to these (regulations), it [shall not be] | legally binding. *vv*
60 || [If any] one [wishes (?)] to accept (for trial) the name of the aforemen-
tioned, his *parents* [his wife,] his children and their descendants | and to
make a capital prejudgment[13] [---] that they as envoys to *our* senate | and
[to] *our* magistrates [and] *promagistrates* can come (themselves) and send
envoys | [about] their own affairs, it pleases us that [the aforementioned

people] shall have that power. Whatever *govern|ment* and [whatever] magistrate [does not do] the things [required by these (regulations), or contrary] to these (regulations) acts or investigates their case before a
65   tribunal ‖ [or agrees to it (?)] or takes pledges from them and in bad faith prevents the aforementioned people from | *being able* [to enjoy] the [privileges] given to them, to the People of the Romans | *let them be liable* to pay (a fine of) one hundred thousand sesterces, and regarding this sum, | let [whoever wishes] have the right *to lay claim to it* and exact it, [whether] in the province before *our* magistrates [and] pro|magistrates or in Rome he
70   wishes to show cause and exact (the fine). And concerning these ‖ [matters] it pleases us that the prosecutor shall put up sufficient sureties.[14] [That] these afore|mentioned (regulations) may be carried out let our *magistrates* [and promagistrates] who therein have juris|diction make the decisions and take particular care. *vv* |
(Letter III) [Year -,] the month Dystros the 15th. Imperator Caesar, son of the god, imperator for the sixth time (31 BC), consul | for the *third* time, (consul) designate for the fourth time,[15] [to the magistrates,] Boule (and)
75   People of Rhosos, holy and inviolate and autonomous (city), ‖ greetings. If you are well, it is good. I myself too with the ar|my am *well*. The envoys sent by you, Seleukos my admiral, Heras (son) of Kalli|[--, --]eros, Symmachos, good men from a good People, our friends and allies, | [having traveled] to Ephesus to me, spoke about the instructions which they had (from you). I accordingly | received the [men,] having found them to be
80   patriotic and good, and I have accepted the honors and the crown, ‖ and I [will try,] when (or if) I come to your area, to be the author of some good to you and to watch over | [the privileges] (given) to your city, and all the more gladly will I do these things because of Seleukos my admiral who campaign|ed with me throughout the whole time of the war and distinguished himself in every way and furnished every proof of his goodwill | [and his] *loyalty*, a man who has never lost an opportunity to come to me on your behalf and | who has *exercised* all his zeal and enthusiasm for your advantage. Farewell. *vv*
85   ‖ (Letter IV) [Year-,] the month Apellaios the 9th. Imperator Caesar, son of the god, imperator for the sixth time, consul for the four|th time (30 BC), to the magistrates, Boule (and) People of Rhosos, holy and inviolate and autonomous (city), greetings. If you are well, | [it is] good. I myself too with the army am well. Seleukos, your citi|zen [and] *my* admiral who has campaigned with me in all the wars and has given many p|roofs of his
90   goodwill and loyalty and bravery, as was fitting ‖ for [those who campaigned with] us and displayed valor in war, has been honored with privileges, | tax-immunity and (Roman) citizenship. I therefore commend him to you, for such men make more eager our goodwill toward their ‖ [cities.] Thus I will do everything possible for you more glad|ly [because of Sel]eukos. Thus assured, send to me for whatever you wish. Farewell.

1 This is the date on which Octavian's letter was entered into the archives at Rhosos. The era of Rhosos began in 42, 41 or 40 BC. Traces of '8' after 'Year' seem possible.

2 According to the arrangements made in 39 BC, Antonius and Octavian decided who would be the consuls for the next eight full years (Dio 48.35.1; Appian, *Bell. Civ.* 5.73). Thus, Octavian was to be consul II in 33 BC and consul III with Antonius in 31 BC. See the remarks of M. P. Charlesworth in *CAH* 10.46, n. 1.

3 See above, no. 83 n. 2.

4 First suggested by de Visscher, basing it merely on the number of letters needed to fill the available space.

5 M. Guarducci, in *Rendiconti della Pontificia Accademia di Archeologia* (1938) 53ff., has 'in the [regions] toward [the east]'; G. Manganaro, in *Siculorum Gymnasium* (1958), 289ff., suggests 'in the [straits] toward [Italy]'; Roussel has 'toward [Thrace]' or 'toward [Sicily]'.

6 The phrase 'his descendants' was accidentally omitted in *RDGE*.

7 Arangio-Ruiz: '[of some city or colony] of Italy, [they are to have permission]'.

8 Arangio-Ruiz: 'was immune in his country'.

9 These lines are too mutilated to yield more than a few terms and phrases of importance: 'the worst of *war contributions* and the publican'; 'for the sake of furnishing military quarters nor *wintering over*'; 'marriage'; 'by the Atilian Law [and the] Julian [law]'.

10 The Greek here translates a Roman legal phrase (litem contestari) which indicates the moment when one party asserts his case and the other denies it: A. H. J. Greenidge, *The Legal Procedure of Cicero's Time* (Oxford 1901) 243–51.

11 E. Schönbauer in *Archiv für Papyrusforschung* 13 (1939) 177–209 adds here '[by Roman laws]' and argues that Seleukos and his family may choose between two kinds of laws rather than two jurisdictions.

12 The interpretation is controversial.

13 The Greek here translates a Roman legal phrase (praeiudicium capitis), meaning a preliminary to a trial involving the status of the person accused.

14 The reference is to the Roman legal procedure whereby the party who loses the case also loses the sureties, i.e. the amount of money, which he put up: Greenidge, *op. cit.* 185.

15 Octavian's fourth consulship was to begin on January 1, 30 BC. His sixth imperial acclamation was granted right after Actium (September 2, 31 BC). Therefore this third letter must have been written between those two dates, in the last four months of 31 BC.

87 Letter of Octavian to Plarasa-Aphrodisias concerning documents relevant to the city's status. Fall of 39 BC or 38 BC.

One marble fragment extant, the rest from an old copy,[1] Aphrodisias.

OGIS 453–4; *RDGE* 28 A; Reynolds, **Aphrodisias*, Document 6. Cf. Tacitus, *Ann.* 3.62.

RDGE pp. 166–9; Reynolds 41–8.

[Imperator Caesar, (?) | son of the god (?) Iulius,[2] consul] desig|nate for
5 the second and [third time,[3]] ‖ triumvir for the constitution of the
10 Republic, | to the Plarasa-Aphrodisian[4] magistrates, ‖ Boule and People,
greetings. | If you are well, it is good. | I myself too am in good health, |
15 along with the ar|my.[5] Solon ‖ (son) of Demetrios, your | envoy, has given

20   most careful thought to the affairs of your city ‖ and not only was content
25   with the arrangements made but also asked us ‖ to dispatch to you copies
      of the edict, the decree of the senate, the oath, and the la|w,[6] all concerning
30   you, ‖ from our public | records (stop). For these actions I have prai|sed
35   Solon and all the mo‖re (gladly) received him, and have held him among
40   my | acquaintances,[7] | and to him I have assigned appropriate privi‖leges,
      having considered him to be a man worthy of honor from us, and I re|joice
45   with you at your having ‖ such a citizen. | Copies of the privileges granted
50   to you are affixed below. ‖ I wish you to register them in your public
      records. | *vv* Letter of Caesar (*leaf*)[8] |

1   The newly found fragment (lines 31–40) was not available for use in establishing the
    text presented in *RDGE*. Reynolds (Pls. V–VI) gives a photograph of it along with
    photographs of the handwritten copy of the material that has never been recovered. This
    document appeared in the first place on the 'archive wall' at Aphrodisias, i.e. on the
    south wall of the north parodos of the theater. Because of the extreme brevity of the lines
    in this document line dividers are used only where such division seemed appropriate.
    The text ends with line 53.
2   The exact title given to Octavian here is not known. He called himself 'Gaius Caesar' as
    late as October 2, 39 BC (see Reynolds, pp. 75–6), and thus did not assume the title of
    'imperator' until after that date, probably not until 38 BC.
3   See above, no. 86, n. 2.
4   For the double name see above, no. 59a, n. 1.
5   See above, no. 82, n. 2.
6   Substantial remains of these documents have been recovered recently from Aphrodisias:
    see Reynolds, *Aphrodisias*, Documents 7–9.
7   Thus, Octavian places Solon in a particular category of his associates. Gaius Gracchus
    is said to have been the first Roman noble to divide his friends into categories for the
    salutatio in the morning (Seneca, *Ben.* 6.34.2): see Reynolds, p. 46.
8   This letter of Caesar is lost, if the phrase is taken to mean that it is a heading of another
    document. Reynolds (pp. 47–8) tentatively suggests that it may mean a kind of
    authentication to introduce 'a valediction in the writer's own hand'. But the natural
    meaning is simply 'letter'. The leaf was a common device to indicate separation or
    punctuation.

88   Marcus Antonius gives foreign territory to Cleopatra, who commemorates the event by adopting a second era. 37–36 BC.
Extract from the Armenian version of Eusebius.

Eusebius Arm. p. 79 Karst (Porphyrios, *FGrHist* 260 F 2.17). Cf. Plutarch, *Ant.* 36.2;
Josephus, *Ant. Jud.* 15.4.1–4, and *Bell. Jud.* 1.18.5; Dio 49.32.

Magie, *RRAM* II 1287, n. 29; Samuel, *PC* 156–60; M. Grant, *Cleopatra* (London 1972) 141.

(Cleopatra's) sixteenth year was also called her first, for after the death of
Lysimachos, king of Chalkis in Syria, the imperator Marcus Antonius
handed over Chalkis and the territory situated around it to Cleopatra.

And from then the following years were described in the same way with the addition of (another) numeral, up to the twenty-second year, which was the end of Cleopatra, so that the twenty-second year of Cleopatra was also her seventh.[1]

1 Cleopatra's years as queen began in 51 BC. Her second year ran from September of 51 to September of 50. Her sixteenth regnal year was 37/6, when she adopted the second era. She died on August 12, 30 BC, in the twenty-second year by the first reckoning, which was also the seventh.

89   Coinage of Antonius and Cleopatra. 34–33 BC (?).

A: Silver tetradrachm issued in Syria (probably Antioch), showing (obverse) Antonius bareheaded, with Greek inscription along the edge, and (reverse) Cleopatra wearing the diadem, earring, pearl necklace and dress embroidered with pearls, with Greek legend: W. Wroth, *Catalogue of the Greek Coins of Galatia, Cappadocia, and Syria* (London 1899, repr. Bologna 1964) p. 158, no. 53 (Plate XIX, 3). **B**: Denarius (silver, minted probably (?) in Antioch), showing (obverse) Antonius bareheaded but with a tiara beside his head, with Latin legend, and (reverse) Cleopatra wearing the diadem, a ship's prow at bottom of her portrait, with Latin inscription along the edge: E. A. Sydenham, *The Coinage of the Roman Republic* (revised edition, London 1952) p. 194, no. 1210; M. H. Crawford, *Roman Republican Coinage* (Cambridge 1974) p. 539, no. 543 (Plate LXIV, no. 543/1).

M. Grant, *Cleopatra* (London 1972) 168–70 (with photos of both coins between pp. 190 and 191, nos. 44 and 46).

A. Wroth, *loc. cit.*

(Obverse) Antonius imperator triumvir.
(Reverse) Queen Cleopatra, Neotera Goddess.[1]

B. Sydenham, *loc. cit.*

(Obverse) Antonius. Armenia defeated.
(Reverse) Of Cleopatra, queen of kings (and) of her sons who are kings.[2]

1 Cleopatra Thea (i.e. 'Goddess') was a Ptolemaic princess who died in 121 BC, famous in Seleucid (Syrian) history, having married in succession three Seleucid monarchs, attesting to Ptolemaic–Seleucid unity at the dynastic level. Cleopatra, calling herself Neotera (i.e. 'Younger Goddess'), now looked upon herself as a similar unifying force. See Grant, *op. cit.* 168–9, for date and background; see T. V. Buttrey, 'Thea Neotera on Coins of Antony and Cleopatra', *American Numismatic Society Museum Notes* 10 (1954) 95–109, for a different interpretation.
2 For the first time the portrait of a foreign woman appears on an official Roman coin containing a Latin inscription and intended for wide circulation. See Grant, *op. cit.* 169–70. Sydenham dates this coin to 32–31 BC, but Grant makes out a case for the Donations

(of land) in 34 BC: pp. 162–5 and 168ff. Her title might illustrate 'her superiority to her son and colleague, the King of Kings Ptolemy Caesar' (Grant).

90   Worship of Isis by a Roman officer, his son and friends. March 28, 32 BC.

Three blocks of a huge pylon, rounded letters carefully engraved, island of Philae in the Nile.

OGIS 196; *IGRR* I 1300; Bernand, **Philae* I 63.

Bernand, *op. cit.* pp. 334–43.

I, Gaius Iulius Papius, prefect,[1] | have come and worshipped our La|dy Isis, along with Iulius my son, and on | behalf of Gaion my younger son,
5   and ‖ also with my friends and fell|ow travelers Symmachos, Eumenes, | Apollonios (son) of Chares and his son Apellas, | and Apion [-- and -- and
10   the] | centurions Rufus, Demetrios, Niger, ‖ Valerius, Labyon, Terentius, | Nikanor (and) Baronas,[2] and (on behalf of) all | my young children. *vv* | *vacat* | *vv* The twentieth year, which is also the fifth, on the thirtieth of Phamenoth.[3]

1   Not, of course, prefect of Egypt. The first prefect of Egypt was C. Cornelius Gallus: below, no. 93.
2   A number of the centurions have Greek names, including Demetrios, Nikanor and Baronas. 'Labyon' is a Roman: Labeo.
3   The double era used by Cleopatra VII produces 33/2 BC: see above, no. 88. The thirtieth (not the first as in *OGIS*) of the Egyptian month Phamenoth is March 28. See the tables in T. C. Skeat, *The Reigns of the Ptolemies* (Munich 1954).

91   Letter of Octavian to the city of Mylasa. 31 BC.

Two stone fragments (A–B) found at Mylasa in Karia.

*SIG*³ 768; **RDGE* 60.

Magie, *RRAM* I 431 and 442; II 1290, n. 39; *RDGE* pp. 310–12.

(A) Imperator Caesar, son of the god Iulius, | *v* designated (?) as consul for the third time (31 BC), | to the Mylasan magistrates, Bou|le (and)
5   People, greetings. *vv* If you are well, it is ‖ good. *v* I too with *my* | army am in good health. *v* For|merly already concerning the misfortune that he|ld you in its grip you sent (an embassy) to | me, *v* and now have come (to me)

10   your ‖ envoys, *vv* Ouliad[es --] (B) [--] of the enemy to have fallen and
     your city overwhelmed, | *v* many of your citizens | lost as prisoners of war,
 5   *v* not a few were murder|ed, *v* and some burned together with the city, ‖ as
     the savagery of the enemy *v* neither from the | shrines nor from the most
     sacred of temples was he|ld back; *v* they (the envoys) informed me of |
     your plundered land *vv* and your | farm-buildings that had been set afire,
10   with the result that ‖ you have fallen into every misfortune; *v* in regard to
     all of these I am *con|scious* that, [having suffered] this, you [are men worthy
     of] | every honor and favor *from* | [the Romans --]

Even before the Battle of Philippi (Fall, 42 BC) Q. Labienus, acting on behalf of Brutus
and Cassius, had negotiated with King Orodes of Parthia to send aid to the cause of the
Liberators. The king hesitated. Finally, in 40 BC, while M. Antonius was absent in Egypt
and then in Italy, he sent a Parthian invasion army into Syria under the command of his
son Pacorus. Labienus, with part of the Parthian forces, advanced into Asia Minor and
entered Karia. It was then that Mylasa and other Karian cities were devastated. In 39 BC
Antonius sent an army under P. Ventidius Bassus to recover Asia. Karia was then liberated and the Parthians thrust out of Asia Minor.

92   Octavian dedicates his camp overlooking the promontory of Actium. 29 BC.

Twenty-six blocks or fragments of blocks once part of his victory monument on a hill near Nikopolis.[1]

J. H. Oliver, *AJP* 90 (1969) 180; J. M. Carter, *ZPE* 24 (1977) 229. Cf. Livy 1.19.3;
Suetonius, *Aug.* 18; Dio 51.1.2–3.

Oliver, *op. cit.* 178–82; Carter, *op. cit.* 227–30.

To [Nep]tune [and Ma]rs, [Imperator Caesa]r, son of the god [Iulius,
having won the] *victory at sea* [in the war] which he *waged* on behalf of the
Republic in this region and having produced peace on land [and sea, has
dedicated,] *while consul* [for the fifth time and] imperator for the *seventh*
time (29 BC), the camp, [decorated] with the *spoils* (of war), [from] which
he marched forth to attack [the enemy].

1 The main problem connected with the text of this inscription is the order of the blocks or
  fragments, for they are so small that often only a few letters of a word suggest its grammatical connection with other words or its place in the dedication. Thus there is no way
  to determine where one line ends and the next begins.

93   Dedication of C. Cornelius Gallus, first Roman prefect of Egypt. April 15, 29 BC.

Stele of rose-colored granite sawn in half vertically, curved at the top, engraved with hieroglyphics,[1] Latin and then Greek, island of Philae in the Nile.

CIL III 14147.5; *OGIS* 654; *IGRR* I 1293; *ILS* 8995; Bernand, **Philae* II 128, pp. 35–7. Cf. Strabo 17.1.53; Suetonius, *Aug.* 66; Dio 53.23–4.

J. G. C. Anderson, *CAH* 10.240–1; J.-P. Boucher, *Caius Cornelius Gallus* (Paris 1966) 38–45; Bernand, *op. cit.* pp. 37–47; L. P. Kirwan, *Proceedings of the British Academy* 63 (1977) 13ff.

(Latin) Gaius Cornelius, son of Gnaeus, Gallu[s,] Roman knight, after the kings | had been defeated by Caesar, son of the god, first prefect of [Alex]andria and Egypt, | victor in [two] *battles* of the Thebaid revolt, conqueror of the enemy within 15 days, capturer of 5 cities, Bores|is, Coptus, Ceramice, Diospolis Mag[na, Op]hieon. Having carried off the
5   leaders of these revolts, ‖ he *led* his army beyond the cataract of the Nile to a place where | [arms] had never been carried before by either the Roman People or the kings of Egypt, subdued the Thebaid, common terror of all | the kings, gave audience to the *envoys* of the king of the Ethiopians at Philae, received the *same* | king under his protection, and set up a ruler over Tria-kontaschoinos within the frontier of Ethiopia. | He has given this gift to the
10   ancestral gods and to Nil[e] the Helper. ‖[2]

1 At the very top of the stele is the figure of a man on a horse striking a prostrate enemy. The hieroglyphics, although badly mutilated, contain the date.
2 Immediately following the Latin appeared a Greek translation which contains a few differences from the Latin: line 3, the Greek adds that 'some' of the five cities were captured 'at the first assault'; lines 6–7, the Greek says that the Thebaid 'had not sub-mitted to the kings' instead of 'common terror of all the kings'.

94   Preparations in Egypt for a military expedition. A few years after the death of Cleopatra (30 BC).

Fragment of a papyrus roll,[1] Oxyrhynchus.

P. Oxy. 2820; N. Lewis, **GRBS* 16 (1975) 298–9.

M. Treu, *Chiron* 3 (1973) 221–33; Lewis, *op. cit.* 295–303.

[--] | he sent for [-] | to revolt, and because of | this he[2] forged [weapons]
5   mo|re than sufficient, ‖ and [the] | *fleet* of [Cleo]patra | (which) after *her* |
10   death, as ‖ was likely, had been neglec|ted, he again e|quipped, <and> he

set up | garrisons at | entrances to the country | and everything that per-
15 tained to ‖ war he made ready, | with the result that [-|--] | *having understood*
20 that | [--] ‖ the Egyptians around Thebes | were more war|like than the
25 others, | he first urged them (to go) willing‖ly on the expe|dition, but
when they did not | [--]

1 The handwriting belongs to the first half of the second century AD.
2 Treu identified this individual as C. Cornelius Gallus, first prefect of Egypt (30–27 or
   26 BC; above, no. 93), but Lewis, using new readings, attacks this interpretation and
   believes 'he' is Aelius Gallus, prefect of Egypt after Cornelius Gallus (26–24 BC). If
   Lewis is right, then the 'expedition' of the papyrus is that of Aelius Gallus into Arabia,
   on which see S. Jameson, *JRS* 58 (1968) 71ff.

95   Legal decision by Augustus and Agrippa, and a governor's letter to Kyme. 27 BC (for the legal decision).

Marble stele broken at the bottom, damaged on the right and left, decorated with a festoon of ivy at the top, Kyme in Asia on the Aeolian coast. The
inscription is in three parts: A (in Greek) is a legal decision by Augustus
and M. Agrippa (27 BC); B (in Latin) is a letter (of unknown date but
later than A) from the governor of Asia to the city of Kyme; C (in Greek)
is a translation of the Latin letter of the governor.

H. W. Pleket, *The Greek Inscriptions in the 'Rijksmuseum van Oudheden' at Leyden* (Leiden 1958)
no. 57 (+ photograph); *SEG* XVIII 555; *RDGE* 61; H. Engelmann, *Die Inschriften von
Kyme* (Bonn 1976) pp. 46ff.

Pleket, *op. cit.* pp. 49–66; K. M. T. Atkinson, *RIDA* 7 (1960) 227–72 (+ photograph); V.
Arangio-Ruiz, *Bullettino dell'Istituto del Diritto Romano* 64 (1961) 323–42; W. Kunkel, *Studi in
Onore di Emilio Betti* II (Rome 1962) 591–620; J. H. Oliver, *GRBS* 4 (1963) 115–22; *RDGE*
pp. 315–20; F. Millar, *The Emperor in the Roman World* (London 1977) 317–18; N. Charbonnel, *RIDA* 26 (1979) 177–225.

A. Greek

Imperator Caesar, son of the god, Augustus [--][1] | (and) [M]arcus
Agrippa, son of Lucius, consuls *v* [---:[2] | If] there are any public or sacred
places in the cities [---][3] | of each city of the province (?),[4] and if there are
5   or will be *any* [dedica‖tions][5] belonging to these places, [nobody] | is to
remove or buy (them) or take them as [mortgaged property | or] gift.
Whatever has been *taken away* from those places | [or] bought and given as
a gift, [whoever may be in charge of the] | province is to see to it that these
10 are restored to the *public* or sacred [account (?)][6] ‖ of the city, and what-
ever may have been given [as legal secur|ity,][7] he is not to use this in his
administration of justice. *vv* |

B. Latin

[-][8] Vinicius, proconsul, sends greetings to the magistrates of Cyme. Apollonides, son of Lucius, from No[race, | your citizen,] came to me and showed that the temple of Liber Pater[9] was by *title | of sale* possessed by

15 Lysias, son of Diogenes, of Tucalla, [your] citizen, ‖ and that *when* the worshippers wished to restore to their god the sacred property, according to the order of Au[gu|s]tus Caesar, by paying the price which is inscribed on the temple, | *it was withheld* (?)[10] by Lysias. I wish you to see to it that, if such is the case, Lysias | accepts the price which [has been] put on the temple and restores to the god the *tem|ple and* that there be inscribed on it

20 'Imperator Caesar, son of the god, Augustus rest‖ored it'. But [if] Lysias denies what Apollonides *de|mands*, let him give sufficient bail (to appear) where I will be.[11] That Lysias *prom|ises* (bail) meets [more (?)] with my approval(?).[11]

C. Greek

In the prytany of Phanites,[12] *vv* [-] Vinicius sends greetings to the magistrates of Kyme. A[pol‖lonid]es (son) of Lucius of Norake, your citizen,

25 ‖ [came to me] and showed that the temple of Dionysos was by *title* [of sale] possessed by Lysias (son) of Diogenes of [Tukal‖la, your citizen,] and that when [the worshippers] *wished* | [---]

1 Perhaps uninscribed? Pleket: 'for the 7th time (?)', i.e. in his seventh consulship (27 BC). Augustus had been consul with Agrippa in both 28 and 27 BC. Atkinson: 'for the 7th time'. Charbonnel: 'imperator for the 7th time', which is too long for the space.

2 Pleket: '[ordered (or) wrote]'. Atkinson: '[wrote]', likewise Charbonnel. Oliver and *RDGE* leave blank, but note the possibilities of '[said]' or '[determined]' or '[ordained]' among others. Oliver and Kunkel believe some word had been used which pointed to a *lex data*, i.e. some kind of a charter.

3 Pleket: '[or in the surrounding area]' etc. Arangio-Ruiz: '[or throughout the] territory of each city', translating the word *eparcheia* as 'territory' instead of 'province'. Oliver: '[when] these localities fall [within the jurisdiction of the] prefecture [protecting] each city's [interests]', (his own translation). Charbonnel: 'in the cities [belonging to a religious guild or] to a city of each province'.

4 The Greek *eparcheia* would normally mean 'province', but Oliver equates it with 'prefecture' or 'domain': *GRBS* and *AJP* 93 (1972) 195. Arangio-Ruiz takes it loosely as 'territory', which is hardly possible. The word 'each' here is grammatically ambiguous, for it could govern either 'province' or 'city'.

5 Atkinson: '[properties]'. Kunkel: '[ornaments]'.

6 Pleket: '[places]', from which they had been taken.

7 Atkinson: '[in this manner]'.

8 Pleket: '[Lucius]', i.e. the consul of 33 BC who became the governor of Asia in 28–27 or 27–26 BC, approved by Syme in *JRS* 45 (1955) 159. Likewise Kunkel, Arangio-Ruiz, and Charbonnel. But Atkinson, with hesitation, believes he was Marcus Vinicius, the consul of 19 BC.

9 I.e. Dionysos.

10 First suggested by Oliver. Pleket punctuates and restores differently: 'and since the worshippers wanted to restore the sacred objects to the god, as Augustus Caesar has ordered, after having paid the price written on the temple of Liber Pater by Lysias, I wish that you see to it that', etc. (Pleket's translation).
11 In saying 'where I shall be' Vinicius refers to his annual circuit of Asia to hold court. At this point in the text there is disagreement about punctuation and restoration, although Pleket correctly saw the intent, explaining (p. 59) that 'whatever the exact wording of this part of the text may have been, its meaning seems to be fairly clear. Lysias must give security to Apollonides, if he opposes Apollonides' claim; afterwards the proconsul himself will devote his attention to settling the affair.' Pleket then suggests: 'But if Lysias opposes the claim which Apollonides makes, that Lysias promise bail to him, with guarantee that he will present himself where I shall be --.' Atkinson, with different punctuation and restoration: 'But [if] Lysias objects, let him hand over as security for his appearance in court the property which Apollonides demands. I approve [of your] sending Lysias to wherever I shall be (sc. holding the assize).' Kunkel added the restoration '[more]'.
12 This phrase introduces the Greek translation of the letter of Vinicius and, thus, uses the local method of dating.

96   An earthquake at Tralles in Asia, and help from Augustus. 26 BC.
Extract from Agathias.

*Agathias, *Historiae* 2.17 (ed. Keydell). Cf. Strabo 12.8.18.

T. R. S. Broughton, *TAPA* 66 (1935) 20–2; Magie, *RRAM* I 469; II 1331, n. 7; Bowersock, *Augustus* Appendix 3, 157–61.

The city of Tralles, situated in the land now called Asia near the river Maeander, which in ancient times was a settlement of the Pelasgians, was struck by an earthquake in the time of Augustus Caesar and completely ruined, and nothing of it was saved. (2) With the city thus lying in a most pitiful condition, they say that a certain peasant, one of the husbandmen by the name of Chairemon, was deeply touched in his heart by the incident, and, unable to endure it, accomplished something extraordinarily astonishing and unbelievable. (3) Fearing neither the length of the journey nor the importance of the embassy nor the fact that, in all likelihood, he would have to face very great dangers, and that all this was fraught with inscrutable fate, nor the separation from his family at home nor anything else of those things which men consider and then change their resolve, he not only arrived at Rome but actually in the land of the Cantabrians on the very shores of the Ocean, for Caesar at that time happened to be at war with one of the tribes.[1] (4) He told him what had happened and so touched the emperor that he immediately selected seven (ex-)consuls from among the noblest and wealthiest men of Rome and sent them with their escort to the settlement, and they, reaching the place as quickly as

possible, contributed the very greatest amount of money and with great
speed rebuilt the city and brought it into the form it has preserved to the
present.[2]

1 Augustus in person directed the campaigns against the Cantabrians in Spain in 26 and
  25 BC: Sir Ronald Syme in *CAH* 10.342–4, *Roman Papers* II 825 ff.
2 Agathias of Myrina was born about AD 530. His narrative continues on to section 8
  where he quotes an elegiac poem which he himself saw inscribed on an altar to honor
  Chairemon.

97   Two decrees of the senate and a treaty with Mytilene. 25 BC.
Fragments of marble blocks from the great monument in honor of
Potamon, Mytilene.

IG XII 2.35, col. b, lines 36–43, and cols. c–d; *IGRR* IV 33, col. b, lines 36–43, and cols.
c–d; *RDGE 26, col. b, lines 36–43, and cols. c–d.

Magie, *RRAM* I 463; II 1330, n. 2; *RDGE* pp. 155–7.

vv Decrees of the senate concerning the treaty.[1] | *In the consulship* [of
Imperator Caesar] Augustus for the ninth time and Marcus (Iunius)
Silanus (25 BC) | [-- proposed (?)[2]] by *order* of Marcus Silanus in accor-
dance with a *decree* of the senate. | [----] of June[3] in the Curia Iulia. (Wit-
40   nesses) *present* at the writing *were*: ‖ [Paullus Aemilius,] son of [Lu]cius,
(of the tribe) Palatina, Lepidus; Gaius Asin[ius, son of Gnae|us -- Pol-
lio;] Lucius Sempronius, son of Lucius, (of the tribe) Fal[erna, A|tra-
tinus; Marcus Teren]tius, son of Marcus, (of the tribe) Papiria, Varro;
Gaiu[s Iu|nius ---Si]lanus; Quintus Acutius, son of Quintus. (Col. c)
Whereas [Ma]rcus Silanus said that a letter [had been sent to Impera-
tor Caesar Augus]|tus,[4] his colleague (in the consulship), [and an
answer had arrived that,] | if it pleased the senate [that a treaty be
made] *with* [the Mytilenaians, | the authority] for this matter [should
5   be entrusted to Silanus] himself, [con‖cerning] this matter [it was
decreed as follows: that Marcus Silanus,] | consul, if it seemed good to
him, [should see to it that the] treaty [be made with the Mytilenaians,
and any|thing] else such as may seem to be in accordance with the
interest [of the Republic and] *his own* [good faith.] | Decreed. *vv* On the
third day before the Kalends of Ju[ne] (or Ju[ly], May 30 or June 29),
10   [in the --.] (Witnesses) *present* [at the writing] *we‖re*: Gaius Norba[nus,
son of] Gai[us, (of the tribe) --, Flaccus; ---, son of Ap]|pius, (of the
tribe) Pala[tina, ---; -- Marcus --, son of -, (of the tribe) --, | C]ensorinus
[---;] | Marcus Va[lerius ---; ---] | son of [--]cus, [--; --] son of [--,] (of
15   the tribe) Clustu‖mina, L[--; Marcus Terentius, son of Marcus, (of the
tribe) Pap]iria, Varro; | Gaius C[---.] | Whereas M[arcus Silanus said

that as to the] decree [of the senate] | *given* to him, [(to wit) that, if it
seemed good to him,] he should see to it that [the treaty of the Myt]ile-
naians be ma|de [and anything else such as may seem to be in accor-
20   dance with the interest of the] *Republic* ‖ and [his own] good faith, he had
obeyed (this decree) in every way and that it remained | [for the details
attendant upon] this [matter to be carried out,] concerning this | matter
[it was decreed as follows: that Marcus Silanus,] consul, if | it seemed
good to him, [should see to it that the treaty be sent to the Mytilenai]ans
as he had arranged | it to be made, [and that this (treaty) and the decrees
25   of the senate which had been passed] about this ‖ *matter* should be engra-
ved [on a bronze tablet --] and | [set up] in a public place. [Decreed.] *vv*
In the consulship of Imperat[or Caesar Augustus for the ninth time
(and) Marc]us Silanus | [---]

(About 30 lines are here missing)

(Col. d: the treaty) The [People] of the Mytilenaians, in regard to the
rule [and the realm which they have up to the present (?),] | they shall
preserve them in the way in which any [rule is exercised over anything
with the best right and according to the best law.] | In regard to the
enemies of the People [of the Romans, the People of the Mytilenaians] |
shall not allow them [to pass through their own] rea|lm with public [con-
5   sent,] to make war upon [the People] ‖ of the Romans or upon those ruled
by [them or upon the allies of the People of the Romans,] | nor [shall they
help] them (i.e. the enemies of the Romans) [with weapons, money, or
ships.] | The People of the Romans [shall not let] the *enemies* [of the People
of the Mytilenaians pass through their own]‖ land and their own realm
[with public consent, to make war] | upon the People of the Mytilena[ians
10   or upon those ruled by them or upon the alli]‖es of the People of the Myti-
len[aians,--- nor shall they] *help* [them (i.e. the enemies of the Mytile-
naians)] | with weapons, money, or ships. *vv* | If anyone takes the initiative
in *making* war [upon the People of the Mytilenaians or upon the People] |
of the Romans [and] the [allies of the People of the Romans, | the People of
the Romans shall help the People of the Mytilenaians, and the People of
15   the Mytilenai‖ans (shall help) the People of the Romans and the allies of]
the People of the Romans | [---][5] and shall be steadfast. [There shall be]
peace | [for all time. *vv* | ---] it shall belong to them. Likewise, | [whatever
possessions --- the people of the Romans] have given to the People of
20   the Mytilenaians ‖ [--] they shall belong to the People of the
Mytilenaians, | [and whatever possessions -- of the Mytilen]aians there
were on the island | [of Lesbos and whatever possessions --- on the --- day
before the Kal]ends of January, which | [---] there were to them either
25   (on) [this | island or any other ---,] as each of these ‖ [---] they ruled over

and possessed | [---] all these they [shall] *poss|ess. vv* | [---] of the Myti-
lenaians they shall establish.

(27 lines are missing)[6]

1 Immediately preceding these words on the monument is a letter of Caesar the Dictator
to Mytilene: above, no. 83, with n. 1, on the nature of Potamon's monument.
2 Arangio-Ruiz (*Acta Divi Augusti* Part 1 (Rome 1945) 232) proposes '[documents pub-
lished]'. This passage, like the preceding line 36, must be a heading to introduce the
senatorial decrees and the treaty.
3 The date may have been a given number of days (up to 16 by our count or 17 by theirs)
'[before the Kalends] of June', in which case the date would have fallen in the month of
May. Otherwise, the date would have been in June, but before the Ides (13th). The
date is probably between May 16 and June 12, with June 1 and June 5 excluded.
4 In 25 BC Augustus was in Spain conducting the war against the Cantabrians. This
entire section, down to line 7, contains a large amount of conjectural restorations, and
should not be accepted without that in mind.
5 Arangio-Ruiz restores: '[as may seem to be appropriate to each of them in accordance
with the treaty]'.
6 After these missing lines col. e concludes the long dossier of documents. Only tiny fragments of it remain, treating of matters, according to Arangio-Ruiz, concerned with the
use of local law and the guarantee of Mytilenaian privileges.

98   M. Vipsanius Agrippa and Julia in the Greek East. 16–13 BC.

A: **IG* II[2] 4122. Inscribed base of huge size that once supported a statue of Agrippa in a
chariot drawn by four horses, Athens. Cf. Day, *Athens* 140. **B**: **IG* XII 2.204; *IGRR* IV 64.
Marble base, Mytilene. **C**: Nikolaos of Damascus (**FGrHist* 90 F 134). Extract from his
Autobiography. Cf. Dio 54.24; Josephus, *Ant. Jud.* 16.26. **D**: *SIG*[3] 776; *IGRR* IV 204; **I.
Ilion* 86, p. 186. Inscribed base, Ilium. **E**: **RDGE* 63. Letter of Agrippa to the Argive
Gerousia, stele from Argos. Cf. *RDGE* pp. 323–4. **F**: *SIG*[3] 1065; *IGRR* IV 1064; L. Moretti,
*Iscrizioni Agonistiche Greche (Rome 1953) 60. Greek athletic contest named after Agrippa:
translated below, no. 109, from Cos.

M. Reinhold, *Marcus Agrippa* (Geneva, N.Y. 1933) 106–23; Magie, *RRAM* I 477–8.

A. *IG* II[2] 4122, Athens

[The] People | (dedicated this statue of) M[arcus] Agrippa, | son of
5 Lu[cius,] | *consul* for the third time (27 BC), their ‖ *benefactor.*

B. *IG* XII 2.204, Mytilene

The People (dedicated this statue of) | Iulia, daughter of Imperator Cae-
sar | god Augustus, wife of Marcus Agrippa, | our benefactress, because of
5 her excellence in every way ‖ and her goodwill toward our city.

C. Nikolaos of Damascus: *FGrHist* **90 F 134**

The citizens of Ilium did not know that Iulia, daughter of Caesar and wife
of Agrippa, had arrived among them at night when the Skamandros
(River) was running high, swollen from much rain, and that she was in
danger of losing her life in crossing it, along with the household slaves who
escorted her. Agrippa became furious at this, because the citizens of Ilium
did not help her, and he fined them one hundred thousand silver (drach-
mai). They were destitute. They had not foreseen the storm, nor the fact
that the young lady was coming in it, but they did not dare to say anything
to Agrippa. When Nikolaos arrived, they begged him to acquire for them
the help and protection of Herodes (the Great). Nikolaos very eagerly
gave his support to them because of the city's fame. He entreated the king
and described the situation for him, that it was unjust for Agrippa to be
angry at them, since he had not told them beforehand that he was sending
his wife to them and since they had been wholly unaware of her arrival at
night. Finally Herodes took up their protection and obtained release for
them from the fine. And since they had already departed because of their
despair over deliverance, Herodes gave the letter about this turn of events
to Nikolaos who was sailing to Chios and Rhodes, where his sons were, for
Herodes himself was going on to Paphlagonia with Agrippa. Nikolaos
sailed from Amisos to Byzantium and from there to the Troad, and he
went to Ilium. When he delivered the letter of release from the fine, both
he and even more the king were greatly honored by the citizens of Ilium.

D. *I. Ilion* **86, p. 186, Ilium**

(This statue of) Marcus Agrippa, kinsman[1] | and patron of our city and |
benefactor, (has been dedicated) for his | piety toward the goddess
5   (Athena) and his ‖ goodwill toward our People.

E. *RDGE* **63, Argos**

Of the Elder Citizens. | Agrippa to the Argive Elder Citizens | Descended
from Danaos and Hypermestra,[2] greetings. | For the continuation of your
5   organization ‖ and the protection of its ancient prestige | I am conscious of
my responsibility, | and also for the return to you | of many of your lost
10   rights, and for | the future I intend [zealously] to provide for you ‖ and [--]

F. Greek athletic contest named after Agrippa

For translation see below, no. 109, line 13.

For other honors paid to Agrippa and Iulia in the Greek East see *IG* V 1.374: inscribed base, Sparta, to Agrippa; *IG* VII 349: marble base, Oropos, to Agrippa; *SEG* I 385: marble base, Samos, to Iulia.

It was in the spring of 16 BC that Agrippa with Iulia and their two little sons set out for the Greek East. He had been formally granted the tribunician power (see below, no. 99) and a proconsular command over the eastern provinces. He returned to Italy in 13 BC and died there the following year.

1 Agrippa is called 'kinsman' because of his marriage to Iulia, which gave him a relationship with the Iulian clan. The Iulian clan traced its lineage back via Aeneas to the Trojans and the Troad.
2 This social organization, called a Gerousia, had its own officials and funds. Because of the prestige and age of its members, it often made its influence felt in public affairs. The members, 'Elder Citizens', sometimes traced their origin back to the mythical past.

99   Greek translation of funeral oration given by Augustus for Agrippa. 12 BC.

Small fragment of a Greek papyrus of the first century BC, from the Fayum in Egypt, now in Cologne.

L. Koenen, *ZPE* 5 (1970) 226 (+ photograph); *P. *Köln* 10. Cf. Dio 54.28.1–5.

Koenen, *op. cit.* 217–83; *idem*, *ZPE* 6 (1970) 239–43; E. W. Gray, *ZPE* 6 (1970) 227–38; M. W. Haslam, *CJ* 75 (1979–80) 193–9; E. Badian, *CJ* 76 (1980–1) 97–109; R. K. Sherk, *ZPE* 41 (1981) 67–9.

[--] the tribunician power for fi|ve years in accordance with[1] a decree of the senate | was given to you when the Lent<ul>i[2] were consuls (18 BC);
5   and | again this (power) for another five-year period[3] ‖ was granted when the consuls were Tiberius (Claudius) Nero[4] | and (Publius) Quin<ti>lius Varus (13 BC), your sons-in-law. | And into whatever | provinces the
10 Republic of the Ro|mans should ever summon you, ‖ it had been sanctioned in a law that your power <was to be> not *less* than (that of) any (other magistrate) in th|ose (provinces).[5] *Having been considered worthy* of the *supreme* | height (of power)[6] and [becoming a colleague] in our [rule,] | by your own <excellent qualities> and [accomplishments[7] | you surpassed] all men.

1 Koenen, *op. cit.* 274, believed that the tribunician power had been given to Agrippa 'by' a decree of the senate alone, but the Greek phrase is a translation of the Latin *ex senatus consulto* and means simply 'in accordance with a decree of the senate'. Thus, as Badian (*op. cit.* 99–101) has argued, the further action was taken by some other body than the senate. He believes that further action could only have been the vote of the Roman People.
2 P. Cornelius Lentulus Marcellinus and Cn. Cornelius Lentulus.
3 The Greek translator used the word 'Olympiad', no doubt in an attempt to translate the Latin *lustrum* or *quinquennium*.
4 He is the future emperor Tiberius.

5 Koenen argues that this means *imperium maius*, but Gray thinks of it as *imperium aequum*.
Imperium was the supreme administrative power in the Republican government in both
the military and the judicial field, duly conferred by law upon a Roman magistrate or ex-
magistrate and confined to a certain sphere of activity called *provincia*. One magistrate's
imperium was neither lesser nor greater than that possessed by another magistrate within
the same rank and it is called *aequum* ('equal') for that reason. Even M. Antonius in 74
BC and Cn. Pompeius in 67 BC possessed *imperium aequum*. In 43 BC, however, a
special grant of *imperium maius*, i.e. 'greater' *imperium*, was given by the senate to Brutus
and Cassius, and in 23 BC a similar grant was given to Augustus. See H. Last, *JRS* 37
(1947) 157–64, and E. Badian, *op. cit.* 105–6, who rightly follows Gray.
6 The 'supreme height of power' is the tribunician power: cf. Tacitus, *Ann.* 3.56.
7 The copyist wrote 'own' twice in line 13. Sherk: 'and [accomplishments]'. Previous editors: 'and [benefactions]'.

100 Letter of Augustus to the Alexandrians and the proceedings of an embassy. 10 or 9 BC.

Papyrus of the early first century AD from Egypt, Oxyrhynchus.

*P. Oxy. 3020.

P. J. Parsons in *P. Oxy.* pp. 69–74.

(Col. 1) Imperator Caesar Augustus, pontifex maximus, | holder of the
tribunician power for the fourteenth time (10/9 BC), imperator | for [the]
twelfth time, to the People[1] of Alexandria, greetings. Those | envoys, whom
you have sent, came to Gaul ‖ to me[2] and gave me your injunctions, | and
the things which seem to have distressed you | in previous *years* they
revealed to me | [---] formerly if ou|r [---]
(Col. 2) The exegetes:[3] 'Caesar, unconquered hero, these [are(?)] | envoys
of Alexandria, and us | [---] we divided up the embassy | [--] each one of
us is able [--‖-] Theodoros concerning Egypt [--] | (and) Ha[rp(?)]o-
krates concerning the Idios Logos[4] [--|-] (and) I concerning the city [--|
we have come (?)] not to defend ourselves but [---]'

1 The absence of any reference to a Boule or to magistrates is noteworthy. Dio (51.17.2–3)
says that Augustus ordered the Alexandrians to conduct their city government without
a Boule. For a summary of the controversy concerning the Alexandrian Boule see P. M.
Fraser, *Ptolemaic Alexandria* (Oxford 1972) I 94–5 with the notes. Cf. H. I. Bell, *Aegyptus*
12 (1932) 173–84.
2 In the period 12–9 BC Roman arms pushed beyond the Rhine River all the way to the
Elbe under the command of Drusus, stepson of Augustus. Augustus himself, as Dio
(54.36.3–4) informs us, spent the years 10–9 BC in Gaul to keep watch on the area. Cf.
Orosius 6.21.22.
3 In Alexandria he was the spokesman for the community.
4 In Ptolemaic times this was the 'private account' of the kings, but in the Roman period it
was the private account of Augustus and the subsequent emperors. Its administrator
was also called Idios Logos and he was appointed directly by the emperor.

101   A new calendar for the province of Asia in honor of Augustus. 9 BC.

Various documents assembled from copies published in different cities of Asia.

Arrangement of the documents:[1]

IV. Edict of the governor of Asia (Greek): lines 1–30 = Pr; lines 4–14 = Ap Gr 1 + 2a; lines 8–20 = Maion; lines 15–25 = Ap Gr 2b; lines 26–30 = Ap Gr 3a, lines 1–6.
V. Appendix to the governor's edict (Greek): lines 1–8 = Ap Gr 3a, lines 6–13; lines 9–10 = Ap Gr 3b, lines 1–2.
VI. First decree of the Koinon of Asia (Greek): lines 30–77 = Pr; lines 30–6 = Ap Gr 3b, lines 3–9; lines 40–51 = Ap Gr 4; lines 51–62 = Ap Gr 5; lines 54–67 = Eum.
VII. Second decree of the Koinon of Asia (Greek): lines 78–84 = Pr.

OGIS 458; *RDGE* 65; U. Laffi, **Studi Classici e Orientali* 16 (1967) 18–23 (+ photographs).

RDGE pp. 328–37; Laffi, *op. cit.* 5–98; Samuel, *GRC* 181–2.

IV. Edict of the governor of Asia, in Greek

[--] | from our ancestors (?) we have received [--|-] goodwill of the gods and [--| whether] more pleasant or *more beneficial* is the most divine Cae-
5   sar's bir‖thday, which we might justly *consider* equal to the beginning of all things. | If not exact from the point of view of the natural order of things, at least from the point of view of the useful, if there is nothing which has fal- len to pieces and to an un|fortunate condition has been changed which he has not restored, he has given to the whole | world a different appearance, (a world) which would have met its ruin with the greatest pleasure, if as the common good | fortune of everyone Caesar had not been born. There- fore (perhaps) each person would justly consider that this (event) has
10   been for himself‖ the beginning of life and of living, which is the limit and end of re|gret at having been born. And since from no day both for | public and for private advantage could each person receive luckier | beginnings than from the one which has been lucky for everyone, and (since), roughly speaking, it happens that | the cities in Asia have the same time for the
15   entrance (of magistrates) into public office, ‖ an arrangement clearly thus preordained according to some divine will, | in order that it should be a beginning of honor for Augustus, and since it is diff|icult to return for his many great benefactions thanks in equal measure, | unless for each of them we think of some manner of repayment, | and more joyfully would
20   men celebrate a birthday common to everyone ‖ if some particular plea- sure through (his? their?) magistracy should come to them, it seems good to me | that one and the same New Year's day for all states should be | the birthday of the most divine Caesar and that on that day all men | should

124

enter into their public office, (the day) which is the ninth day before the
Kalends of October (September 23), in order that | in an even more extra-
ordinary manner the day may be honored by acquiring in addition from
25 without a certain religious observance and ‖ (thus) may become better
known to everyone. I think this (observance) will render the greatest service
| to the province. A decree by the Koinon of Asia will ha|ve to be written to
include all his excellent qualities, in order that the plan formu|lated by us
for the honor of Augustus may remain forever. I will ordain | that the dec-
ree, engraved on the stele, be erected in the temple (of Roma and Augus-
30 tus in Pergamum), pre‖ceded by my edict written in both languages.[2]

V. Appendix to the governor's edict, in Greek

[--] the | [--] the number | [--] from the | [ninth day before the Kalends of
October, and the birthday] of Caesar as ‖ [--|--|--|--] | and it will not be a
single day, with an interval of two [years] ‖ according to the Roman practice.[3]

VI. First decree of the Koinon of Asia, in Greek

It has been decreed by the Greeks of Asia | on the motion of the high-priest
Apollonios (son) of Menophilos the Aizanian: | since Providence, which
has divinely disposed our lives, having employed zeal | and ardor, has
arranged the most perfect (culmination) for life | by producing Augustus,
35 whom for the benefit of mankind she has fill‖ed with excellence, as if [she
had sent him as a savior] for us and our descendants, | (a savior) who
brought war to an end and set [all things] in order; [and (since) with his
appearance] | Caesar *exceeded* the hopes of [all] those who received [glad
tidings] before us, | not only *surpassing* those who had been [benefactors]
before him, | but not even [leaving any] hope [of surpassing him] for those
40 who are to come in the future; ‖ and (since) the beginning of glad tidings
on his account for the world was [the birthday] | of the god, and since Asia
decreed in Smyrna, when the proconsul | was Lucius Volcacius Tullus[4]
and the secretary was Pap[ion] from Dios Hieron, | that the person who
found the greatest honors for the god should have a crown, | and Paulus
45 Fabius Maximus[5] the proconsul, as benefactor of the province ‖ having
been sent from that (god's) right hand and mind together with the other |
men through whom he bestowed benefits on the province, the size of
which benefits no speech | would be adequate to relate, has found some-
thing unknown until now to the Gre|eks for the honor of Augustus, that
from Augustus' birth|day should begin the time for life – for this reason,
50 with good luck and for (our) salvation, it has been de‖creed by the Greeks
in Asia that the New Year's first month shall begin for all | the cities on the
ninth day before the Kalends of October (September 23), which is the

birth|day of Augustus; in order that each time the day might correspond
in ea|ch city, (the Greeks) shall use the Greek day along with the Roman; |
they shall make the first month – (called) 'Caesar', as previously decreed –
55 be‖gin with the ninth day before the Kalends of October, the birthday | of
Caesar; and the crown decreed for the one who found the greatest | honors
for Caesar shall be given to Maximus the proconsul, and he shall each
time | be publicly proclaimed (as having won it), at the gymnastic festival
in Pergamum (held in honor) of Roma (and) | Augustus, (as follows:)
60 'Asia crowns Paulus Fabius Maximus who found the most pi‖ous manner
of honoring Caesar'; there shall be a similar proclamation | at the festivals
for Caesar in the individual cities; | the message written by the proconsul
and the decree of Asia shall be engraved | on a stele of white marble, which
shall be set up in the precinct of Roma and | Augustus; and the ekdikoi[6] of
65 this year shall see to it that ‖ in the cities at the head of the judicial districts[7] on stelai of white marble the message of Maximus and the decree of
Asia be engraved, | and that these stelai be set up in the temples of Caesar.
The computation | of the months shall be as follows: Caesar, 31 days;
Apellaios, 30 days; | Audnaios, 31 days; Peritios, 31 days; Dystros, 28;
70 Xandikos, 31; ‖ Artemision, 30 days; Daisios, 31; Panemos, 30; Loos, 31;
Gorpiaios, 31; | Hyperberetaios, 30. Total of days: 365. For this year,
because of the intercalated day, | Xandikos shall be computed at 32 days.
In order that from the present there may be a correspondence | of months
and days, the current month of Peritios shall be counted up to the | 14th,
but on the ninth day before the Kalends of February (January 24) we shall
75 count the first day of the month ‖ of Dystros, and for each month the begin-
ning of the new month shall be the ninth day | before the Kalends. The
intercalated day shall always be that of the intercalated Ka|lends of the
month of Xandikos, with an interval of two years (between intercala-
tions). |

VII. Second decree of the Koinon, in Greek

Decreed by the Greeks in Asia on the motion of the high-priest Apollonios
(son) of | Menophilos the Aizanian: since the New Year's day always
80 ought to fall on the same (day) ‖ for everyone for the entrance into public
office according to the edict of Paulus Fabius Maximus the pro|consul and
the decree of Asia, and since (this) arrangement of time causes difficulties |
over the announcement of the results of the elections, the procedures con-
nected with the election of magistrates shall take place | in the tenth
month, as has been laid down in the Cornelian Law,[8] within | the first ten
days (of the month).

This series of documents deals with the introduction into the province of Asia of a solar
calendar of twelve months, of which seven had 31 days, four had 30, and one had only 28.

There was a periodic intercalation of one day. The first day of the year for this calendar was to be on September 23, the birthday of Augustus.

1 The text here translated is a composite text assembled from fragments of copies which originally had been set up in many different cities of Asia: Priene (Pr): the largest fragment, containing eighty-four lines in Greek, on two blocks; 2. Apamea Kibotos (Ap Lat and Ap Gr 1, 2a–b, 3a–b, 4, 5): fragments of marble blocks, one of which (Ap Lat) contains four lines in Latin with a fifth in Greek, while the others (Ap Gr 1–5) contain fragments of Greek text; 3. Dorylaion: two small fragments in Latin; 4. Maionia (Maion): one fragment of a marble block, text in Greek, corresponding to lines 8–20 of Pr; 5. Eumeneia (Eum): one fragment, text in Greek, corresponding to lines 54–67 of Pr. In his publication of these fragments Laffi has arranged them in the order I–VII. The first (I) is the edict in Latin of the governor of Asia, Paulus Fabius Maximus; the second (II) is an appendix in Latin to the governor's edict; the third (III) is a preface to the Greek redaction of the documents. These three exist only in fragments, and the longest of them (nine lines of Latin of the governor's edict) is full of both small and large errors because of the Greek engraver's unfamiliarity with Latin. They are omitted in the present translation. For a comparison of the Latin of the governor's edict and the corresponding redaction into Greek see *RDGE* pp. 207–9.

2 The author of this edict is, of course, Paulus Fabius Maximus: document VI, line 44, and VII, line 80.

3 The restoration of '[years]' is assured by line 77. A two-year interval between intercalations (i.e. a leap-year every third year instead of every fourth) was an error committed by the Roman pontifices between 42 and 9 BC. Corrective measures were then taken by Augustus. See *RDGE* pp. 335–6 and Samuel, *GRC* 155–8.

4 He was consul in 33 BC and governor of Asia in either 30/29 or 29/28 BC, according to Laffi, *op. cit.* 59–62. Atkinson, *Historia* 312–14, placed his governorship in 26/5 BC.

5 The date of his governorship of Asia depends on the fact that after 9 BC intercalations in the calendar were no longer made in the erroneous manner of every third year, as described in these documents, and on the fact that he had been consul in 11 BC. Laffi, *op. cit.* 27–34, fixes his governorship to 10/9 BC.

6 These were annually elected 'advocates' who represented the Koinon of Asia in its negotiations with the emperor or other high dignitaries and magistrates.

7 See above, no. 77, n. 5.

8 This seems to be some law concerning Asia that is unknown to us, but perhaps of Augustan date.

102 Five edicts of Augustus and a decree of the senate. 7/6 and 4 BC.

Marble stele over two meters high, complete on all sides, in the agora of Cyrene.

SEG IX 8; F. de Visscher, *Les Édits d'Auguste découverts à Cyrène* (Louvain-Paris 1940) 16–26 (+ photograph); *FIRA* I 68; *RDGE* 31 (Edict V and the decree).

De Visscher, *op. cit.* 31–210 (full commentary); *RDGE* pp. 174–82.

EDICT I

Imperator Caesar Augustus, pontifex maximus, holding the tribunician |
power for the seventeenth time (7/6 BC), imperator for the fourteenth
time, | *vv* DECLARES[1] *vv* | Since I find that all the Romans in the province
5   of Cyrene ‖ are two hundred and fifteen of every age *v* | who have a census
valuation of twenty-five hundred denarii or more, | from whom the judges
are (chosen), and that there are conspiracies among these (Romans) | – so
the embassies of the cities from the province have complained – which
have oppre|ssed the Greeks in capital cases,[2] the same people taking turns
10   as ac‖cusers and as witnesses for each other, and (since) I myself have
found that some in|nocent people in this way have been oppressed and
brought to the ulti|mate penalty, until the senate may decide about this |
or I myself may find something better, *vv* the fair and appropriate course
of action, it seems to me, | would be for those who govern the province of
15   Crete and Cyrene to set up (a list) in the ‖ province of Cyrene of Greek
judges of the highest census valuati|on, equal in number to the Roman
(judges), none of them younger than twenty-five years, Roman | or Greek,
with a census valuation and property, if there is a sufficient number of
such m|en, of no less than seventy-five hundred denarii, or, if in this way |
20   the number of judges which ought to be listed cannot be filled, ‖ they shall
list those people who have half and no less than half of this census valua-
tion to be judges in | capital cases of the Greeks. *vv* If a Greek is on tri|al,
one day before the accuser begins to speak he shall be given the pow|er (to
decide) whether he wishes his judges to be Romans or | half of them
Greeks. If he chooses half Greeks, then, after the balls have been
25   weighed[3] ‖ and the names inscribed on them, from the one ur|n the names
of the Romans, and from the other the names of the Greeks shall be drawn
by lot, | until in each group twenty-five have been selected. Of these names
| the accuser, if he wishes, shall reject one from each group, but the defen-
dant (may reject) three of all the names, | *vv* on condition that he reject
30   neither all Romans nor all Greeks. Then ‖ all the others shall be sent to
cast their votes and they shall cast their votes, | the Romans separately
into one basket, the Greeks separately into another. Then, when the
counting has been finished sep|arately for the votes in each group, what-
ever the majority of all shall have | decided the praetor (i.e. governor) shall
declare publicly (as the verdict). And since unjust deaths, for | the most
part, the relatives of victims do not allow to go unavenged, and it is likely
35   that ‖ Greek accusers will not be lacking in procuring justice for the guilty
on behalf of their murdered | relatives or (fellow) citizens, *vv* the correct
and appropriate course of action, it seems to me, wou|ld be if the future
governors of Crete and Cyrene, | in the province of Cyrene, would not per-
mit a Roman to be the accuser of a Greek in a case of the murder of a Greek

man or woman, | except that someone who has been honored with Roman citizenship may go to court on behalf of the death of one of his relatives or
40 (fellow) citizens. || *vv*

EDICT II

Imperator Caesar Augustus, pon|tifex maximus, holding the tribunician power for the seventeenth time (7/6 BC) *v* DECLARES:[1] *v* Ill-will and blame | ought not be (directed) to(ward) Publius Sextius Scaeva[4] because he saw to it that Aulus Stlaccius, son of Lu|cius, Maximus and Lucius Stlaccius, son of Lucius, Macedo and Publi|us Lacutanius, freedman of
45 Publius, Phileros, *vv* when they || said that they knew and wished to tell something that pertained to my safety and to the Republic, | were sent in chains to me from the Cyrenaica, | for in this Sextius acted properly and with vi|gilance. *v* Moreover, since they know nothing of matters that pertain to me and the Republic | and stated and made it clear[5] to me that this,
50 which they said in the province, had been a fa||brication and a falsehood, I have set them free | and released them from custody. *vv* But (as for) Aulus Stlaccius | Maximus, whom envoys of the Cyreneans accuse of removing statues from | public places, among them being the one beneath which the city has inscribed my name, until | I have formed an opinion about this
55 matter, I forbid him to leave (Rome) without my order. || *vv*

EDICT III

Imperator Caesar Augustus, pontifex maximus, holding the tribunician power | for the seventeenth time (7/6 BC) *vv* DECLARES:[1] *vv* If any people from the Cyrenaican provin|ce have been honored with (Roman) citizenship, I order them to perform the personal (?)[6] liturgies, nevertheless, in their role[7] | as Greeks, *vv* with the exception of those to whom in accordance with a law or decree of the senate | (or) decree of my father or of myself, immunity from taxation has been granted along with the citi-
60 zenship. || And it pleases me that these men to whom immunity has been given *vv* shall have exemption only for that pro|perty which they had at the time (of the grant). For all newly acquired property | they shall pay the taxes. *vv*

EDICT IV

Imperator Caesar Augustus, ponti|fex maximus, holding the tribunician power for the seventeenth time (7/6 BC) *vv* declares: *vv* Whatever | dis-
65 putes shall arise between Greeks in the Cyrenaican province, || except for those who are liable for capital offenses, in whose case the one who governs the province | has the duty of conducting the investigation and rendering

judgments himself or establishing a list of judges, | – for all other matters
it pleases me that Greek judges be granted to them, unless some | defen-
dant or accused wishes to have Roman citizens for judges. For the parties
| to whom Greek judges will be given in consequence of this decree of mine,
70   it pleases me that no judge should be given || from that city from which the
plaintiff or accuser comes, or th|*vv*e defendant or accused. *vv* | *vacat* |

EDICT V

Imperator Caesar Augustus, pontifex maximus, | holding the tribunician
power for the *vv* 19th time (5/4 BC) *vv* d e c l a r e s:[1] | A decrec of the senate
was passed in the consulship of Gaius Calvisius (Sabinus) and Lucius
75 || Passienus (4 BC). I was present and par|ticipated in its writing, and since
it pertains to the security of the allies of the People | of the Romans, in
order that it might be known | to all those under our care I have decided to
send it to the provinces and | to append it to this, my edict, from which it
80   will be clear to all || inhabitants of the provinces how much concern | I and
the senate have that no one of our sub|jects may suffer unduly any harm or
extortion. *vv* | *vv* DECREE OF THE SENATE *vv* | Whereas Gaius Cal-
85   visius Sabinus and Lucius Passie||nus Rufus, consuls, spoke about mat-
ters which *vv* Imperator Caesar *vv* Augustus, our Princeps,[8] | after con-
sultation with the Advisory Board which he had drawn by lot from the
senate,[9] | wished to be introduced to the senate by us because they pertain
to | the security of the allies of the People of the Romans, it has been
90   de||creed by the senate: *vv* Our ancestors have passed laws for legal action
| in the recovery of money[10] in order that our allies | more easily might be
able to begin proceedings for the wrongs done to them and to recover the
money of which they have been de|prived. But because the form of such
court ac|tions sometimes is very burdensome and disagreeable to those
95   very people for whom the law was writ||ten, poor people and those weak
with illness or old age | being dragged from far-off provinces as witnesses,
it plea|ses the senate: If any of our allies after the passage of this | decree
of the senate either publicly or as individuals have been deprived of money
and wish to reco|ver it, without introducing a capital charge against the
100   extorter,[11] and if they present themselves about || these matters and
declare them to any one of our magistrates who has the power to con|vene
the *senate*, the magistrate shall introduce these people as quickly as pos-
sible into the senate | and give them an advocate who will speak on their
behalf before the senate, any | (advocate) they might ask for, but no one
shall unwillingly serve as advocate to whom in accordance with our laws |
an exemption from this public duty has been given. *vv* In order that the
105   (trials) may be heard (?) || for those people who may bring charges in the

senate,[12] whatever magistrate gives them access to the | senate shall, on
the same day in the presence of the senate with no less | than two hundred
being present, draw by lot four of all the consulars who are either in Rome
itself | [or] within twenty miles of the city; likewise three of all the prae|-
110 torians who are in Rome itself or within twenty miles of the ci‖ty; likewise
two of the rest of the senators or of all those who have the right to express
their o|pinion before the senate, who may then be either in Rome or within
twenty | miles of the city. Nobody shall be chosen who is seventy or | more
years old or who holds a magistracy or is in an official position[13] or is a
president of a cou|rt or is in charge of the grain supply or is a person whom
115 illness prevents from performing this public du‖ty and who so swears
before the senate and produces | three members of the senate to swear to it,
or who is a person who is re|lated by kinship or marriage to him (i.e. the
accused) so that by the Julian Judiciary Law[14] he may not be forced to
testify as a witness | against his will in a public court, or is a person who the
accused swears before the senate | is hostile toward him; but he shall not
120 reject on oath more than three. Of the nine men ‖ drawn by lot in this way
the magistrate who does the drawing shall see | to it that within two days
those seeking recovery of money and the person from whom | they seek it
take turns in rejection, until five are left. | Whoever of these judges may die
before the case is decided or if any other reason pre|vents him from decid-
125 ing and his excuse is approved by five men under oath fro‖m the senate,
then the magistrate, in the presence of the judges and those seek|ing recov-
ery of money and the person from whom they are seeking it, shall draw by
lot a substitute from (among) those | men who are the same rank and have
held the same magistracies as that man happen|ed to hold into whose
place they are being assigned by lot as a substitute, on condit‖ion that he
does not as|sign a man who cannot be assigned against the accused by this
130 decree of the sen‖ate. *v* Those who have been chosen as judges shall only
about those matters he|ar and render decisions concerning which some-
one is accused of having, at the expense of the public or of an individual,
ap|propriated (funds), *vv* and whatever sum of money his accusers may
sho|w has been taken from them privately or publicly, just so much shall
they order to be restored, | on the condition that the judges render their
135 decision within thirty days.[15] Those (judges) who must ‖ decide about
these cases and pronounce their decision, until they do decide and pro-
nounce | their decision, shall be relieved of every public liturgy except
public wor|ship. *vv* And it pleases the senate that the magistrate who has
conducted the drawing by lot | of the judges or, if he is unable, the consul
who has priority,[16] | shall preside over this investigation and for the sum-
140 moning of witnesses who are in Ita‖lly shall grant power, on condition that
to a man seeking recovery as a private individual (it shall be) no mo|re

than five (witnesses), and to those in a public capacity no more than ten (that) he shall give permission to summon. | Likewise it pleases the senate that the judges who are chosen by lot in accordance with this <decree of the senate> | shall pronounce openly what each of them has decided, *vv* | and whatever the majority pronounces shall stand (as the decision).

1 In extra large letters on the stone. Cf. lines 41 and 56. In line 73 the letters merely have more space between them.
2 I.e., in cases involving the death penalty and not the loss of civil rights.
3 They must all weigh the same to prevent a particular name from being singled out in the selection process.
4 Governor of Crete-Cyrene.
5 Textual observations made by J. H. Oliver in *Memoirs of the American Academy in Rome* 19 (1949) 107–8, are followed here.
6 This is a celebrated crux, and the solution given by A. Wilhelm in *Wiener Anzeiger* 80 (1943) 2–10 and accepted later by many others is followed here. De Visscher has a text which means: 'I order that they, nevertheless, following their turn, should hold the personal liturgies of the Greeks'. Oliver, in *Hesperia* 29 (1960) 324–5, felt an addition was necessary: '<financial and> personal liturgies'. But K. M. T. Atkinson, *Studies Presented to Victor Ehrenberg on his 75th Birthday* (Oxford 1966) 21–36, believes that no emendation of the text or additions to it are necessary, and instead of 'personal' liturgies she sees a more specific reference to military service. See also Sherwin-White, *Citizenship*[2] 334–6, for further discussion.
7 A. Wilhelm (above, n. 6) thus interprets this difficult phrase. De Visscher and others have accepted his view. It is a question of double citizenship: see Sherwin-White, *Citizenship*[2] 295–306.
8 Augustus speaks of himself as *princeps* three times in his *Res Gestae* (13; 30; 32).
9 The existence of such an imperial Advisory Board to be used by Augustus is known from Dio (53.21.4) and Suetonius (*Div. Aug.* 35.3). See J. Crook, *Consilium Principis* (Cambridge 1955) 8ff. See the Glossary *s.v.* Advisory Board.
10 For these earlier laws: de Visscher, *op. cit.* 156–83; A. N. Sherwin-Shite, *PBSR* 17 (1949) 5–25; P. A. Brunt, *Historia* 10 (1961) 189–99.
11 A controversy exists over this phrase. Was extortion in itself a capital offense in previous legislation? What if the accuser does wish to introduce a capital charge? See the works cited above, n. 10.
12 There are textual and grammatical difficulties in this clause, although the general meaning is clear enough. Oliver, *op. cit.* above, n. 5, 109–13, follows the word order on the stone: 'In order that <there might be judges> for these (trials) to be heard for those who bring charges in the senate'. De Visscher and others have inverted two words of the original.
13 The Greek contains a word that might render the Latin *potestas*, i.e. 'power'. See de Visscher, *op. cit.* 145–6.
14. It is not known whether the reference is to legislation of Julius Caesar or of Augustus.
15 This is not an exclusionary clause. The judges are expected to give their decision within thirty days.
16 Explained by de Visscher as the consul who has the fasces at that particular time: see Aulus Gellius 2.15.4ff., and de Visscher, *op. cit.* 149, and cf. J.-L. Ferrary in *Mélanges de l'École Française de Rome* 89 (1977) 647–52. Cf. above, no. 55 A, B5.

103   Letter of Augustus to Knidos. Last half of 6 BC.

Marble stele broken on lower right side and bottom, found at Astypalaia.[1]

IG XII 3.174; *SIG*[3] 780; *IGRR* IV 1031; *FIRA* III 185; **RDGE* 67.

RDGE pp. 343–5; F. Millar, *The Emperor in the Roman World* (London 1977) 443.

[When] Kairogenes (son) of Leu[ka]theos (?) was the [demi]orgos.[2] |
Imperator Caesar, son of the god, Augustus, pontifex maximus, | consul
designate for the twelfth time[3] | and holding the tribunician power for the
5   eighteenth time (6 BC)[4] ‖ to the magistrates, Boule and People of Knidos,
greetings. Your en|voys Dionysios {II} and Dionysios II (sons) of Diony|-
sios met me in Rome, gave me your decree, | and accused Euboulos (son)
10   of Anaxandridas, now de|ad, and his wife Tryphera, present here, ‖ of the
murder of Euboulos (son) of Chrysippos. I | ordered my friend Asinius
Gallus[5] to interrogate | those of the household slaves who were involved in
the accusation under | torture, and I learned that Phileinos (son) of
Chrysippos for three ni|ghts in succession had attacked the house of
15   Eubou‖los and Tryphera with violence and in the manner of a sie|ge; that
on the third night he also brought his bro|ther Euboulos along with him;
and that the owners of the house, Eubou|los and Tryphera, neither by
20   negotiating with | Phileinos nor by erecting barricades against his atta‖cks
were able to find safety in their own house; | and they gave instructions to
one of their household slaves not to ki|ll them, as perhaps one might be
driven to do out of justifiable anger, | but rather to drive them off by scat-
tering their (the household's) excrement over them; and that the | slave,
25   along with what he poured over them – either intentionally ‖ or uninten-
tionally, for he himself remained steadfast in his denial – | let go of the
chamber pot, *and* Euboulos fell down under it. It would have been more
ju|st for him to have been saved than his brother. I have sent you also the |
interrogation reports themselves. I would have been amazed at how much
| the interrogation of their slaves in your city was feared by the defen-
30   ‖dants, if you had not seemed to be toward them excessively | harsh and
to be turning your hatred of crime in the wrong direction (?), since at
those who deserved to suffer every punishment, who had attacked
another's | house three times at night with violence and force | and were
destroying the common security of all of you, (at those people) you did
not become angry ‖ but (rather) at those who had suffered misfortune
35   even *when* | they defended themselves and had committed no crime at
all. | But now you would seem to me to act correctly, if to my decision
[in this | matter] you paid attention and made the records in your *public*
| *archives* agree (with it). *vv* Farewell.

1 On the same stele is engraved a letter of Hadrian to the Astypalaians.
2 He was the eponymous magistrate at Astypalaia.
3 Augustus held his twelfth consulship in 5 BC, from January until the end of April.
4 It spans the period July 1 of 6 BC to June 30 of 5 BC.
5 C. Asinius Gallus was the son of C. Asinius Pollio (consul in 40 BC), one of the leading personalities of the Augustan age. Gallus himself became consul in 8 BC and governor of Asia two years later. His wife was Vipsania, whom he married after Tiberius was forced to divorce her in 12. See *RDGE* pp. 344–5 and A. B. Bosworth, *AJAH* 2 (1977) 173–92.

104   Gaius, son of Augustus, is honored at Sardis. 5 BC.

Huge stele of bluish marble with pediment, within which the first five lines are inscribed, complete at top and bottom and damaged near the middle of the right side, with a break across the face near the bottom. The stele contains twelve documents listing honors for the prominent Sardian citizen Menogenes. Found near the temple of Artemis in Sardis.

A: The first document: the Koinon of Asia and the city of Sardis decree that the day on which Gaius assumed the toga of manhood is to be an annual holiday: *IGRR* IV 1756, lines 1–21; W. H. Buckler and D. M. Robinson, **Sardis* VII 1 (Leiden 1932) no. 8, lines 1–21 (+ photograph of the whole stele). **B**: The second document: a letter of Augustus to Sardis: *IGRR* IV 1756, lines 22–7; Buckler-Robinson, **op. cit.* no. 8, lines 22–7; *RDGE* 68.

Magie, *RRAM* I 481; *RDGE* p. 347.

A. *Sardis* VII 1, no. 8, lines 1–21

The Koinon | of the Greeks in Asia | and the People of the Sardi|ans and
5   the Elder Citizens[1] honored Menoge‖nes (son) of Isidoros (grandson) of
Menogenes by what is written below. | Metrodoros (son) of Konon, Klei-
nias, Mousaios, and Dionysios, the strategoi,[2] introduced the motion: |
Whereas Gaius Iulius Caesar, the eldest of the sons of Augustus, | has put
on the toga most earnestly prayed for (and) radiant with every decoration,
in place of the one with purple border,[3] and there is joy among all | men to
see the prayers that have been awakened everywhere (by this event) to
10   Augustus on behalf of his sons, and o‖ur city on the occasion of such great
good fortune has decided that the day which completed his transition from
boy to man | shall be a holy day, on which each year all our people in their
brightest clothing shall wear wreaths, and (on which) sacri|fices shall be
performed by the strategoi of the year to the gods, and prayers offered
through the | sacred heralds for his (i.e. Gaius') safety, and (on which) his
image shall be jointly consecrated and set up in his father's | temple, and
on that (day) on which our city received the glad tidings and this decree
15   was passed, on that day too wr‖eaths shall be worn and most splendid

sacrfices performed to the gods; and (whereas our city has decided) that an embassy | concerning these things be sent to go to Rome and to congratulate him and Au|gustus, it is decreed by the Boule and the People to send forth envoys selected from among the foremost me|n to carry greetings from our city and to give him a copy of this de|cree sealed with the public seal, and to speak with Au‖gustus about matters of common interest to Asia and our city. Chosen as envoys were Iollas (son) of Metrodoros | and Menogenes (son) of Isidoros (grandson) of Menogenes. | *vv*

B. *Sardis* **VII 1, no. 8, lines 22–7**

Imperator Caesar, son of the god, Augustus, pontifex maximus, holding the tribunician power for the 19th time (5 BC) | to the Sardian magistrates, Boule (and) People, greetings. Your envoys, Iollas (son) of Metrodoros and | Menogenes (son) of Isidoros (grandson) of Menogenes, met with me in Rome and ‖ gave me the decree from you by means of which you disclosed what had been decreed by you concerning yourselves and rejoiced with me at the trans|ition to manhood of the elder of my sons. I praise your zeal | in showing your gratitude to me and all my (family) for the benefits given (to you) by me.[4] Farewell.

Gaius Iulius Caesar was the eldest son of Agrippa and Iulia, daughter of Augustus. He was born in 20 BC and adopted by Augustus as his son in 17 BC. He died in AD 4.

1 This association of Elder Citizens (Gerousia) was essentially social in nature: see above, no. 98 E.
2 These were annually elected magistrates in Sardis forming a board with civil functions.
3 The *toga praetexta* (purple-bordered toga) was put aside by boys for the *toga virilis* (toga of manhood) in a solemn ceremony, normally at age 15.
4 One expects this sentence to be followed by the usual statement that the writer, in this case Augustus, will be the author of some good for the city in the future. Its omission is noteworthy.

105   Oath of loyalty sworn in Paphlagonia to Augustus and his descendants. March 6, 3 BC.

Stele of sandstone, Phazimon.

IGRR III 137; *OGIS* 532; *ILS* 8781; F. Cumont, *Studia Pontica* III no. 66; P. Herrmann, **Der Römische Kaisereid*, Hypomnemata 20 (Göttingen 1968) no. 4, pp. 123–4.

Magie, *RRAM* I 465; Herrmann, *op. cit. passim.*

Of Imperator Caes[ar,] | son of the god, Augustus the twelfth consulship (5–3 BC), | third year (of the province, 3 BC),[1] *on the day before* | the Nones

5   of March (March 6) in Gangra in [camp (?),]² the oa‖th completed by *the inhabitants* of [Pa]|phlagonia [and the] R[omans] *who do business among* | them: *v* | I swear by Zeus, Earth, Sun, all the gods [and] *god|desses*, and

10 Augus[t]us himself that I will be favorably disposed toward [Cae]‖sar Augustus and his *children and descendants* | all the time of my [life] in *wo|rd* and deed and thought, considering as *friends* | those whom they may consider (friends) and *holding* as enemies | those whom they may judge to be

15 (enemies), and for things that are of interest *to them* ‖ I will spare neither my body [nor] | my soul nor my life nor my children, but in *every* | way for the things that *affect* them | I will undergo every danger; and whatever I

20 might *perceive* | or hear against them being *sa‖id* or plotted or done, | I will report it and *I will be* an enemy to *the* | person saying or plotting or doing [any of] *the|se* things; and whomever they may judge to be their enemies,

25 *the|se*, on land and sea, with arms and ‖ steel will I pursue and ward off. | If I do anything contrary to this [oath] | or anything not in agreement with what I have *sw|orn*, I pray that there may come upon myself, my *bod|y* and

30 soul and life, my *chil‖dren* and all my *family* | and whatever is of use to us, destruction, total *destructio|n* till the end of all *my* line [and] | of all my descendants, and may neither the [bodies] | of my family or of my descen-

35 dants by earth or [se‖a] be received, nor may (earth or sea) bear fruit [for them.] | In the same words was this oath sworn by all the [inhabitants of the land] | in the *tem|ples* of Augustus throughout the districts (of the province) by the altars [of Augustus.] | And likewise the Phazimonians living

40 in what is [now] called [Neapo]‖lis [swore the oath,] | all of them, in the temple of Augustus by the [altar of] | Augustus. *v*

Other examples of loyalty oaths from the Greek East are to be found in: Assos in the Troad (*IGRR* IV 251; *SIG*³ 797); Samos (*Athen. Mitt.* 75 (1960) 70ff.); Palaipaphos on Cyprus (*JRS* 50 (1960) 75; *SEG* XVIII 578). All of these can also be examined in Herrmann, *op. cit.* pp. 123–6.

1 The provincial era of Paphlagonia began when Paphlagonia was attached to the province of Galatia, in 6/5 BC.
2 Cumont has 'in [camp]', but Dittenberger (in *SIG*³) and Dessau (in *ILS*) have 'in the [agora]'.

106   Roman legionaries guard the government grain during its transportation down the Nile to Alexandria. 2 BC.
Text on a terracotta jar, Oxyrhynchus in Egypt.

O. Guéraud, **Journal of Juristic Papyrology* 4 (1950) 106–11 (+ photograph); *SB* 9223; S. Daris, *Documenti per la storia dell'esercito romano in Egitto* (Milan 1964) no. 66.

Guéraud, *loc. cit.*

From the Ox(yrhynchite) nome.[1] *vv* | Ammonios (son) of Ammonios,
pilot of a public boat whose emblem is [--,] through the agency of
marine escort Lucius Oclatius, soldier | of the legion XXII (Deiotari-
ana), cohort II, century of Maximus Stoltius, and Hermias (son) of
Petalos, pil(ot) of another boat | whose emblem is Egypt, through the
agency of marine escort Lucius Castricius, soldier of the legion XXII

5 (Deiotariana), cohort IV, century of‖ Titus Pompeius. This is a sample[2]
of what we have put on board from the prod(uce) of the 28th (year) of
Caesar (3 BC): Ammonios, (loaded) up to the bulwarks | with 433¼
(artabai)[3] (of wheat), and Hermias likewise with 433¼ (artabai) (of
wheat), all together, loaded through the agency of Leonidas and Apol-
lonios the sito(logoi)[4] of the east(ern) | part of the lower toparchy,[1]
866½ (artabai) (of wheat), and we made an additional measurement of
½ (artabe) (of wheat) per hundred artab(ai) (as tax). The loading was
do|ne by us from the 2nd of Hathyr to the 4th of the sam(e) month, and we
have sealed (this jar) with bo(th) of our seals, that of Ammo(nios) | whose
figure is Ammon, and that of Hermias whose figure is Harpokrates.

10 (Year) 29 of Caesar (2 BC), Hathyr 4. ‖ (Second hand) We, Hermias and
A<m>moni<o>s, have sealed the samples. (Year) <29> of Caesar,
Hathyr 19.

In documentary texts of this nature many abbreviations and symbols are used. An
attempt is made in this translation to indicate the abbreviations by means of round ( )
brackets, except that the following are additions by the translator: (Deiotariana), (son),
(loaded), (as tax), (this jar), (Second hand), (3 BC), (2 BC). '(Year)' is the translation
of a special symbol.

1 Egypt was divided into many administrative districts called nomes, which in turn
   were divided into toparchies.
2 The jar itself contained this sample of wheat from the Oxyrhynchite nome, to be
   opened and compared with the cargo at Alexandria to ensure its purity.
3 An artabe was an Egyptian measure of capacity, containing about 40 liters. See
   Wilcken, *Grundzüge* pp. LXVIIIff., and J. Shelton in *ZPE* 42 (1981) 99–106.
4 The sitologos in Egypt was the collector of the grain tax at the local granary.

107 Restoration of sacred writings to the archives of Nysa. 1 BC.
A copy made from a stone long lost, Nysa on the Maeander.

*SIG*³ 781 I; **RDGE* 69 I.

RDGE pp. 348–50.

(I) [--] | when the priest of Roma and of Imperator Caesar Augustus was
[Hera|kl]eides (son) of Herakleides from Mastaura, when the stephane-
phoros | was Diom[e]des (son) of Athenagoras (son) of Diom[e]des, (who

was) priest | of Jupiter Capitolinus for life, in the month of Gorpiaios the
5 nine‖teenth, on the day before the Ides of August (August 12), in the
consulship of Cossus [C]o[r]nelius Lentulus | and Lucius (Calpurnius)
Piso (1 BC), when the secretary of the People was Heli|odoros (son) of
Maiandrios (son) of Theodotos, who was priest of Tiberius Clau|dius
Nero[1] for life, Artemidoros, (son) of Demetrios, Papas | (member) of the
10 city's (board) of generals cared for the restora‖tion to the archives of the
holy writings concerned with the gods | and their inviolability and (their
right of receiving) suppliants and the tax-exempt status for their tem|ple,[2]
after he had reported this to <G>naeus Lentulus Augur the procon|sul[3] and
returned the attached letter.[4] |

1 It should be noted that at this early date there is already a cult of the future emperor
Tiberius in the Greek East.
2 This was the temple of Pluto and Kore. Nearby was a sacred cave in which miraculous
cures were often experienced by the sick: Strabo 14.1.44.
3 Cn. Cornelius Lentulus Augur had been consul in 14 BC, but did not become governor
of Asia until 2/1 BC: Atkinson, *Historia* 327–8.
4 There follows, in the copy of the inscription, the beginning of this letter by Cn. Cornelius
Lentulus Augur to Nysa, but only the salutation and a few mutilated phrases survive.

108   Letter of a governor of Asia concerning a point of law. About AD 4/5 or soon afterwards.
Stone found in Chios.

SIG[3] 785, *IGRR* IV 943; *SEG* XXII 507; **RDGE* 70; cf. Appian, *Mithridatic Wars* 46–7;
61.

RDGE pp. 351–3; A. J. Marshall, *GRBS* 10 (1969) 255–71.

[--] he having been *petitioned* by A[--] | of Staphylos, [--] to the Chian
envoys (and) read alo|ud a letter of Antistius Vetus,[1] my predecessor as
5 proconsul, | a most distinguished man. Following my general proce‖dure
of preserving the written files of my predecessors in the proconsulship, to
keep | safe also the letter of Vetus, which had been produced concerning
this case, | I considered sensible. And later each party in oppo|sition
concerning their claims met with me separately, and I lis|tened to them,
and according to my usual practice requested from each party more
10 care‖fully written memoranda. When I received [these,] I appro|pria-
tely fixed my attention on them and the oldest (document) I found, in
order of time, was a sealed copy of a decree of the senate passed when
Lucius Sulla was consul for the se|cond time (80 BC), in which, after the
Chians had testified to the actions that they on behalf of the Romans had
ta|ken bravely against Mithridates and to their suffering at his hands,

15   the sen‖ate specifically confirmed that they were to enjoy the laws and
customs and rights | which they had when they entered into friendship
with the Romans, and that they should not be subject to any ruling
whatsoever | of (Roman) magistrates or promagistrates, and that the
Romans among them | should obey Chian laws.[2] And a letter of Impera-
tor, son of the god, Au|gustus, consul for the eighth time (26 BC), written
20   to the Chians [--‖--] the *freedom* for the city | [--]

1 C. Antistius Vetus, consul in 6 BC and governor of Asia about AD 2/3 or 3/4:
    Atkinson, *Historia* 328.
2 This is a striking point, that resident Romans should be subject to local Chian laws:
    see Marshall, *loc. cit.* And unfortunately the present letter is incomplete, making it
    impossible to know the exact nature of the case brought before the unknown governor
    who wrote this letter. It may have concerned an infringement of the city's freedom or it
    may have involved a Roman citizen who refused to recognize the jurisdiction of a
    Chian court.

109   Greek athletic contests named in honor of Augustus and his family. About AD 5.
Base of gray marble, Cos.

*SIG*³ 1065; *IGRR* IV 1064; L. Moretti, **Iscrizioni Agonistiche Greche* (Rome 1953) no. 60.

Moretti, *op. cit.* pp. 156–9.

[--] |[1] *victor* at the Nem[ean Games] in the men's | pentathlon; | [at the]
Great [Ac]tian Games[2] of the Imperial family (victor) in the young |
5   men's pentathlon, first of the Coans to do so; ‖ at the Games of [R]oma and
Augustus established by | the Koinon of Asia in Pergamum[3] | (victor) in
the Pythian boys'[4] pentathlon; | at the Great Games of Asklepios (victor)
10   in the Isthmian boys' | pentathlon; at the Games of the Im‖perial family
established for Gaius Cae|sar (victor) in the Isthmian boys' stadi|on-race[5]
and pentathlon on the same da|y; at the games of Agrippa[6] (victor) in the
Isthmian (boys') penta|thlon; at the Games of Apollo in Myndos (victor)
15   in the Isthmian bo‖ys' stadion-race; at the Dorian Games | in Knidos
(victor) in the Pythian boys' | pankration;[7] at the Games of the Imperial
family in Hali|karnassos (victor) in the Isthmian boys' | pentathlon; at
20   the Games of Herakles in Iasos ‖ (victor) in the Isthmian boys' pentathlon; at the Games of Dionysos in Teos (victor) in the Pythian (boys')
pen|tathlon; at the Games of the Imperial family in Sardis | (victor) in the
Isthmian boys' pentathlon.

1 In one of the preceding lines would have appeared the name of the athlete being honored
    by his native city of Cos.
2 These were games established by Augustus, perhaps in 28 or 27 BC, to celebrate his

victory at Actium over Antonius and Cleopatra: see Dio 51.1 and Suetonius, *Aug.* 18. For the date of these games see Moretti, *op. cit.* pp. 205–6.

3 The worship of Augustus was simply associated with the older cult of the goddess Roma: see above, no. 18.

4 'Pythian' and 'Isthmian' in this context refer to age-groups of the athletes. Youngest were the 'Pythian boys' from 12 to 14 years, then the 'Isthmian boys' 14–17 years, and the 'young men' of 17–20. Those who were older were simply 'men'.

5 A foot-race the length of the Greek stadium, either half a lap or a full lap.

6 I.e. M. Vipsanius Agrippa, who was well known to the Greeks because of his proconsular command over the eastern provinces in 16–13 BC: see above, no. 98.

7 The pankration was personal combat similar to wrestling: cf. H. A. Harris, *Sport in Greece and Rome* (Ithaca, N.Y. 1972), 25–6.

110   Early Roman organization of mines and quarries in Egypt. AD 11.

Rectangular stone block over four feet high, decorated with a representation of the Egyptian god Mîn (called Pan by the Greeks) on the upper right side, Wâdi Semna in the eastern desert of Egypt.

AE (1910) 207; L. A. Tregenza, *Bulletin of the Faculty of Arts, Fouad I University* (Cairo) 13 (1951–2) p. 40 (+ drawing and photograph); *SB* 10123; *SEG XX 670, lines 1–22. Cf. Strabo 17.1.45.

J. Lesquier, *L'Armée romaine d'Égypte d'Auguste à Dioclétien* (Cairo 1918) 239–43, 427ff.; Tregenza, *op. cit.* 41–6; M. G. Raschke in *ANRW* 2.9.2, 648–9.

In the 40th year of Caesar (AD 11), Payni 1. | With good luck. When
5   Publius | Iuventius Rufus (was) tribu|ne of the Third Le‖gion (Cyrenaica) and prefect of Berenike[1] | and chief superintendent | of the emerald and
10 to|paz mines and the pearls and | all the mines ‖ of Egypt, there was dedicated | a temple in Ophiates | to Pan the greatest god | by (?)[2] Publius
15 Iuventius | Agathopous, *his* freedman, ‖ (on behalf of?)[2] himself, procurator and super|visor and benefactor | of all the mines | of Egypt. *vv* The act
20 of adoration of Ptolemai‖os,[3] curator of the cohort of Flo|rus, of the century of Bassus,[4] who also | set up (the work).[5]

1 This prefect was in charge of the whole area between Koptos on the Nile and the Red Sea.

2 The Greek grammar in this whole section is confused. The translation here is of only one possibility for what may have been meant. It is not clear who actually set up the inscription, although it would appear to be the freedman Agathapous. There is even a good possibility that Ptolemaios (lines 19–20) set it up.

3 His name is spelled 'Tholemaios' on the stone.

4 Each Roman legion was composed of ten infantry cohorts, and each cohort was organized into six centuries. Each of the legion's sixty centuries was under the command of a centurion. Thus, Ptolemaios was not the permanent commander of a cohort, since, as 'curator', he was only in temporary command in the absence of Florus. Ptolemaios was

merely a simple legionary soldier in the century commanded by the centurion Bassus, but at the present time he was acting-commander of a cohort.
5 The 'acts of adoration' of two other men follow this one. They are called 'architects who set up the work'.

111 Minutes of an audience in Rome given by Augustus with his Advisory Board to envoys from Alexandria. First half of AD 13.

Verso of a papyrus of the early first century AD,[1] Oxyrhynchus in Egypt.

P. Oxy. 2435, lines 29–61 (+ photograph).

E. G. Turner on *P. Oxy.* 2435, pp. 102–12; A. K. Bowman, *JRS* 66 (1976) 154.

30 [Roll no. -,][2] *column* 80. Year 42 of Caesar (AD 13), ‖ (month of) [--] the 4th (or 24th), the 9th hour. Au[gustus] sat | in the temple of Apollo | [in the R]oman Library and *lis|tened* to the envoys of the Alexan|[drians,]
35 and seated with him were Tib[e]rius ‖ [Caesar] and D[r]usus the (son) of Caesar,[3] | [and Va]l[e]rius Messalinus Corvinus[4] | [--]us and Ti[--]us Den(?)[--]tor, | [--]us Ma[s]o[ni]us, Titus [--]inus | [--]o,[5]
40 Marcus Avidius Org<ol>anius,[6] ‖ [--]sianus (?) T[--.] Alexandros gave (him) the | *decrees* and said, | ('-- my city sent me | [--] to present to
45 you | [--] and to deliver the decrees ‖ [--] and of Livia | [--] and [of
50 Tibe]rius (?) [Caes]a[r --|--|--] | *envoys* between [--‖-] whose *justice* you decided, we as|k you [--] victory [--|--'] *v* Augustus (said), 'I have seen it.' | (Shouts)[7] 'Good luck! Good luck!' After | [this] Timoxenos the
55 orator (said), 'As much ‖ [--] as you grant to the [--|--,] lord Augustus, just so mu|ch also we beg you to grant to *your* A[l]exandrians | today, for (although) in a manner of speaking | we are here to make a request of
60 you, the truth is ‖ that with all zeal [our city] is worshipping your most sacred | [Fortune] and [--']

1 The recto of this papyrus contains a speech, punctuated by applause, of an unnamed 'imperator' to the citizens of Alexandria. He is almost certainly Germanicus Caesar, adopted son of Tiberius.
2 The present document was merely one of very many others included in a papyrus roll, which was itself one of a large collection of such rolls.
3 These two are the future emperor Tiberius and his natural son Drusus.
4 This is the consul of 3 BC, the son of the famous orator M. Valerius Messalla Corvinus (consul in 31 BC) who had fought at Philippi on the side of Brutus and Cassius but had later joined Octavian. The son, after his consulship, became governor of Illyricum and campaigned with Tiberius against King Maroboduus, winning the ornamenta triumphalia ('triumphal decorations').
5 All names in lines 37–8 are uncertain.
6 The editors decided to treat the papyrus reading 'Organios' as an error for 'Orgolanios',

making him the father or brother of the Urgulania in Tacitus (*Ann.* 2.34; 4.21–2) who was an intimate of the Imperial family.

7 Perhaps from the envoys or, more likely, from bystanders. These shouts are familiar from the later so-called Acts of the pagan martyrs: see H. A. Musurillo, *The Acts of the Pagan Martyrs* (Oxford 1954).

112   Augustus sets up the final report of his accomplishments in the Greek East. Composed AD 12–14.

Extract from his Res Gestae.

J. Gagé, *Res Gestae Divi Augusti*[3] (Paris 1977) (+ photographs); H. Volkmann, *Res Gestae Divi Augusti*[3] (Berlin 1969) Chapters 26–33.

(Col. 5, lines 18ff.; chapter 26, section 5) By my order and under my auspices there were led | [two][1] armies at almost the same time into
20 Aethiopia and Ar[a]bia, which is ca‖lled Blessed, and *great forces* of the enemy from both nations | were cut down in battle and *many* towns were captured: in Aethiopia it was as far as the *to|wn* of Nabata that they advanced, next to which is Meroe.[2] In Arabia it was as far | as the frontier of the Sabaei, to the town of Mariba that the army marched.[3] | (27, 1) I added Egypt to the empire of the [Ro]man People. (27, 2) Greater Armenia, at
25 the assassi‖nation of its king Artaxes, *when* I could have made it a province, I preferred, | following the example of our ancestors, to hand it over as a kingdom to Tigranes, son of King Artavasdes and grandson | of King Tigranes, acting through T[iberius Ne]ro,[1] who was at that time my stepson.[4] | This same nation when it later revolted and rebelled, but was pacified by Gaius, | my son, I handed over to King Ariobarzanes, son of
30 King Artabazus of the Medes, to be ru‖led (by him) and after his death by his son Artavasdes. When he was assassinated, I sent Tig[ra]|nes,[1] who was sprung from the royal family of the Armenians, into that kingdom.[5] (27, 3) The pro|vinces, all those which lie to the east across the Hadriatic Sea, as well as Cyre|ne, with kings possessing them for the most part, and even earlier Sicily and | Sardinia, which had been seized in the Slave War,
35 (all these) I recovered. ‖ (28, 1) I established colonies of soldiers in Africa, Sicily, [M]acedonia, the two Spains, Achai[a,] Asia, S[y]ria, | Gallia Narbonensis, and Pi[si]dia. (28, 2) And Italy has 28 *coloni|es* which have become very much frequented and populous during my lifetime, (all) by my [authority][1] | established. | (29, 1) Very many military standards,
40 *lost* by other commanders, I *recovered*, after defeating the enemy, ‖ from Spain and [Gaul and the Dalm]atians.[1] (29, 2) I forced the Parthians to *return* three Roman armies' | spoils and standards[6] to me and to beg as suppliants for the friendship of the Roman People. | And these standards to the inner shrine, which is in the temple of Mars the Avenger, | I restored. | (30, 1) The tribes of the Pannonians, whom before me as leader of

45   the Roman People an army[7] had ne‖ver approached, were conquered (by
me) through Tiberius [Ne]ro, who was at that time my stepson and
legate, | and I added them to the empire of the Roman People and exten-
ded the frontier of Illyricum to the bank of the River | Danube.[8] (30, 2)
When an army of [D]a[cians][1] crossed to this side of that (river), under
my *auspices* it was defeated and utterly destroy|ed, and later *my army*
crossed the Dan[u]be and [forced][1] the Da[cian] | tribes [to submit to][1]
50   the commands of the R[oman][1] P[eople.][9] ‖ (31, 1) To me [embassies of
kings were often sent][1] from In[dia, not seen before this][1] *age* | in the
presence of *any commander* of the R[omans.][1] (31, 2) Our *friendship* was
sought | through envoys by the B[a]starnians and [Scythians][1] and by
kings of the Sarmatians, who live [on this side of][1] the River | Tanais
(Don) [and] beyond it, and by the king of the [Alba]nians[1] and of the
Iberians *and* [of the Medes.][1] | (32, 1) To me kings fled as suppliants: of
the Parthians, Tirida[te]s and later Phrat[es,] ‖ (Col. 6) son of King
Phrate[s;] of the Medes, Ar[tavasdes; of the Adiabenians,[1] A]rtaxa|res;
of the Britons, Dumnobellaunus and Tin[commius; of the Sugambr]ians,[1]
| Maelo; of the Mar[c]omanian Suebians, [--rus.][1] (32, 2) To [me the]
king of the Parthians, | Phrates son of Orodes, sent all his sons [and]
5   grandsons into Italy, not ‖ (because he was) conquered in war, but be-
cause he sought our friendship through the pledges | of his *children.*[10] (32, 3)
And very many other nations made *trial* of the good faith [of the Roman
People,][1] under me as their lea|der, for which earlier [there had existed
no][1] exchange with the Roman People of embassies | and friendship. |
(33, 1) From me the nations of the Parthians and Medes, [through
10   envoys][1] (composed of) the leading men of their na‖tions, received their
kings when they asked for them: the Par[thians, Vonones][1] son of [King
Ph]rates,[1] | grandson of King Orodes; the Medes, Arioba[rzanes][1] son of
King Artavazdes, | grandson of King Ariobarzanes. |

When Augustus died on September 19, AD 14, at Nola in Campania at the age of 76, a
meeting of the senate was called by Tiberius, and various papers written by Augustus were
read aloud. These included, among several other items, an account of his Res Gestae
('Accomplishments'): Suetonius, *Aug.* 101; Dio 56.33. In these papers Augustus specified
that his Res Gestae were to be engraved on bronze tablets and set up before his mauso-
leum. These tablets have never been found, but copies of the text have come to light in the
province of Galatia. The fullest of these copies was discovered in the sixteenth century at
Ancyra, and it included the Latin along with a translation into Greek. Further fragments
since then have been found at Pisidian Antioch (Latin only, very fragmentary) and at
Apollonia, also in Pisidia (Greek only, very fragmentary). The translation given here was
made from the Latin copy found at Ancyra, which extended over six columns of text
engraved on the inside wall of the pronaos of the temple of Roma and Augustus. The
Greek translation was engraved on the outside of the right temple wall. Only those chapters are presented here which pertain to the Greek East, but there are thirty-five chapters
in all. Modern citation is regularly by chapter and section rather than by column and line

number, but both methods are employed here. The best modern commentary is the one by Gagé. The edition of the Latin with translation and short commentary by P. A. Brunt and J. M. Moore (*Res Gestae Divi Augusti* (Oxford 1967)) should be used with great caution because of the authors' failure to present a proper text.

1 The restoration is assured by the remains of the Greek translation.
2 This is the campaign of C. Petronius, while prefect of Egypt, in 24–22 BC: Strabo 17.1.54; Dio 54.4ff.
3 This is the campaign of Aelius Gallus, prefect in Egypt, in 25–24 BC: Strabo 16.4.22–4; Dio 53.29.3ff.
4 Tacitus, *Ann.* 2.3; Suetonius, *Tib.* 9; Dio 54.9.4ff.
5 Suetonius, *Aug.* 21; Dio 55.10a.4–8; Tacitus, *Ann.* 2.4.
6 These were lost in 53 BC with the defeat of Crassus, in 40 BC with the death of Decidius Saxa, and in 36 BC with the retreat of Marcus Antonius.
7 Alternate translation: 'no army of the Roman People before me as leader', but see L. W. Wickert in *ANRW* 2.1.16–25.
8 The first Pannonian campaign of 12–9 BC which brought the ornamenta triumphalia ('triumphal decorations') to Tiberius: Velleius Paterculus 2.96.3; Suetonius, *Tib.* 9.2; Dio 54.31.4; and 55.2.4.
9 Dio 54.36.2; Strabo 7.3.11; Suetonius, *Aug.* 21.1; Suetonius, *Tib.* 7; Florus 2.28.19.
10 Suetonius, *Aug.* 21.3; 43.4; Strabo 6.4.2; 16.1.28; Velleius Paterculus 2.94.4; Tacitus, *Ann.* 2.1.

Advisory Board. Roman magistrates regularly sought the advice of the senate before making important public decisions. Thus, the senate acted as a *consilium publicum* ('Public Advisory Board'). Magistrates away from Rome and promagistrates formed smaller boards from the members of their staff and entourage. Sometimes the senate itself supplied a magistrate with such a board for use on a particular occasion. Augustus also instituted a different kind of Advisory Board for his own use, consisting of senators who served as a standing committee for six months and whose main business was the preparation of agenda for presentation to the senate. This latter type of board was discontinued under Tiberius. See J. Crook, *Consilium Principis* (Cambridge 1965).

Agora. The open square at the heart of a Greek city, where people could gather for political or commercial activity. In it were located the main public buildings.

Amphictiones ('Those dwelling around'). These were religious associations or unions connected with temples and their cults. Largest and most important politically was the Amphictionic League, the council of which, composed of representatives from various Greek states, met at Delphi. See Ehrenberg, *State* 108–12.

Bireme. A Greek ship (Greek *dikrotos*) with two banks of oarsmen. See J. S. Morrison and R. T. Williams, *Greek Oared Ships* (Oxford 1968) 194 and 310.

Boule ('Council'). Best known is the one at Athens, which in classical times consisted of 500 members selected by lot from the demes, each of the ten tribes being represented by 50 men in the Boule. Its chief task was to prepare the agenda for the Ekklesia ('Assembly'). The increase in the number of Athenian tribes to twelve in 307/6 BC raised the membership to 600. At that time a few other administrative changes were made, but the basic mechanism of the Boule working with the Ekklesia was retained. In 83 BC Sulla caused a change to be made in the government, which permitted the Boule to take decisions unilaterally without final approval by the Ekklesia. Outside Athens most of the Greek cities had a Boule or an equivalent institution as long as they remained democratic. The duties and functions were similar to those of the Athenian Boule, although the number of members, the length of their tenure, and other details varied considerably. For Athens: P. J. Rhodes, *The Athenian Boule* (Oxford 1972), and D. J. Geagan, *The Athenian Constitution after Sulla, Hesperia*, Supplement XII (Princeton 1967); for outside Athens: Busolt, *Staatskunde* I 465ff.

Capitolium. One of the hills of Rome, with two summits. On one of them, overlooking the Tiber to the west and the Forum to the east, was the temple of Jupiter, Juno, and Minerva. It was the very heart and soul of Rome, where the consuls took their vows, and triumphal generals climbed its heights to approach the temple. On its northern summit was the temple of Juno Moneta with an adjoining building that served as the mint.

Censor. These magistrates relieved the consuls of taking the census, which came to include control over the moral life of the Roman people. The two censors held office for eighteen months, with an interval of four or, later, normally five years before the next election. Re-election was forbidden. After taking the census, they saw to the proper registration of all citizens in their tribes and centuries. They also compiled the lists of senators and equites and could remove men from those lists for reasons stated. Another of their important functions was to let out state contracts with the publicans for public works and the collection of public revenue. Eventually the office became one of even greater dignity than the consulship itself, and, with hardly any exceptions, was held only by ex-consuls. See Greenidge, *Public Life* 115–16; Meyer, *Staat* 71–2, 164–70, 183–5; J. Suolahti, *The Roman Censors* (Helsinki 1963).

Centurion. Each Roman legion had sixty non-commissioned officers called centurions, their relative rank depending on their position in the legion's ten cohorts and on their own seniority.

Cognomen. See Appendix on Roman names.

Comitium. An open area for political assembly in Republican Rome, located just north of the Forum proper. One of its central features was the Rostra, i.e. the Speaker's Platform.

Consul. The highest regularly elected magistrates of the Roman Republic. Two were elected annually by the People, giving their names to the year. The minimum age, fixed by the Villian Law of 180 BC, was forty-two, and in the late Republic a ten-year interval was required before the office could be held a second time. Their imperium (military and civil authority) in the field was unrestricted, but in the city of Rome it was defined or limited by specific statutes and in practice by the assignment of special functions to other magistrates. After Sulla (81 BC) the consuls usually remained in Rome or Italy, and the foreign commands were usually given to promagistrates. See Greenidge, *Public Life* 196–202; Meyer, *Staat* 156–8.

Demes. These were townships in Attica or wards within the city of Athens and its suburbs. By the Hellenistic period the number of Attic demes reached about 170. Since membership in a deme was necessary for citizenship, the deme was included in a citizen's full name (cf. no. 23, lines 12–13). Although best known at Athens, the institution existed elsewhere in the Greek world, especially in the Ionian cities. See Busolt, *Staatskunde* I 262–72; J. S. Traill, *Political Organization of Attica, Hesperia*, Supplement XIV (Princeton 1975).

Denarius. A Roman silver coin which in the course of the second century BC came to be regarded as equivalent to the Attic drachma. It became the standard silver piece of Republican Rome and weighed about one-seventh of an ounce (3.90 grams).

Dictator. In the early and middle Republic he was a magistrate superior to the consuls, appointed in emergencies or for a special and limited purpose, and never in office for more than six months. The dictatorship was weakened in 217 BC when it was granted by election instead of by consular appointment, and after 202 BC no dictator in the old sense was ever appointed. By a bill introduced into the Roman Assembly Sulla was made dictator with special powers to reorganize the Roman constitution: 81–79 BC. After Caesar's march on Rome and down to his death (49–44 BC) the dictatorship was given to Caesar four times, the fourth dictatorship for life. He made it the foundation of his arbitrary power to control the state. After his assassination the dictatorship was banned forever. See H. Last in *CAH* 9.282–4 (Sulla); F. E. Adcock in *CAH* 9.731–5 (Caesar); E. S. Staveley, *Historia* 5 (1956) 101ff.

Dionysiac Artists. These were professional actors and musical performers who presented the great dramas and comedies in Athens at the various religious festivals. In the Hellenistic age they organized themselves into a guild called the Synodos of Dionysiac Artists in Athens. They traveled over all Attica and elsewhere in central Greece to perform at the festivals. Similar guilds or associations developed quickly alongside the Athenian, including one in Egypt and another in Asia Minor. Each had its own headquarters in a Greek city, and all of them enjoyed a wide variety of privileges and immunities. Since they lived in or side by side with Greek cities, each was a kind of state within a state. See Sir Arthur Pickard-Cambridge, *The Dramatic Festivals of Athens*[2] (Oxford 1968), Chapter 7.

Drachma A standard of weight as well as of silver coinage. The smallest unit of weight and coinage was the obol (on the Attic-Euboic standard about 0.72 grams), and there were six obols to a drachma, 100 drachmas to a mina, and 60 minas to a talent. Its value in the Hellenistic age varied greatly from place to place and time to time. The drachma came to be regarded as equivalent to the Roman denarius.

Ekklesia ('Assembly'). The sovereign body of a Greek democratic state, best known to us at Athens. It acted upon the agenda placed before it by committeemen (prytaneis) from the Boule, approving, amending or rejecting the proposals. In the Hellenistic age it was still the sovereign body, but after Sulla's measures in 83 BC meetings of the Athenian Ekklesia were no longer necessary until 48 BC, since the Boule in that period could make decisions on its own. Caesar restored democratic government, but Antonius suppressed it. Outside of Athens the institution existed in all Greek democratic states, although each city had its own development, its own nomenclature, and its own procedures, often different from the model in Athens. See P. J. Rhodes, *The Athenian Boule* (Oxford 1972) *passim*, and D. J. Geagan, *The Athenian Constitution After Sulla, Hesperia*, Supplement XI (Princeton 1967); for outside of Athens see Busolt, *Staatskunde* I 442ff.

Ephebes. Young men (18–20) of citizen families in a Greek city, undergoing organized military and gymnastic training. In Athens this training began about 335 BC. In the Hellenistic age this Athenian institution was gradually transformed into a peacetime school of a single year's duration, in which the sons of wealthy citizens received their physical and intellectual education. From Athens it spread quickly to other Greek states. The central feature was the gymnasium, the director of which was called the *kosmetes* in Athens but the gymnasiarch in most other cities. The gymnasiarch was generally one of the wealthiest citizens of the city, for the position came to require the expenditure of private funds for the school and was, thus, a liturgy. The school itself was sometimes called a palaestra ('wrestling ground'), but more often simply the gymnasium. Alongside this institution there were also young men's clubs called Neoi, which had their own schools. See C. A. Forbes, *Greek Physical Education* (New York 1929); *idem, Neoi, A Contribution to the Study of Greek Associations* (New York 1933); H. I. Marrou, *A History of Education in Antiquity* (Toronto 1956) 151–64; J. Delorme, *Gymnasion: Études sur les monuments consacrés à l'éducation en Grèce* (Paris 1960).

Equites ('Knights'). The old Republican order of Equites was an elite body of 1800 cavalrymen recruited from the aristocratic families. By the second century their military role had been reduced largely to ceremony, but the social prestige remained. The growth of non-senatorial wealth caused the emergence of a middle class whose members called themselves Equites, although they did not belong to the 1800. Many of them were publicans or negotiatores ('businessmen'), but others simply lived as country gentlemen, while still others entered politics and became senators. In the late Republic they were almost equal to the senators in social prestige, and Augustus found a place for them in the new political structure. See H. Hill, *The Roman Middle Class in the Republican Period* (Oxford 1952); C. Nicolet, *L'ordre* I–II; Badian, *Publicans* 82ff.

Forum. The main public square in Rome, surrounded by the great public buildings and temples, bounded on the south by the Palatine Hill and on the west by the Capitoline.

Gymnasiarch. See under Ephebes.

Glossary

Hieromnemon. A religious official with various functions in different parts of the Greek world. He was usually one of a group such as those who represented their cities at meetings of the Amphictionic League at Delphi. In some cities he seems to have been an eponymous magistrate.

Ides. See Appendix on Greek and Roman chronology.

Imperator. A generic title for Roman commanders which became a special title of honor. After a victory in the field, the general was hailed as imperator by his soldiers, and he held the title until the end of his magistracy or until his triumph in Rome. Occasionally the senate seems to have given or confirmed the title. The growing power of the army in the late Republic made the title a symbol of military authority. Caesar was the first to use it permanently, and Augustus adopted it as a praenomen. Later it became part of the nomenclature of every Roman emperor. See R. Syme, *Historia* 7 (1958) 172–88 (*Roman Papers* I 361–77); R. Combès, *Imperator: Recherches sur l'emploi et la signification du titre d'Imperator dans la Rome republicaine* (Paris 1966).

Kalends. See Appendix on Greek and Roman chronology.

Koinon. A general term (pl. *koina*) for almost any kind of association, public or private. When used to describe a government or a federal state it means 'Commonwealth'. Often it conveys the notion of 'Confederacy' or 'League'. The term implies an organization of size with provisions for meetings, regular officials, secretaries, etc. Of particular importance were the provincial koina, which were assemblies of delegates from the constituent cities or tribes within a Roman province (such as Asia) or of several associated provinces which earlier had belonged to independent kingdoms or states (such as Bithynia or Lycia). The nature and function of such provincial koina varied from province to province, but their delegates ordinarily met once a year in some central city and their primary function in the late Republic came to be the worship of the goddess Roma (cf. no. 18) and finally of Roma and Augustus. Games and festivals were often associated with the religious ceremonies. These provincial koina also played a political and diplomatic role, serving as avenues of communication between Rome and the provinces. See J. A. O. Larsen, *Representative Government in Greek and Roman History* (Berkeley 1955) 23–5; Ehrenberg, *State* 110, 121–4; J. Deininger, *Die Provinziallandtage der römischen Kaiserzeit* (Munich 1965).

Legate. The Republican legati ('ambassadors' of the senate and the Roman People) were regularly senators not in office who accompanied provincial governors or generals in the field and who often had personal connections with them. Various kinds of duty – military, judicial or administrative – were delegated to them by their superior. An innovation took place in 67 BC when, under the Gabinian Law, Pompey was entitled to appoint *legati pro praetore* (legates with praetorian imperium) for his campaign against the pirates. See B. Schleussner, *Die Legaten der römischen Republik*, Vestigia 26 (Munich 1978).

Liturgy. Liturgies were public services performed by the wealthy citizens in Greek cities. They were compulsory and often very expensive, the incumbents defraying the costs out of their own funds. But ambitious politicians often volunteered to perform them out of turn. They varied from city to city, but could include choregoi to pay for the training of choruses for musical and dramatic festivals, envoys to represent the cities on missions to foreign states, gymnasiarchs to employ and pay trainers for the gymnasium, etc. The number of these liturgies grew larger in the course of the Hellenistic age. See H. Michell, *The Economics of Ancient Greece*[2] (Cambridge 1957) 375ff.; Magie, *RRAM* I 61–2, 651–8.

148

Glossary

Nomen. See Appendix on Roman names.

Nones. See Appendix on Greek and Roman chronology.

Palaestra See under Ephebes.

Patron. From Rome's early history the weak or deprived turned to the strong or wealthy for protection. When such a 'client' found such a 'patron' to satisfy his needs, a series of strong mutual duties bound them together, each pledged to help the other in his own way. One of the most common ways of forming this relationship was the freeing of slaves by their master, the *liberti* ('freedmen') then becoming the legal clients of their former master. The relationship was hereditary. The duties, based on moral ties, included mutual trust, protection, friendship, and support in the world of politics and law. This patron–client relationship played an important role in the means by which the aristocratic nobles gained and held political power. During the last two centuries of the Republic the institution spread over the provinces, when Roman senators became patrons of whole cities or communities as well as of individuals outside of Italy and especially in the Greek East. The Roman ruling class was very successful in exploiting these foreign connections to its own advantage. Cf. Dion. Hal. 2.9–11; Twelve Tables 8.21; Terence, *Andria* 924ff., and *Eunuchus* 1039ff. See M. Gelzer, *The Roman Nobility*, trans. R. Seager (Oxford 1969) 62ff.; R. Syme, *The Roman Revolution* (Oxford 1939) *passim*; Badian, *FC* 1ff.; Bowersock, *Augustus* 1ff.

People. See under Ekklesia.

Pontifex Maximus. The chief priest of the Roman state religion, elected (in the late Republic) by tribal vote for life. Among his other duties, he presided over the college of pontifices, chose the Vestal Virgins, and presided over the Curiate Assembly. He had an office in the Regia, on the traditional site of the house of the Roman kings, at the eastern end of the Roman Forum. Both Caesar and Augustus were elected to the office, and thereafter it was held by each of the emperors until Christianity became the state religion. See Lily Ross Taylor, *Party Politics in the Age of Caesar* (Berkeley 1961) 90–7.

Praenomen. See Appendix on Roman names.

Praetor. Originally the name given to the two eponymous Roman magistrates who were later (perhaps toward the end of the fourth century BC) officially called consuls. In 366 BC a further praetor (*praetor urbanus*, i.e. 'city praetor') was first elected who was not eponymous and he was made responsible for the administration of justice in Rome. He also possessed and sometimes used the right of military command; he could summon the Roman People to Assembly and initiate legislation; he could summon the senate to a meeting and also supervise the defense of Rome in the absence of the consuls. About 242 BC a second praetor (*praetor peregrinus*, i.e. 'peregrine praetor') was created to handle lawsuits involving foreigners. Both of them were elected annually by the People. Because of the acquisition of overseas provinces the activities of the praetors were expanded, so that in 227 BC their number was increased from two to four, to provide for the government of Sicily and Sardinia, and to six in 197 BC, to govern Spain. The Villian Law of 180 BC fixed their minimum age at 39. By exercising the supreme authority in the provinces, the praetors once more became military magistrates, and gradually the difference of power between them and the consuls decreased, although they always remained subordinate to the consuls. Sulla increased their number to eight and made all of them stay in Rome, permitting them to become provincial governors only as promagistrates after the expiration of their year in office. His reform was abolished in the age of Augustus. See Greenidge, *Public Law* 120–1 and 202–8; Meyer, *Staat* 86–8 and 161–4; E. S. Staveley, *Historia* 5 (1956) 90ff.

Princeps. A term used to describe a leading personage within the Roman Republican ruling class. Augustus adopted the term to describe his own role within the constitution, i.e. as 'first man' or 'Leader', distinguishing him from any ordinary magistrate in office. See M. Hammond, *The Augustan Principate* (Cambridge, Mass. 1933); L. Wickert in *RE s.v.* Princeps, cols. 1998ff., and in *ANRW* 2.1.3ff.

Proconsul. See under Promagistrate.

Procurator. Literally 'manager' or 'deputy in charge', the term designated an individual given a wide variety of functions or duties by and on behalf of another or others. As the emperor's property and business began to coalesce with the State's, the procurators came to be appointed for some public posts and their numbers and duties increased steadily. Cf. no. 110. See A. N. Sherwin-White in *PBSR* 1939, 11ff.; H. G. Pflaum, *Les procurateurs équestres* (Paris 1950); for their careers, as far as then known, see the same author's *Les carrières procuratoriennes équestres sous le Haut-Empire romain* (4 vols., Paris 1960–1); A. H. M. Jones, *Studies in Roman Government and Law* (New York 1960) 19ff.

Promagistrate. The use of promagistrates was a device which allowed the Romans to increase the number of qualified men in military commands without adding to the number of annually elected magistrates in office. By a legal fiction an ex-magistrate was originally given the power to act as if he were a consul or praetor or quaestor in office. As proconsul or propraetor or proquaestor his services were used in a variety of ways, usually in some military command. The practice began in 326 BC and was used there-after whenever necessary for military purposes and it became routine for the senate alone to approve it. After 146 BC, when the number of provinces was greatly increased, some provincial governors were either proconsuls or propraetors. In 52 BC Pompey saw to the passage of a law which required that between a magistracy and a pro-magisterial command an interval of time had to elapse, perhaps as long as five years (Dio 40.46). This had the result of making the promagistracy virtually independent of the magistracy itself, a condition similar to what happened in 210 BC when the young P. Cornelius Scipio (later Africanus) was elected proconsul, although pre-viously he had never held any office higher than that of aedile. Caesar claimed that Pompey's move was unconstitutional, but Augustus adapted Pompey's idea to his own system of senatorial provinces administered by proconsuls, whether they were of praetorian or consular rank. See W.F. Jashemski, *The Origins and History of the Proconsular and Propraetorian Imperium* (Chicago 1950).

Proxenos. A citizen of a Greek city could be made proxenos ('public friend' or state 'guest') to represent the interests of a foreign state in his own city. He would be chosen to act as proxenos by the foreign state and would usually be granted certain honors and privileges in return. It was a status much respected in the fifth and fourth centuries throughout the Greek world, but already in the fourth century it had begun to lose some of its original significance. In Hellenistic times it gradually degenerated into a reward for previous actions, often only as a conventional honor granted to important foreigners, although occasionally it was still felt to exist for its original purpose. See F. Gschnitzer in *RE s.v.* Proxenos, Supplement XIII (1973) cols. 629–730.

Prytany. See Appendix on Greek and Roman chronology.

Publicans. Non-senatorial citizens who bought the state contracts for public works and for collecting the revenues. With the great profits made (especially) in the overseas pro-vinces they formed a large part of the new middle class in Roman society and in the first century BC called themselves Equites. By re-investing their profits they became extre-mely wealthy and by the second century BC had already begun to exert political pres-sure. In the first century they were the most powerful pressure group outside the senate. They formed companies and expanded their operations to almost all areas of the Republican empire. See G. Ürögdi in *RE s.v.* Publicani, Supplement XI (1968) cols. 1846ff.; Badian, *Publicans*.

Quaestor. Roman magistrates elected annually by the People. Originally two, they were gradually increased until Sulla raised the number to twenty. Caesar raised it to forty, but Augustus returned it to twenty. They were basically in charge of finance, the two urban quaestors in Rome being in charge of the aerarium ('treasury'), but they could be given other duties of a civil, military or judicial nature. With the acquisition of overseas provinces their services were required to handle the provincial funds. Although normally lacking the military power of imperium, a quaestor was sometimes endowed with it as quaestor pro praetore and left in a position of authority, in case of the death or early departure of a provincial governor, until his successor could arrive. See Greenidge, *Public Life* 80–1, 212–16, 369; Meyer, *Staat* 38–9, 87–8, 177–8.

Savior and Benefactor. Originally applied to the gods by the Greeks, the word *soter* ('savior') was later used to describe men who were thought to have saved or delivered their city or people from some danger. In Hellenistic times it was most often used of the kings in Ptolemaic Egypt and elsewhere in the Greek East. Although it was used to honor these kings, it did not imply divinity in and of itself. It was often coupled with the word *euergetes* ('benefactor') to add still greater honor. With the advance of Rome and the end of the Hellenistic monarchies, these same words were given by the Greeks to their new masters: men like T. Quinctius Flamininus (no. 6), Pompey (no. 75), Julius Caesar (no. 79), and Augustus. See A. D. Nock, *Essays on Religion and the Ancient World* II, ed. Z. Stewart (Cambridge, Mass. 1972) 720–35.

Senate. The Republican senate was a council of 300 members down to the time of Sulla, who increased it to 600. Caesar added 300 more, but Augustus again reduced it to 600. Entrance was regulated by the consuls and later by the censors, but from the time of Sulla the holding of the quaestorship brought with it a seat in the senate. Meetings were called by a consul, praetor or dictator who then became the presiding officer. As an advisory body, the senate voted on whatever proposals the presiding officer brought before it. Its decision was called a *senatus consultum* ('decree of the senate'). In strict law, such decrees were not binding, but because of the senate's prestige, they were felt to be binding and were acted upon as if they were. The senate thus gave advice to the magistrates about all important matters such as foreign and domestic policy, religion, finance and legislation to be proposed to the People. Foreign envoys were brought before it to lodge complaints or to make requests. It appointed special commissions to organize new territorial acquisitions or to arbitrate between cities or groups foreign and domestic. It made the practical decisions of war and peace, even though formal declarations of war and the ratification of treaties belonged to the People. Meetings were in private, but the doors were open. Freedom of speech was unlimited, but a strict order of speaking was followed according to the rank of the senators. Voting was done by the division of members into two bodies, one for and one against the proposal. Each decree was carefully recorded and deposited in the state archives, the aerarium Saturni. As the body from which the candidates were selected for the holding of all the higher magistracies, the senate thus occupied a position of great power and authority over almost all branches of the government. See Greenidge, *Public Life* 261ff., 377ff.; O'Brian Moore in *RE s.v.* Senatus, Supplement VI (1935) cols. 660ff.; Meyer, *Staat* 202–15.

Sestertius. A Roman silver coin and unit of account, four of which were equal to the denarius.

Stele. A square or rectangular slab of stone, placed in an upright position for public viewing, with a smooth front surface for the engraving of epitaphs, decrees, laws or other material of a public or private nature. A stone stele containing an important text often reproduces in miniature the architrave of a temple with acroteria, pediment and molding, and may contain engraved reliefs of various kinds. Like the lettering itself, these stelai show patterns of style and development along geographical and chronological lines. See J. Kirchner, *Imagines inscriptionum Atticarum*[2] (Berlin 1948), and, for the archaeological criteria, Möbius in *RE s.v.* Stele, cols. 2307–20.

Stephanephoros ('wreath-wearer'). This official was an eponymous magistrate in the Greek East, especially common in the Ionian cities of the western parts of Asia Minor and on the islands of the Aegean. He is best known to us at Miletus, where the inscriptional remains are sufficient to allow some chronological deductions. See Magie, *RRAM* II 836–9, n. 23; A. Rehm, *Das Delphinion in Milet* (Milet 3) (Berlin and Leipzig 1914) 241ff.

Stoichedon. A style of Greek engraving in which the letters are in both vertical and horizontal alignment and are placed at equal intervals along their alignment, with each line falling letter by letter underneath the line above, as on a typewritten page. It survived well into the third century, although after *c.* 200 BC only isolated examples occur, most of them outside Athens. See R. P. Austin, *The Stoichedon Style in Greek Inscriptions* (Oxford 1938), and the additional observations of M. J. Osborne in *ZPE* 10 (1973) 249–70.

Strategoi. From the very early times the strategos ('general') was a most important official in almost every Greek city-state, and in Athens during the fifth century he had political as well as military power. In the Hellenistic age many Greek cities, especially in Asia Minor, had a board of strategoi, originally in charge of military affairs but gradually transformed into civil officials whose duties differed from city to city. Apart from these city strategoi, the Hellenistic monarchs also appointed strategoi with a wide range of duties. The heads of Greek leagues were often called strategoi. And the word was also used to translate into Greek the Latin 'praetor'. See Hignett, *Athenian Constitution* 244–51; D. J. Geagan, *The Athenian Constitution After Sulla, Hesperia*, Supplement XII (Princeton 1967) 18–31; H. Bengtson, *Die Strategie in der Hellenistischen Zeit* I–III (Munich 1937–52).

Tetradrachma. A four-drachma silver coin, the most common silver coin in the Hellenistic age.

Tribes. The Roman tribes were territorial divisions of the citizens, four of them (Suburana, Esquilina, Collina, Palatina) in the city of Rome itself and the remaining thirty-one originally in the rest of Italy. The number of thirty-five was reached in 241 BC and was never increased. The territorial expansion of the Republican empire in Italy and then overseas simply resulted in an extension of already existing tribal territories, often without regard for contiguity. Each citizen had to belong to a tribe (cf. no. 86, line 24), and the tribal designation was part of his full name, placed before the cognomen. It was through the tribal organization that voting and other civic duties were performed: the tribes were used for census, taxation and the military draft. See W. Kubitschek, *De Romanorum tribuum origine ac propagatione* (Vienna 1882); Lily Ross Taylor, *The Voting Districts of the Roman Republic*, American Academy in Rome: Papers and Monographs XX (Rome 1960).

Tribune of the Plebs. These were officials elected annually by the Roman plebeians, originally to defend them and to help them obtain civic rights. Ten in number, they enjoyed personal inviolability, had the right of veto against any act of the state or its magistrates with the exception of the dictator, and had the power of enforcing their actions on behalf of the plebeians. They summoned plebeians to their assemblies and presided over them, passing most Roman routine legislation. In the third century they acquired the right to convene the senate, and by the late second century election to the tribunate qualified the holder to become a member of the senate (cf. no. 16, lines 1–2). Because of the power of their veto and their control over legislation they were regularly courted or abused by the contending factions in Roman politics from the time of the Gracchi to the end of the Republic. See Greenidge, *Public Life* 93ff.; Meyer, *Staat*, Index, *s.v.*; J. Bleicken, *Das Volkstribunat der klassischen Republik*[2] (Munich 1968).

Tribune of the Soldiers. In the Republican army each legion had six military tribunes, officers elected annually by the People, whose duties were primarily administrative and who rarely ever commanded troops in the field. In the Caesarian period these tribunes were mainly of equestrian origin, and only the tribunes of the four *legiones urbanae* ('city legions') were elected by the People, the remainder being appointed by the various commanders. Their importance declined with the growing use of legionary legates.

Tribunician Power. The 'power of the (plebeian) tribune' included all the rights enjoyed by the tribunes of the plebs (see above). Augustus, who (as a Patrician) could not be tribune of the plebs, recognized its political potential within the structure of his new order, and in 23 BC his possession of it became annual by a law of the People (*Res Gestae* 10.1). Thereafter it was found to be a convenient way of dating documents and coins. In 18 BC Augustus used the tribunician power to introduce a series of Julian Laws, and in that same year caused the senate to grant it to Agrippa. It was later conferred on Tiberius as his designated successor. Subsequent emperors held and used it as a means to express their imperial position and to date the years of their reign. See W. K. Lacey, *JRS* 69 (1979) 28–34.

Trireme. A Greek warship (Greek *trieres*), light in weight, with slim lines, about 115–120 feet long and 16–20 feet wide, drawing less than four feet of water, so called because there were three oarsmen to each rowing station. See J. S. Morrison and R. T. Williams, *Greek Oared Ships* (Cambridge 1968).

Triumviri ('Board of Three'). The title was given by the Romans to various boards of three men who held certain public positions, such as those in charge of the mint or those in charge of the assignment of particular areas of land. But in November of 43 BC a new use of the old title appeared, when M. Antonius, M. Lepidus and Octavian were appointed triumvirs for five years 'for the constitution of the Republic' by a bill passed into law by the People. This gave each of them the absolute power of a dictator such as Sulla and Caesar, and it was later renewed for a second term of five years, although by then Lepidus had *de facto* dropped out. These years are usually called the Triumviral period. Cf. Augustus, *Res Gestae* 1 and 7; Appian, *Bell. Civ.* 4.2–3; Dio 46.54–6; Livy, *Per.* 120. See T. Rice Holmes, *Architect of the Roman Empire* I (Oxford 1928) 72ff., 231ff.; R. Syme, *The Roman Revolution* (Oxford 1939) 188ff.; F. Millar, *JRS* 63 (1973) 50–4.

Roman names

A Roman citizen's official name by the late Republic normally had five parts, arranged in a particular order: praenomen, nomen, filiation, tribe, and cognomen. The praenomen was given to infants by their parents on the ninth day after birth, and there were not very many of these praenomina to choose from. Among the Roman ruling class only the following were in common use:

A.	= Aulus	M.	= Marcus	Sex. = Sextus
Ap.	= Appius	M'.	= Manius	Sp. = Spurius
C.	= Gaius	Mam.	= Mamercus	T. = Titus
Cn.	= Gnaeus	P.	= Publius	Ti. = Tiberius
D.	= Decimus	Q.	= Quintus	
L.	= Lucius	Ser.	= Servius	

This praenomen, regularly abbreviated in official documents, was followed by the nomen, which was the clan name. The clan (gens) was a group of families linked together by a common name and their belief in a common ancestor. Since the clan formed the basis for the organization of political life in the Republic, the nomen is perhaps the single most important part of a Roman citizen's nomenclature.

After the nomen comes the filiation, always abbreviated in official documents: f(ilius) = 'son' and sometimes n(epos) = 'grandson'. Thus: L.f.(L.n.) = 'son of Lucius, (grandson of Lucius)'. In the case of a freedman, the word lib(ertus) = 'freedman' was preceded by the praenomen of the patron, who had freed him: e.g., C. lib. = 'freedman of Gaius'.

Since every Roman citizen had to belong to a tribe, the tribal affiliation regularly became part of his official name, and stood at this point in it. For the tribes see the Glossary.

The fifth and last part of a Roman's normal official name was the cognomen. Some Romans, in the period covered in this volume, never had cognomina. Others, who did have them, did not include them in official documents on a regular basis. Their inclusion in such documents does not become common until the first century BC. They were personal names and had specific meanings, concerned with physical pecularities (e.g. Laevinus = 'left-handed'), individual characteristics (Cato = 'sagacious'), occupations (Pictor = 'painter'), etc. These were normally, but not always, hereditary. To these cognomina members of the ruling class sometimes added a 'triumphal' name, such as Asiaticus or Africanus, when a man's accomplishments were thought to warrant it. These too could become hereditary. In the cases of adoption, when a man received his adoptive father's name, he officially added his old nomen in an adjectival form after his new cognomen. E.g., when C. Octavius was adopted by the dictator C. Iulius Caesar in Caesar's testament, he became officially C. Iulius Caesar Octavianus.

The full use of these names in the prescribed form was the hallmark of a Roman citizen. Non-citizens who acquired the citizenship had to conform to the official usage: see Badian, *FC* 253ff., for details on this point.

In the late Republic members of the ruling class sometimes introduced deliberate variations into this official structure of a Roman name, to stress their distinction. See R. Syme in *Historia* 7 (1958) 172–88 (*Roman Papers* I 361–77).

APPENDIX II

Roman consuls

The standard work on the chronology of the consuls and the other magistrates during the Republic is T. R. S. Broughton, *The Magistrates of the Roman Republic*, Philological Monographs published by the American Philological Association, Vol. I (1951), Vol. II (1952), Supplement (1960). For the period of the Empire it is A. Degrassi, *I fasti consolari dell'impero romano* (Rome 1952).

When a consul in office died, another consul was appointed to take his place. This new consul was called a 'consul suffectus' and his name could not be used to date the year in official records, even though he would be entered on the official list of consuls. During the period of the triumvirate and then (from the last part of Augustus' reign) under the Empire the suffect consulship became a regular institution. The first pair of consuls were then called *ordinarii*, who might hold office for only a few months and then be replaced by another pair.

The following is a list of consuls covering the period 200 BC–AD 14, reproduced from Broughton down to 31 BC and from Degrassi from 30 BC to AD 14. After 30 BC the list covers only the *ordinarii*. A few corrections have been inserted.

BC

200	P. Sulpicius Ser. f. P. n. Galba Maximus II	C. Aurelius C. f. C. n. Cotta
199	L. Cornelius L. f. L. n. Lentulus	P. Villius Ti. f. Ti. n. Tappulus
198	Sex. Aelius Q. f. P. n. Paetus Catus	T. Quinctius T. f. L. n. Flamininus
197	C. Cornelius L. f. M. n. Cethegus	Q. Minucius C. f. C. n. Rufus
196	L. Furius Sp. f. Sp. n. Purpurio	M. Claudius M. f. M. n. Marcellus
195	L. Valerius P. f. L. n. Flaccus	M. Porcius M. f. Cato
194	P. Cornelius P. f. L. n. Scipio Africanus II	Ti. Sempronius Ti. f. C. n. Longus
193	L. Cornelius L. f. Merula	Q. Minucius Q. f. L. n. Thermus
192	L. Quinctius T. f. L. n. Flamininus	Cn. Domitius L. f. L. n. Ahenobarbus
191	P. Cornelius Cn. f. L. n. Scipio Nasica	M'. Acilius C. f. L. n. Glabrio
190	L. Cornelius P. f. L. n. Scipio Asiaticus	C. Laelius C. f. C. n.
189	M. Fulvius M. f. Ser. n. Nobilior	Cn. Manlius Cn. f. L. n. Vulso
188	M. Valerius M. f. M'. n. Messalla	C. Livius M. f. M. n. Salinator
187	M. Aemilius M. f. M. n. Lepidus	C. Flaminius C. f. C. n.
186	Sp. Postumius L. f. A. n. Albinus	Q. Marcius L. f. Q. n. Philippus
185	Ap. Claudius Ap. f. P. n. Pulcher	M. Sempronius M. f. C. n. Tuditanus
184	P. Claudius Ap. f. P. n. Pulcher	L. Porcius L. f. M. n. Licinus
183	M. Claudius M. f. M. n. Marcellus	Q. Fabius Q. f. Q. n. Labeo
182	Cn. Baebius Q. f. Cn. n. Tamphilus	L. Aemilius L. f. M. n. Paullus
181	P. Cornelius L. f. P. n. Cethegus	M. Baebius Q. f. Cn. n. Tamphilus
180	A. Postumius A. f. A. n. Albinus Luscus *Q. Fulvius Cn. f. M. n. Flaccus* suff.	C. Calpurnius C. f. C. n. Piso
179	Q. Fulvius Q. f. M. n. Flaccus	L. Manlius L. f. L. n. Acidinus Fulvianus
178	M. Iunius M. f. L. n. Brutus	A. Manlius Cn. f. L. n. Vulso
177	C. Claudius Ap. f. P. n. Pulcher	Ti. Sempronius P. f. Ti. n. Graccus
176	Cn. Cornelius Cn. f. L. n. Scipio Hispallus	Q. Petillius C. f. Q. n. Spurinus

C. Valerius M. f. P. n. Laevinus suff.

175	P. Mucius Q. f. P. n. Scaevola	M. Aemilius M. f. M. n. Lepidus II
174	Sp. Postumius A. f. A. n. Albinus Paullulus	Q. Mucius Q. f. P. n. Scaevola
173	L. Postumius A. f. A. n. Albinus	M. Popillius P. f. P. n. Laenas
172	C. Popillius P. f. P. n. Laenas	P. Aelius P. f. P. n. Ligus
171	P. Licinius C. f. P. n. Crassus	C. Cassius C. f. C. n. Longinus
170	A. Hostilius L. f. A. n. Mancinus	A. Atilius C. f. C. n. Serranus
169	Q. Marcius L. f. Q. n. Philippus II	Cn. Servilius Cn. f. Cn. n. Caepio
168	L. Aemilius L. f. M. n. Paullus II	C. Licinius C. f. P. n. Crassus
167	Q. Aelius P. f. Q. n. Paetus	M. Iunius M. f. M. n. Pennus
166	M. Claudius M. f. M. n. Marcellus	C. Sulpicius C. f. C. n. Galus
165	T. Manlius A. f. T. n. Torquatus	Cn. Octavius Cn. f. Cn. n.
164	A. Manlius A. f. T. n. Torquatus	Q. Cassius L. f. Q. n. Longinus
163	Ti. Sempronius P. f. Ti. n. Gracchus II	M'. Iuventius T. f. T. n. Thalna
162	P. Cornelius P. f. Cn. n. Scipio Nasica (Corculum)	C. Marcius C. f. Q. n. Figulus
	P. Cornelius L. f. L. n. Lentulus suff.	*Cn. Domitius Cn. f. L. n. Ahenobarbus* suff.
161	M. Valerius M. f. M. n. Messalla	C. Fannius C. f. C. n. Strabo
160	L. Anicius L. f. L. n. Gallus	M. Cornelius C. f. C. n. Cethegus
159	Cn. Cornelius Cn. f. Cn. n. Dolabella	M. Fulvius M. f. M. n. Nobilior
158	M. Aemilius M'. f. M'. n. Lepidus	C. Popillius P. f. P. n. Laenas II
157	Sex. Iulius Sex. f. L. n. Caesar	L. Aurelius L. f. L. n. Orestes
156	L. Cornelius Cn. f. L. n. Lentulus Lupus	C. Marcius C. f. Q. n. Figulus
155	P. Cornelius P. f. Cn. n. Scipio Nasica (Corculum) II	M. Claudius M. f. M. n. Marcellus II
154	Q. Opimius Q. f. Q. n	L. Postumius Sp. f. L. n. Albinus
		M'. Acilius M'. f. C. n. Glabrio suff.
153	Q. Fulvius M. f. M. n. Nobilior	T. Annius T. f. Luscus
152	M. Claudius M. f. M. n. Marcellus III	L. Valerius L. f. P. n. Flaccus
151	L. Licinius Lucullus	A. Postumius A. f. A. n. Albinus
150	T. Quinctius T. f. T. n. Flamininus	M'. Acilius L. f. K. n. Balbus
149	L. Marcius C. f. C. n. Censorinus	M'. (M.?) Manilius P. f. P. n.
148	Sp. Postumius Sp. f. Sp. n. Albinus Magnus	L. Calpurnius C. f. C. n. Piso Caesoninus
147	P. Cornelius P. f. P. n. Scipio Africanus Aemilianus	C. Livius M. Aemiliani f. M. n. Drusus
146	Cn. Cornelius Cn. f. L. n. Lentulus	L. Mummius L. f. L. n.
145	Q. Fabius Q. f. Q. n. Maximus Aemilianus	L. Hostilius L. f. L. n. Mancinus
144	Ser. Sulpicius Ser. f. P. n. Galba	L. Aurelius L.? f. C. n. Cotta
143	Ap. Claudius C. f. Ap. n. Pulcher	Q. Caecilius Q. f. L. n. Metellus Macedonicus
142	L. Caecilius Q. f. L. n. Metullus Calvus	Q. Fabius Q. f. Q. n. Maximus Servilianus
141	Cn. Servilius Cn. f. Cn. n. Caepio	Q. Pompeius A. f.
140	C. Laelius C. f. C. n. (Sapiens)	Q. Servilius Cn. f. Cn. n. Caepio
139	Cn. Calpurnius Piso	M. Popillius M. f. P. n. Laenas
138	P. Cornelius P. f. P. n. Scipio Nasica Serapio	D. Iunius M. f. M. n. Brutus (Callaicus)
137	M. Aemilius M. f. M. n. Lepidus Porcina	C. Hostilius A. f. L. n. Mancinus
136	L. Furius Philus	Sex. Atilius M. f. C. n. Serranus

135	Ser. Fulvius Q. f. Flaccus	Q. Calpurnius C. f. C. n. Piso
134	P. Cornelius P. f. P. n. Scipio Africanus Aemilianus II	C. Fulvius Q. f. Cn. n. Flaccus
133	P. Mucius P. f. Q. n. Scaevola	L. Calpurnius L. f. C. n. Piso Frugi
132	P. Popillius C. f. P. n. Laenas	P. Rupilius P. f. P. n.
131	P. Licinius P. f. P. n. Crassus Dives Mucianus	L. Valerius L. f. L. n. Flaccus
130	L. Cornelius Lentulus	M. Perperna M. f. L. n.
129	C. Sempronius C. f. C. n. Tuditanus	M'. Aquillius M'. f. M'. n.
128	Cn. Octavius Cn. f. Cn. n.	T. Annius T.? f. T.? n. Rufus
127	L. Cassius Longinus Ravilla	L. Cornelius L. f. Cinna
126	M. Aemilius Lepidus	L. Aurelius L. f. L. n. Orestes
125	M. Plautius Hypsaeus	M. Fulvius M. f. Q. n. Flaccus
124	C. Cassius Longinus	C. Sextius C. f. C. n. Calvinus
123	Q. Caecilius Q. f. Q. n. Metellus (Baliaricus)	T. Quinctius T. f. T.? n. Flamininus
122	Cn. Domitius Cn. f. Cn. n. Ahenobarbus	C. Fannius M. f. C.? n.
121	L. Opimius Q. f. Q. n.	Q. Fabius Q. Aemiliani f. Q. n. Maximus (Allobrogicus)
120	P. Manilius P.? f.	C. Papirius C. f. Carbo
119	L. Caecilius L. f. Q. n. Metellus (Delmaticus)	L. Aurelius Cotta
118	M. Porcius M. f. M. n. Cato	Q. Marcius Q. f. Q. n. Rex
117	L. Caecilius Q. f. Q. n. Metellus Diadematus	Q. Mucius Q. f. Q. n. Scaevola (Augur)
116	C. Licinius P. f. Geta	Q. Fabius (Q. Serviliani f. Q. n.?) Maximus Eburnus
115	M. Aemilius M. f. L. n. Scaurus	M. Caecilius Q. f. Q. n. Metellus
114	M'. Acilius M'.? f. L.? n. Balbus	C. Porcius M. f. M. n. Cato
113	C. Caecilius Q. f. Q. n. Metellus Caprarius	Cn. Papirius C. f. Carbo
112	M. Livius C. f. M. Aemiliani n.? Drusus	L. Calpurnius (L. f. C. n.?) Piso Caesoninus
111	P. Cornelius P. f. P. n. Scipio Nasica Serapio	L. Calpurnius Bestia
110	M. Minucius Q. f. Rufus	Sp. Postumius Albinus
109	Q. Caecilius L. f. Q. n. Metellus (Numidicus)	M. Iunius D. f. D. n. Silanus
108	Ser. Sulpicius Ser. f. Ser. n. Galba	L. (Q.?) Hortensius *M. Aurelius Scaurus* suff.
107	L. Cassius L. f. Longinus	C. Marius C. f. C. n.
106	Q. Servilius Cn. f. Cn. n. Caepio	C. Atilius Serranus
105	P. Rutilius P. f. Rufus	Cn. Mallius Cn. f. Maximus
104	C. Marius C. f. C. n. II	C. Flavius C. f. Fimbria
103	C. Marius C. f. C. n. III	L. Aurelius L. f. L. n. Orestes
102	C. Marius C. f. C. n. IV	Q. Lutatius Q. f. Catulus
101	C. Marius C. f. C. n. V	M'. Aquillius M'. f. M'. n.
100	C. Marius C. f. C. n. VI	L. Valerius L. f. L. n. Flaccus
99	M. Antonius M. f. M. n.	A. Postumius Albinus
98	Q. Caecilius Q. f. Q. n. Metellus Nepos	T. Didius T. f. Sex. n.
97	Cn. Cornelius Cn. f. Cn. n. Lentulus	P. Licinius M. f. P. n. Crassus
96	Cn. Domitius Cn. f. Cn. n. Ahenobarbus	C. Cassius L. f. Longinus

95	L. Licinius L. f. C. n. Crassus	Q. Mucius P. f. P. n. Scaevola
94	C. Coelius C. f. C. n. Caldus	L. Domitius Cn. f. Cn. n. Ahenobarbus
93	C. Valerius C. f. L. n. Flaccus	M. Herennius M. f.
92	C. Claudius Ap. f. C. n. Pulcher	M. Perperna M. f. M. n.
91	L. Marcius Q. f. Q. n. Philippus	Sex. Iulius C. f. L.? n. Caesar
90	L. Iulius L. f. Sex. n. Caesar	P. Rutilius L. f. L. n. Lupus
89	Cn. Pompeius Sex. f. Cn. n. Strabo	L. Porcius M. f. M. n. Cato
88	L. Cornelius L. f. P. n. Sulla (Felix)	Q. Pompeius Q. f. A.? n. Rufus
87	Cn. Octavius Cn. f. C. n.	L. Cornelius L. f. L. n. Cinna
		L. Cornelius Merula suff.
86	L. Cornelius L. f. L. n. Cinna II	C. Marius C. f. C. n. VII
		L. Valerius C.? f. L.? n. Flaccus suff.
85	L. Cornelius L. f. L. n. Cinna III	Cn. Papirius Cn. = Cn. f. C. n. Carbo
84	Cn. Papirius Cn. f. C. n. Carbo II	L. Cornelius L. f. L. n. Cinna IV
83	L. Cornelius L. f. L. n. Scipio Asiaticus (Asiagenus)	C. Norbanus
82	C. Marius C. f. C. n.	Cn. Papirius Cn. f. C. n. Carbo III
81	M. Tullius M. f. A. n. Decula	Cn. Cornelius P. f. L. n. Dolabella
80	L. Cornelius L. f. P. n. Sulla Felix	Q. Caecilius Q. f. L. n. Metellus Pius
79	P. Servilius C. f. M. n. Vatia (Isauricus)	Ap. Claudius Ap. f. C. n. Pulcher
78	M. Aemilius Q. f. M. n. Lepidus	Q. Lutatius Q. f. Q. n. Catulus
77	D. Iunius D. f. M. n. Brutus	Mam. Aemilius Mam. f. Lepidus Livianus
76	Cn. Octavius M. f. Cn. n.	C. Scribonius C. f. Curio
75	L. Octavius Cn. f. C. n.	C. Aurelius M. f. Cotta
74	L. Licinius L. f. L. n. Lucullus	M. Aurelius M. f. Cotta
73	M. Terentius M. f. Varro Lucullus	C. Cassius L. f. Longinus
72	L. Gellius L. f. L. n. Publicola	Cn. Cornelius Cn. f. Lentulus Clodianus
71	P. Cornelius P. f. P. n. Lentulus Sura	Cn. Aufidius Cn. f. Orestes
70	Cn. Pompeius Cn. f. Sex. n. Magnus	M. Licinius P. f. M. n. Crassus
69	Q. Hortensius L. f. Hortalus	Q. Caecilius C. f. Q. n. Metellus (Creticus)
68	L. Caecilius C. f. Q. n. Metellus (*Servilius*) *Vatia* suff.	Q. Marcius Q. f. Q. n. Rex
67	C. Calpurnius Piso	M'. Acilius M'. f. M'. n. Glabrio
66	M'. Aemilius M'. f. Lepidus	L. Volcacius Tullus
65	L. Aurelius M. f. Cotta	L. Manlius L. f. Torquatus
	(Both elected after conviction for bribery of consuls designate P. Cornelius P.? f. L. n. Sulla and P. Autronius L. f. Paetus)	
64	L. Iulius L. f. L. n. Caesar	C. Marcius C. f. C. n. Figulus
63	M. Tullius M. f. M. n. Cicero	C. Antonius M. f. M. n. (Hibrida)
62	D. Iunius M. f. Silanus	L. Licinius L. f. L. n. Murena
61	M. Pupius M. f. Piso Frugi Calpurnianus	M. Valerius M. f. M'. n. Messalla (Niger)
60	Q. Caecilius Q. f. Q. n. Metellus Celer	L. Afranius A. f.
59	C. Iulius C. f. C. n. Caesar	M. Calpurnius C. f. Bibulus
58	L. Calpurnius L. f. L. n. Piso Caesoninus	A. Gabinius A. f.
57	P. Cornelius P. f. L.? n. Lentulus Spinther	Q. Caecilius P. f. Q. n. Metellus Nepos
56	Cn. Cornelius P. f. Lentulus Marcellinus	L. Marcius L. f. Q. n. Philippus
55	Cn. Pompeius Cn. f. Sex. n. Magnus II	M. Licinius P. f. M. n. Crassus II
54	L. Domitius Cn. f. Cn. n. Ahenobarbus	Ap. Claudius Ap. f. Ap. n. Pulcher

53   Cn. Domitius M. f. M. n. Calvinus   M. Valerius Messalla (Rufus)
52   Cn. Pompeius Cn. f. Sex. n. Magnus III   Q. Caecilius Q. f. Q. n. Metellus Pius
                                          Scipio Nasica

51   Ser. Sulpicius Q. f. Rufus   M. Claudius M. f. M. n. Marcellus
50   L. Aemilius M. f. Q. n. Lepidus Paullus   C. Claudius C. f. M. n. Marcellus
49   C. Claudius M. f. M. n. Marcellus   L. Cornelius P. f. Lentulus Crus
48   C. Iulius C. f. C. n. Caesar II   P. Servilius P. f. C. n. Isauricus
47   Q. Fufius Q. f. C. n. Calenus   P. Vatinius P. f.
46   C. Iulius C. f. C. n. Caesar III   M. Aemilius M. f. Q. n. Lepidus
45   C. Iulius C. f. C. n. Caesar IV   no colleague
     Q. Fabius Q. f. Q. n. Maximus suff.   *C. Trebonius C. f.* suff.
     C. Caninius C. f. C. n. Rebilus suff.
44   C. Iulius C. f. C. n. Caesar V   M. Antonius M. f. M. n.
     P. Cornelius P. f. L.? n. Dolabella suff.
43   C. Vibius C. f. C. n. Pansa Caetronianus   A. Hirtius A. f.
     C. Iulius C. f. C. n. Caesar suff.   *Q. Pedius M. f.* suff.
     P. Ventidius P. f. Bassus suff.   *C. Carrinas C. f.* suff.
42   M. Aemilius M. f. Q. n. Lepidus   L. Munatius L. f. L. n. Plancus
41   L. Antonius M. f. M. n. (Pietas)   P. Servilius P. f. C. n. Isauricus
40   Cn. Domitius M. f. M. n. Calvinus   C. Asinius Cn. F. Pollio
     L. Cornelius L. f. Balbus suff.   *P. Canidius P. f. Crassus* suff.
39   L. Marcius L. f. C. n. Censorinus   C. Calvisius C. f. Sabinus
     C. Cocceius Balbus suff.   *P. Alfenus P. f. Varus* suff.
38   Ap. Claudius C. f. Ap. n. Pulcher   C. Norbanus C. f. Flaccus
     L. Cornelius Lentulus suff.   *L. Marcius L. f. L. n. Philippus* suff.
37   M. (Vipsanius) Agrippa L. f.   L. Caninius L. f. Gallus
                                     T. Statilius T. f. Taurus suff.
36   L. Gellius L. f. L. n. Publicola   M. Cocceius Nerva
     L. Nonius L. f. T.? Asprenas suff.   *-Marcius-* suff.
35   Sex. Pompeius Sex. f. Sex.? n.   L. Cornificius L. f.
     P. Cornelius P.? f. Scipio? suff.   *T. Peducaeus* suff.
34   M. Antonius M. f. M. n. II   L. Scribonius L. f. Libo
     L. Sempronius L. f. L. n. Atratinus suff.
     Paullus Aemilius L. f. M. n. Lepidus
     C. Memmius C. f. L. n.
     M. Herennius (M.? f. T.? n. Picens?)
33   Imp. Caesar Divi f. II   L. Volcacius L. f. Tullus
     L. Antonius P. f. L. n. Paetus suff.
     L. Flavius
     C. Fonteius C. f. Capito
     M. Acilius M'. f. Glabrio
     L. Vinicius M. f.
     Q. Laronius
32   Cn. Domitius L. f. Cn. n. Ahenobarbus   C. Sosius C. f. T. n.
     L. Cornelius Cinna suff.
     M. Valerius Messalla
31   M. Antonius M. f. M. n. III (design.)   Imp. Caesar Divi f. III
     M. Valerius M. f. M. n. Messalla Corvinus
       suff.
     M. Titius L. f.
     Cn. Pompeius Q. f.
     (From 30 BC, only ordinary consuls are listed here, without filiation)

30	Imp. Caesar Divi f. IV	M. Licinius Crassus
29	Imp. Caesar Divi f. V	Sex. Appuleius
28	Imp. Caesar Divi f. VI	M. (Vipsanius) Agrippa II
27	Imp. Caesar Divi f. VII	M. (Vipsanius) Agrippa III
26	Imp. Caesar Divi f. Augustus VIII	T. Statilius Taurus II
25	Imp. Caesar Divi f. Augustus IX	M. Iunius Silanus
24	Imp. Caesar Divi f. Augustus X	C. Norbanus Flaccus
23	Imp. Caesar Divi f. Augustus XI	A. Terentius Varro Murena
22	M. Claudius Marcellus Aeserninus	L. Arruntius
21	M. Lollius	Q. Aemilius Lepidus
20	M. Appuleius	P. Silius Nerva
19	C. Sentius Saturninus	Q. Lucretius (Cinna?) Vespillo
18	P. Cornelius Lentulus Marcellinus	Cn. Cornelius Lentulus
17	C. Furnius	C. Iunius Silanus
16	I. Domitius Ahenobarbus	P. Cornelius Scipio
15	M. Livius Drusus Libo	L. Calpurnius Piso Frugi (Pontifex)
14	M. Licinius Crassus Frugi	Cn. Cornelius Lentulus (Augur)
13	Ti. Claudius Nero	P. Quinctilius Varus
12	M. Valerius Messalla Barbatus Appianus	P. Sulpicius Quirinius
11	Q. Aelius Tubero	Paullus Fabius Maximus
10	Africanus Fabius Maximus	Iullus Antonius
9	Nero Claudius Drusus	T. Quinctius Crispinus (Sulpicianus)
8	C. Marcius Censorinus	C. Asinius Gallus
7	Ti. Claudius Nero II	Cn. Calpurnius Piso
6	D. Laelius Balbus	C. Antistius Vetus
5	Imp. Caesar Divi f. Augustus XII	L. Cornelius Sulla
4	C. Calvisius Sabinus	L. Passienus Rufus
3	L. Cornelius Lentulus	M. Valerius Messalla Messallinus
2	Imp. Caesar Divi f. Augustus XIII	M. Plautius Silvanus
1	Cossus Cornelius Lentulus	L. Calpurnius Piso (Augur)

AD

1	C. Caesar	L. Aemilius Paullus
2	P. Vinicius	P. Alfenus Varus
3	L. Aelius Lamia	M. Servilius
4	Sex. Aelius Catus	C. Sentius Saturninus
5	L. Valerius Messalla Volesus	Cn. Cornelius Cinna Magnus
6	M. Aemilius Lepidus	L. Arruntius
7	Q. Caecilius Metellus Creticus Silanus	A. Licinius Nerva Silianus
8	M. Furius Camillus	Sex. Nonius Quinctilianus
9	C. Poppaeus Sabinus	Q. Sulpicius Camerinus
10	P. Cornelius Dolabella	C. Iunius Silanus
11	M'. Aemilius Lepidus	T. Statilius Taurus
12	Germanicus Caesar	C. Fonteius Capito
13	C. Silius A. Caecina Largus	L. Munatius Plancus
14	Sex. Pompeius	Sex. Appuleius

APPENDIX III

Greek and Roman chronology

A. The Greeks. For the reckoning of time year by year all the Greek states in the Hellenistic age continued to use the old method of eponymous magistrates, i.e. annually elected magistrates after whom the year was named. There was no uniformity in the title of such magistrates, however: in many cities he was called the archon; in others the stephanephoros; in still others the prytanis; and in some he was a priest. The duties of these magistrates or priests had been diluted in the passage of time until they were merely ceremonial in most cases, and the real political power lay elsewhere. Lists of these magistrates were kept locally, but the only one known to us with any fullness is the archon list of Athens to the end of the fourth century BC. In the Hellenistic age that list in some parts is fragmentary and bristling with problems. Some parts of other lists, like those of Delphi and Miletus, can be put together only for short stretches of time.

The only Greek calendar known in some detail is the Athenian. It normally had twelve months of 29 or 30 days each. Their official sequence was:

Hekatombaion	Gamelion
Metageitnion	Anthesterion
Boedromion	Elaphebolion
Pyanopsion	Mounychion
Maimakterion	Thargelion
Poseideon	Skirophorion

This so-called Archon's calendar (or 'calendar according to the goddess') was based on a lunar year of only 354 days, the addition (intercalation) of an extra month being required every few years to keep the months in line with the seasons. The new year (Hekatombaion 1) began in the evening of the first observed new moon after the summer solstice (i.e. after June 22).

For Athenian administrative purposes there was a second way of dividing the year, not based on the moon's phases, but on the time periods (called prytanies) during which committees (called by the same term) of the Boule took turns, in an order determined by lot, preparing and administering the business that came before it. In the period of the ten Athenian tribes (down to 307/6 BC) there were ten prytanies to the year, each committee composed of fifty men from one of the tribes. The official order of the tribes was:

I Erechtheis	VI Oineis
II Aigeis	VII Kekropis
III Pandionis	VIII Hippothontis
IV Leontis	IX Aiantis
V Akamantis	X Antiochis

In the Hellenistic age tribes were sometimes added or abolished for political reasons. In 307/6 BC two tribes were added, Antigonis and Demetrias, which were given places in that order at the head of the list. In 224/3 BC a thirteenth tribe, Ptolemais, was added and placed between Leontis and Akamantis. In 201–200 BC the tribes Antigonis and Demetrias were abolished, but almost immediately another tribe called Attalis (cf. no. 24) was created (200 BC). It was placed at the end of the list, and thereafter no changes were made until the second century AD.

Outside of Attica our knowledge of Hellenistic Greek calendars is often nothing more than (at best) the names of the months. The calendar in widest use was the Macedonian, i.e. the Seleucid, which consisted of the following months, in order:

Artemisios	Dios
Daisios	Apellaios
Panemos	Audnaios
Loios (Loos)	Peritios
Gorpiaios	Dystros
Hyperberetaios	Xandikos

The search for precise equivalents of ancient dates in modern terms is controversial and risky.

In Egypt a unique situation developed when the Greeks under Ptolemy I consolidated their control of the country. The Egyptian civil calendar was solar and had a year of 365 days, but the Egyptians never corrected for the extra one-fourth of a day by means of inter-calation. Over long stretches of time this caused gradual rotation of the months through the seasons. But since that rotation was regular and predictable, modern tables can be constructed to account for it, and modern dates can be determined for Egyptian dates. The Greeks in control of Egypt accepted this Egyptian solar year, although for a long time they tried to apply the Macedonian system to it, month by month. Beginning with the fourth year of the reign of Ptolemy V (205–180 BC), however, they no longer did this. Thereafter the Macedonian month names in Egypt were simply alternative names for the Egyptian months. Down to 119/8 BC the equations were:

Dystros = Thoth	Gorpiaios = Phamenoth
Xandikos = Phaophi	Hyperberetaios = Pharmouthi
Artemisios = Hathyr	Dios = Pachon
Daisios = Choiach	Apellaios = Payni
Panemos = Tybi	Audnaios = Epeiph
Loios = Mecheir	Peritios = Mesore

But in 119/18 BC the equivalents were changed:

Dios = Thoth	Artemisios = Phamenoth
Apellaios = Phaophi	Daisios = Pharmouthi
Audnaios = Hathyr	Panemos = Pachon
Peritios = Choiach	Loios = Payni
Dystros = Tybi	Gorpiaios = Epeiph
Xandikos = Mecheir	Hyperberetaios = Mesore

This system, with the first day of Thoth the beginning of the Egyptian year, continued in use into the Roman period. See Samuel, *GRC* and *PC*, as well as E. J. Bickerman, *Chronology of the Ancient World* (Ithaca, N.Y. 1980). Tables for the conversion of Egyptian dates into modern equivalents will be found in T. C. Skeat, *The Reigns of the Ptolemies* (Munich 1954).

B. The Romans. The pre-Julian calendar, i.e. the one before the reforms of Julius Caesar, was lunar with a total of 355 days: March, May, July, and October had 31 days each, while February had 28 and all the rest 29 days each. To keep the months in line with the seasons it had been the practice to add (intercalate) an extra month during February every few years, but the Romans, like the Greeks, never did this with regularity. Each month was divided into three parts by means of special days called the Kalends, Nones and Ides. Since the frame of reference was always one of looking forward to the arrival of these days, each of the other days was given a number reflecting how many days had to pass before they did arrive. The Kalends were always the first day of each month, the Nones were either the seventh day (of March, May, July, and October) or the fifth (of all the rest), while the Ides were either the fifteenth day (of March, May, July, and October) or the thirteenth (of all the rest). The Roman method of counting these days was inclusive. Thus, e.g., the Roman date 'on the third day before the Ides of January' is by our method of counting actually the second day before the Ides of that month (January 11).

This calendar was changed by Julius Caesar in 45 BC to one based on the sun, following the Egyptian model, but with proper intercalation. Thereafter the number of days in the months were: September, April, June, and November had 30 days; February had 28; all the rest had 31. The rules governing the days on which the Kalends, Nones, and Ides fell remained the same. This Julian year had 365 days, with one intercalated day to be added in February every fourth year. See Samuel, *GRC*; Bickerman, *op. cit.*; and A. K. Michels, *The Calendar of the Roman Republic* (Princeton 1967).

INDEXES

All references are to numbers of items and, where applicable, of numbered lines or sections of items. References to explanatory notes are marked 'n'. Names occurring as patronymics are not listed.

I. Personal Names

A. GREEKS

Ablouporis, 64.24
Abroupolis (Thracian king), 19.15–16
Adaios son of Adaios, 48.50
Aeneas, 59 n.1
Agasias son of Menophilos, 47 C2, D6
Agelaos, 12 B35
Akornion son of Dionysios, 78.44
Alexandros, 111.40; 62 A4
Alexidemos son of Theodoros, 70.18
Ammonios, 106.2
Amphikrates son of Eurynomos, 6 A
Amyntas son of Dies, 48.50
Amyon son of Epikouros, 26.2
Androsthenidas, 12.4
Antilakos son of Simides, 9.2
Antiochos, 59a A4
Antiochus III, 3 B; 8.4; 13.6; 18 n.2; 34 n.2; 55 n.1
Antipatros son of [-]stos, 59b B2
Apollodoros, 5.71; 30.7
Apollodoros son of Hermokrates, 57.51
Apollonios son of Chares, 90.7
Apollonios son of Lucius, 95.12,24
Apollonios son of Menophilos, 101 VI 31, VII 79
Apollonios son of Zethos, 82.2
Arathes, 56.1
Archelaos (Mithridates' general), 56.6; 68.5
Archelochos son of Aristophantes, 51.1,10
Archias, 44.7
Ariarathes, 21 B1,9; 56.1
Ariobarzanes (King), 47 H1; 112, chapters 27.2 and 33.1
Aristainos son of Timokades, 6 b
Aristeides, 14.4
Aristogeiton son of Patron, 57.49
Aristomachos son of Aristokleides, 6 A
Aristonikos (of Pergamum, pretender to the throne), 43 n.1–2; 44.15
Arsinoe III, 1.2
Artemidoros, 59a B9
Artemidoros son of Artemidoros, 57.49
Artemidoros son of Demetrios, 107.8

Artemidoros, son of Myon, 59b B9
Artaxas (King), 112, chapter 27.2
Artavasdes (King), 112, chapters 27.2, 32.1, and 33.1
Arthetauros, 19.28
Asklepiades son of Philinos of Klazomenai, 66.5 and *passim* in 66
Athanokles, 17.12
Athena (name of a ship), 71 E–F
Athenaios (brother of Eumenes II), 23.6
Athenaios son of Stratonikos, 82.3
Athenais (Queen), 47 H2
Athenodoros (pirate), 71 C
Attalos son of Menandros, 59a A6
Attalus I, 7 n.2; 13.1
Attalus II, 23.15; 29.1; 32.9
Attalus III, 35.8; 39.3; 40.13,16; 43 n.2; 45 n.; 80 A6
Attis, 29.1

Biadas, 74.15
Bithys (son of King Perseus), 26 n.2
Boulon, 15.2; 16.9
Burebista (King), 78.22,34

Chairemon (of Tralles), 96.2
Chairemon son of Pythodoros, 60 A2; B3,9; C2
Charmides, 28.1
Charopeinos, 85.10
Chloros, 29.8
Cleopatra I, 31.4; 47 A6
Cleopatra VII, 88; 89; 94.8

Damarmenos, 74.11
Damokrita, 21.48
Damon son of Alkisthenes, 11.8
Damosthenes son of Archelas, 16.3
Danaos and Hypermestra, 98 E3
Demainetos son of Theoteles, 20.18
Demetrios, 28.5,23
Demetrios son of Kleonymos, 83.15
Dies, 14.3
Dies son of Matrokles, 83.15

I. Index of personal names

Diomedes son of Athenagoras, 107.3
Dionysios, 14.3–4; 44.6,60
Dionysios son of Dionysios, 103.6
Dionysios son of Iason, 65.10, 28
Dionysios son of Menis, 59b B10
Diophanes, 17.12
Dorotheos son of Hegesandros, 75 A8
Dumnobellaunus (Celtic king, in Britain), 112, chapter 32,1

Euboulos, 103.8 and *passim* in 103
Eudemos, 14.4
Eukles, 44.60
Eumenes, 90.6
Eumenes II, 7 A1, B1; 13.5; 19.29; 23.15
Eunikos, 23.2

Glauketas, 38.4

Harmoxenos son of Lysandros, 38.14
Hegesias, 5.11 and *passim* in 5
Hekataios, 63.25
Heliodoros son of Maiandrios, 107.6
Heraion son of Pasion, 73.1
Herakleides son of Herakleides, 107.2
Herakleios, 30.11
Herakleitos, 34.40
Heras, 86.76
Hermias son of Petalos, 106.2
Hermippos son of Menoites, 57.51
Hermodoros son of Olympichos, 70.16,50
Herodes ('The Great'), 98 C
Herodes son ofKleon, 83.15
Herodotos son of Herodotos, 30.9
Herostratos son of Dorkalion, 58.6
Herys son of Eudoros, 16.3
Hierokles son of Iason, 65.10,28
Hieronymos son of Boethos, 23.3
Hikesion son of Artemidoros, 57.47

Iollas son of Metrodoros, 104 A20,B23

Kairogenes son of Leukatheos, 103.1
Kalliphanes, 23.8,33
Kleëmporos son of Timasion, 76.8
Kleinias, 104.6
Kotys (King), 26.7,24
Kratinos, 41 A10
Krinagoras, 83.16
Kriton son of Ameinias, 38.3
Kyllanios, 50.5

Lachares, 74.7
Lamachos son of Demetrios, 82.2
Lampromachos son of Politas, 38.15
Leon, 50.1
Leon son of Hagesippos, 38.2

Leonippos (satrap), 60 B1
Lochos son of Kallimedes, 47 A5
Lysanias son of Kaibon, 9.18
Lysias son of Diogenes, 95.14
Lysimachus (King of Chalkis), 88
Lyson son of Philotas, 48.50

Matrios, 30.11
Medeios, 38.27
Megathymos son of Athenaios, 26.3
Menalippos, 47 H6
Menandros, 44.8
Menekrates son of Diodoros, 57.54
Menekrates son of Menekrates, 57.50
Menes, 14.4
Menestratos son of Apollodoros, 39.1
Menippos, 8.4
Meniskos son of Eirenaios, 66.6 and *passim* in 66
Menogenes, 29.4
Menogenes son of Isidoros, 104 A5,21, B24
Menophanes, 56.7
Metrodoros son of Konon, 103.6
Mikas son of Mikas, 64.2
Mikkylion, 12 B6
Mithridates V, 49.2
Mithridates VI (the Great), 47 n.7; 56.1 and *passim* in 56; 60 B1; 61.4,12; 63.6,46; 51.84,94; 64n.; 68.5; 69.4; 71 A–B; 72.25,29,36; 108.14
Mithridates son of Menodotos, 80 A4,B1
Mnasis, 21.47
Moschos, 14.4
Mousaios, 104.6

Nabis (King), 6 n.4; 7 A2,B4
Nikanor, 44.5
Nikaretidas, 74.52
Nikatas, 38.37
Nikolaos of Damascus, 98C
Nikomachos son of Artemidoros, 71 F
Nikomedes son of Nikomedes, 56.6ff.

Orestas, 15.2; 16.9
Orophernes, 32.4
Orthagoras, 18 n.1
Ouliades, 91.9

Paionios son of Hierokles, 63.24
Pamphilos son of Pamphilos, 76.7
Papion, 101 VI 42
Parthenos (name of a ship), 71 D
Patron, 12 B36
Pereitas, 59a A3; 59b B2
Perseus (King), 19.7; 24.1; 26 n.2
Phainias son of Phainias, 83.14
Phanites, 95.23

I. Index of personal names

Pharnakes (King), 30.10,31
Phileinos son of Chrysippos, 103.13
Philetairos (third brother of Eumenes II), 23 n.3
Philetairos son of [-], 53.19
Philip V, 5.65; 7 n.; 19.16
Philopoimen, 35.8
Philoxenos son of Dionysios, 76.9
Phleinos, 74.9
Phoinix son of Phoinix, 57.54
Phrates (King), 112, chapter 32.1
Polykles son of Pheidippos, 38.4
Polystratos son of Menon, 44.9
Polystratos son of Polyarkos, 66.6 and *passim* in 66
Poseidonios, 43 A20,B28,40
Poseidonios son of Poseidonios, 57.48
Potamon son of Lesbonax, 83.14
Ptolemaios IV, 1.1
Ptolemaios V, 3 A–C
Ptolemaios VI, 31 n.1
Ptolemaios VIII, 31.3; 47 A4
Pyllos, 38.28
Python son of Chairemon, 60 B7–8
Pythodoros, 34.40; 60 B7

Rhodokles son of Antimachos, 53.20
Rhoimetalkes, 64.24

Satyros, 23.8; 68.5
Seleukos son of Theodotos, 86.2 and *passim* in 86
Silenos, 68.5
Sokrates the Good, 56.5
Solon son of Demetrios, 87.12,33

Sosandros, 29.4
Sosikrates son of Pythion, 77.58
Sosos son of Tauromenes, 50.8ff.
Staphylos, 108.2
Stratokles, 50.2
Symmachos (1), 86.77
Symmachos (2), 90.6

Teimokles son of Zenon, 59b.B10
Telemnestos son of Aristeides, 10.3
Terpheos son of Dies, 83.15
Theodoros, 78.3
Theon, 44.1
Theophrastos son of Herakleitos, 47 B1
Thessalos son of Thrasymedes, 38.6
Thrasykles, 15.2; 16.9
Tigranes I, 56.4
Tigranes II, 112, chapter 27.2
Timokles son of Anaxagoras, 77.58
Timokrates, 74.33
Timotheos son of Nikias, 50.23
Timoxenos, 111.54
Tincommius (Celtic king, in Britain), 112, chapter 32.1
Tipas (King or chief in Thrace), 48.22
Tryphera, 103.9 and *passim* in 103
Tuta (King or chief in Thrace), 64.25

Vonones, 112, chapter 33.1

Xenopithis, 21.47

Zoilos son of Epigenes, 83.16
Zopyros, 76.5

B ROMANS

Arrangement is by *nomen* when known, otherwise by *cognomen*. The number in parenthesis after the *nomen* is the reference number of Pauly-Wissowa-Kroll.

Acilius, M'., 21.4
Acilius (35) Glabrio, M'. (cos. 191), 12 nn. 1–2; 17.10ff.
Acutius, Q., 97.43
Aelius (59) Gallus (prefect of Egypt), 94 n.2
Aelius (152) Tubero, P. (one of the commissioners of 189–188), 18 n.2
Aemilius (72) Lepidus, M. (cos. 78), 66.1,24,28
Aemilius (82) Lepidus, Paullus, 97 b40
Aemilius (114) Paullus, L. (cos. 168), 24.1
Aemilius, M. (praetor), 34.35,49,61
Aemilius (68) Lepidus, M. (cos. 187 and 175), 3 C–D
Ancharius (3), Q., 74.26
Annaeus, C., 70.11
Annius, M. (quaestor), 48.3,37
Antistius (48) Vetus, C. (cos. 6), 108.3
Antius, C. (trib. pl.), 72.2

Antonius (28), M. (cos. 99), 54.3
Antonius Artemidorus, M., 85.6
Antonius (19), C. (cos. 63), 72.2 (trib. pl.), 78.16
Antonius (30), M. (the triumvir), 85.1 (letter of;) 88 (gives territory to Cleopatra); 89 A–B
Antonius (29) Creticus, M. (praetor), 74.33
Appius (one of the Commissioners of 189–188?), 18.64
Aquillius Florus, L. (quaestor), 42 B3
Aquillius (11), M'. (cos. 101), 56.7
Aquillius (10), M'. (cos. 129), 42 A1,4, B1,2, C1,4; 43 A1, B31; 45.9,18
Asinius (15) Gallus, C. (cos. 8), 103.11
Asinius (25) Pollio, C., 97 b40
Atinius, C., 15 (Decree) 3
Aurelius (107) Cotta, M. (cos. 74), 71 A

I. Index of personal names

Autronius (7) Paetus, P., 74.16,23
Avidius Urgulanius, M., 111.39

Baronas (centurion), 90.11

Caecilius (22 or 86), Q. (trib. pl.), 72.2
Caecilius, Q., 45.23
Caecilius (87) Metellus, Q. (cos. 69), 47 F1
Caepio, Q., 43 B21,25
Calpurnius (74) Piso, L. (cos. 1), 107.6
Calvisius (14) Sabinus, C. (cos. 4), 102.74,84
Cascellius, Aulus, 70.13
Cassius, C., 60.3
Cassius, M., 70.8
Cassius (58) Longinus, C. (cos. 73), 70.64
Castricius, L. (soldier), 106.4
Censorinus, *see* Marcius
Claudius (23), L., 70.16
Claudius, M., 21.15
Claudius (165) Glaber, C., 70.7
Claudius (226) Marcellus, M., 70.7
Claudius, Ti., 28.21
Claudius (245) Nero, Appius (one of the Commissioners of 189–188), 18 n.2
Claudius Nero, Ti. (the future emperor Tiberius), 99.5; 107.7; 111.34; 112, chapter 27.2 and 30.1
Cloatius, M., 74.1,42
Cloatius, Numerius, 74.1,42
Cornelius, C., 73.1
Cornelius (24), Cn. (trib. pl.), 72.2
Cornelius (134) Dolabella, Cn. (cos. 81), 64.1
Cornelius (164) Gallus, C., 93.1; 94 n.2
Cornelius L.f. Lentulus, 27 A3
Cornelius (216) Lentulus, Cn. (cos. 72), 72.4
Cornelius (181) Lentulus Augur, Cn. (cos. 14), 107.12
Cornelius (182) Lentulus, Cossus (cos. 1), 107.5
Cornelius (228) Lentulus Marcellinus, Cn. (cos. 56), 76.1
Cornelius (214) Lentulus, P., 18 n.2
Cornelius Philo, L., freedman of Lucius, 27 A6
Cornelius (337) Scipio, L. (cos. 190), 14.1
Cornelius (336) Scipio Africanus, P. (cos. 205 and 194), 9.2 and *passim* in 9; 14.2
Cornelius (374) Sisenna, L. (praetor 78), 66.2
Cornelius (392) Sulla, L. (the dictator), 56.6,10; 61 A2; 63 *passim*; 64.14; 70.20 and *passim* in 70; 108.12

Demetrius (centurion), 90.9
Didius (5), T., 55 A (B) 28, B IV 10
Domitius (18 or 20), Cn. (cos. of 192 or of 122), 11.7
Domitius (27) Ahenobarbus, Cn. (cos. 54), 70.24

Domitius (20) Ahenobarbus, Cn. (cos. 122), 43 A16, B21,33,38; 46(?)
Drusus (son of Tiberius), 111.35

Egnatius, Cn., 36.2

Faberius (2), L., 66.4
Fabius (102) Maximus, Paulus (proconsul of Asia), 101 VI 44,58
Fabius (111) Maximus, Q. (cos. 116), 49.1; 50.3
Fannius (8), C., 63.21
Fonteius (1), 34.39
Fonteius, M'., 28.23
Fulvius (91) Nobilior, M. (cos. 189), 16.10
Fundanius (1), C., 63.22; 72.3

Gallius (3), C., 74.26
Gavenius, C., 76.11
Gellius (17) Publicola, L. (cos. 72), 72.4
Gerillanus, Maraius, 47 D2

Hostilius, L. (trib. pl.), 72.2
Hostilius (16) Mancinus, Aulus (cos. 170), 22.6
Hostilius (18) Mancinus, C. (praetor), 38.8,68

Iulia (daughter of Augustus), 98 B–C
Iulius (131) Caesar, C. (the dictator), 74.23; 76.10 (in Aquileia); 79 (statues of); 80 A–B (letter to Pergamum); 82.9; 83.6–7 (letter of), 24; 97 n.1
Iulius (132) Caesar Octavianus, C. (Augustus), 86.2 (letter of); 87.1 (letter of); 9.1. (letter of); 92 (dedication by); 93.2; 95 A1 (legal decision by); 96.1; 97 b37, c1,c26; 98 B2,C; 100.1; 101 *passim*; 102 *passim*; 104 A9,16,19, B22 (letter of); 105.1 (oath of loyalty to); 103.2; 107.2; 111 *passim*; 112 (Res Gestae), *passim*
Iulius Caesar, C. (son of Augustus), 104 *passim*; 112, chapter 27.2
Iulius (142) Caesar, L. (censor 89), 59.2
Iulius (151) Caesar, Sex. (cos. 91), 72.16
Iulius Papius, C., 90.1
Iulius Satyros, C., 82.5
Iunius (53) Brutus, M., *see* Servilius Caepio Brutus, Q.
Iunius, P., 71 E
Iunius (157) Silanus, C., 97 b42
Iunius (172) Silanus, M. (cos. 25), 97 b37 and *passim* in 97
Iuventius Agathopous, P., 110.14
Iuventius Rufus, P., 110.2

Labienus (5), Q., 91 n.
Labyon (centurion), 90.10
Lacutanius Phileros, P., freedman of Publius, 102.44

I. Index of personal names

Lartius (1), L., 70.10
Licinius (60) Crassus, P. (cos. 171), 20.2
Licinius (88) Geta, C. (cos. 116), 49.1
Licinius (104) Lucullus, L. (cos. 74), 71 A
Licinius (154) Sacerdos, C., 70.9
Livia, 111.45
Livius (29) Salinator (cos. 188), C. (?), 16.1
Livius (17) Drusus, M. (cos. 112), 52 n.
Lucilius Hirrus, C., 54.5
Lucius, 1.4
Lucretius (23) Gallus, C. (praetor 171),
    21.22,51
Lutatius (12), Cn., 38.12
Lutatius (8) Catulus, Q. (cos. 78), 66 *passim*

Maenius (14), Q. (praetor 170), 21.1,10,39
Maenius (16), T., 70.15,60
Magulnius, 27 C7
Mallius (10), T. 34.39 (he is probably a
    'Manlius')
Manlius (91) Vulso, Cn. (cos. 189), 14 n.; 18 n.2
Marcilius (1), L., 74.16
(Marcius) Censorinus, 97 C12
Marcius (75) Philippus, L. (cos. 91), 72.14
Marcius (76) Philippus, L. (cos. 56), 76.2
Marcius (31), Q. (trib. pl.), 72.2
Marius (14), C. (cos. 107, 104–100, 86), 27 B4;
    47 C1 (?) ; 55 A (B) 20; 56.6
Minucius (54) Rufus, M. (cos. 110), 52.1
Minucius (24, cf. 23), Q. (praetor), 28.15
Minucius (67) Thermus, Q., 70.14
Minucius (67?) [--] Thermus, Q., 27 C5
Mucius, P., 21.15
Mucius (22) Scaevola, Q. (cos. 95), 57.26
Mummius (7a), L. (cos. 146), 35.7ff.
Mutius Erun[--], C., freedman of Gaius, 27 A7

Niger (centurion), 90.9
Nikanor (centurion), 90.11
Norbanus (9a) Flaccus, C. (cos. 38), 97 C10
Numisius, T., 21.5

Oclatius, L. (soldier), 106.2
Octavius (17), Cn. (cos. 165), 1 n.1; 22.1,9
Octavius(22), Cn. (cos. 76), 27 C2
Oppius (20), Q. (procos. 88), 59a B1,6; 59b A1
Orbius, L., 14.16

Pandosinus, Cn., 21.54
Passienus (6) Rufus, L. (cos. 4), 102.74,84
Petilius (6), Q., 66.5
Pompeius, Sex. (praetor), 48.13
Pompeius, T. (centurion), 106.5
Pompeius (31) Magnus, Cn., 75 A–E; 78.31
Pompeius (42) Rufus, Q., 70.12
Popilius (15?), C. (trib. pl.), 72.2
Popillius (17), C. (praetor), 40.11
Popillius (18) Laenas, C. (cos. 172), 22 n.2

Porcius (4), P., 28.20
Porcius (5) Cato, C. (cos. 114), 52 n.
Porcius (10) Cato, M. (cos. of 118?), 55 B III 4
Postumius (44) Albinus, Spurius (praetor 189),
    15.1
Ptolemaeus (Roman soldier), 110.19
Publicius (25) Scaeva, M., 70.15
Publius (one of the Commissioners of 189–
    188?), 18.65

Quinctilius (20) Varus, P. (cos. 13), 99.6
(Quinctius (43) Flamininus, L.) (cos. 192), 5.18
Quinctius (45) Flamininus, T. (cos. 198), 4.1
    (letter of); 5.69; 6 *passim*; 38.52,64

Rancius (1),C., 70.61
Rufus (centurion), 90.9
Rutilius (34) Rufus, P. (cos. 105), 53.5,9,15

Salluvius (1) Naso, C., 69.1
Scribonius (10) Curio, C. (cos. 76), 27 C3
Sempronius (3), A., 38.13
Sempronius (92) Tuditanus, C. (cos. 129), 45.9
Sempronius (26) Atratinus, L., 97 b41
Sergius (16),M'., 21.16
Servilius Caepio Brutus, Q. (the tyrannicide),
    84 A–B
Servilius (67) Isauricus, P. (cos. 48 and 41),
    81.2
Servilius (93) Vatia, P. (cos. 79), 67 A
Sextius Scaeva, P., 101.42
Stallius, C., 47 H5
Stallius, M., 47 H5
Statilienus (1), Q., 38.11
Stlaccius Macedo, L., 102.43
Stlaccius Maximus, A., 102.42,51
Stoltius Maximus (centurion), 106.2

Terentius (centurion), 90.10
Terentius (86) Varro,M., 97 b42, C15
Terentius (= Licinius 109) Varro Lucullus, M.
    (cos. 73), 70.1,64; 73.4
Titius (18), M. (cos. 31), 47 G2
Tullius (29) Cicero, M. (cos. 63), 70.12; 77.38
    (the orator?)

Valerius (centurion), 90.10
Valerius (69), M. (trib. pl.), 72.2
Valerius L[--], M., 97 C13
Valerius (176) Flaccus, L. (cos. 100),
    55 A (B) 20
Valerius (252) Messalla, M. (cos. 188), 8
    (letter of)
Valerius (264) Messalinus Corvinus, M.
    (cos. 3), 111.36
Valerius (363) Triarius, C., 71 A–F
Vinicius (L. or M., governor of Asia), 95 B1

III. Index of geographical names

Vipsanius (2) Agrippa, M. (cos. 37, 28, 27),
95.2; 98 A–F; 109.13
Visellius (3) Varro, C., 70.63

Volcacius (9) Tullus, L. (cos. 33), 101 VI 42
Voluscius (1), L., 70.10

II.Gods and Goddesses

Amphiaraos, 70 *passim*
Aphrodite, 79 D4
Apollo, 6 E; 15.4 (Pythian); 16.23; 19 n.1; 22.17
Lykaios); 47 A7,D5; 52.5; 74.54; 75 B3;
84 C4; 109.14 (Games of); 111.31
(Temple of, in Rome)
Ares, 79 D4
Artemis, 6 D (Temple of); 17.8 (Brauronia);
46.5 (Temple of A. Tauropolos); 47 D5;
60 C5 (Temple of); 61.17 (Temple of)
Asklepios, 51.13 (Temple of); 57.50; 109.7
(Games of)
Athena, 7 A3 (Nikephoros); 13.8; 53.49; 59.6
(Ilias); 98 D4

Ceres, 21 n.1 (Temple of)
Cybele, 29 n.2

Darzalas, 78.10 (= 'Great god')
Demeter, 44.30,50
Dionysos, 37.3; 78.14,45 (Games of); 80 C3;
95.25 (Temple of); 109.20 (Games of).
See also 'Dionysiac Artists'

Hekate, 63.57,113 (Temple of)

Hera, 46.7
Herakles, 109.20 (Games of)

Isis, 90.2

Jupiter, 25.14 (Temple of); 31.24; 44.24; 53.49;
55 A (C) 13; 107 4

Kore, 44.50 (Demeter and)

Leto, 47 D5
Liber Pater, 95.13

Neptune, 92

Pan, 110.12

Roma, 18.71,76; 41 A3,17,24, B24,29; 53.50;
25.15 (statue of); 44.51; 101 IV 29
Roma and Augustus); 107.2 (Roma and
Augustus); 109.5 (Games of)

Sarapis, 78.12

Zeus, 11.10; 30.12; 41 A12; 105.7

III. Geographical Names

Listing is by geographical designation, but no attempt is made to distinguish between country
and inhabitants within separate entries.

Abbaitis, 43 A 5; 69.3
Abdera, 26.1,28; 64.13
Achaia (Phthiotis), 38.46
Achaia, 11.1; 13.4; 17.12; 22.5; 35.7ff.; 50.10
Adiabenians, 112, chapter 32.1
Adramyttium, 45 n.1; 77.46
Aetolia, 2 *passim*; 12 n.1; 16.15; 21.57
Aigeira, 11.5
Aigion, 11.4
Alabanda, 77.44
Albanians, 112, chapter 31.2
Alexandria, 3 A,C; 47 A3,C2; 55 A (B) 9;
55 A (B) III 40; 93.2 (prefect of); 100.3;
111.33
Amaseia, 56.6
Apameia, 29.5; 60.5
Aphrodisias, 59a–b *passim*; 65.20. *See also*
Plarasa
Aquileia, 76.10
Arabia, 112, chapter 26.5
Araxa, 18.67
Argedauon, 78.6

Argos, 7 n.; 22 (decree of); 47 E2,F3; 48.12 (in
Macedonia)
Armenia, 89 B; 112, chapter 27.2
Ascheion, 11.4
Asia, 40.7,17; 45.15; 55 *passim*; 56.8; 58.1; 63
passim; 65.24,27; 66.23,29; 75 C6; 86.48;
96.1; 101 IV 14,VI 41; 104 A20; 112,
chapter 28.1. *See also* 'People and Tribes
in Asia' and 'Koinon'
Astypalaia, 53.2 and *passim* in 53
Athens, 28.28; 54.5; 57.40; 74.12; 75 B1; 84 C1

Balbura, 25 n.1
Bargylia, 43
Bastarnians, 112, chapter 31.2
Berenike, 110.5 (prefect of)
Bessi, 52.3
Bithynia, 19 n.; 56.5–6,8
Boiotia, 35.9–10
Boresis, 93.3
Boura, 11.5

III. Index of geographical names

Britons, 112, chapter 32.1
Bubon, 25 n.1
Byzantium, 98 C

Caicus R., 44 n.1
Cantabrians, 96.3; 97 n.4
Capitolium, 21.33; 51.8; 53.7,11,48 (Capitoline Temple); 63.32,127; 66.25; 83.17,21; 86.5
Cappadocia, 56.1; 61.4; 71 A
Caucasus, 56.3
Ceramice, 93.4
Chalkis (in Euboia), 6 n.1; 21.47; 56.10
Chalkis (in Syria), 88
Chersonesos, 30.15,19; 30.13 and *passim* in 30; 55 A (B) 28, B IV *passim*
Chios, 98 C; 108
Chrysaoris, 63 n.2
Chyretiai, 4.2
Cilicia, 54 n.1; 55 A (B) 7, B III 35; 67 A
Comitium, 15.1; 21.2; 28.17; 34.38; 66.4
Coptos, 93.4
Corcyra, 2 n.1
Corinth, 35 *passim*; 50 n.3
Corycus, 67 A
Cos, 62 A4; 109
Crete, 71 A–B
Cyprus, 31 n.1; 55 A (B) 8, B III 39
Cyrene, 55 A (B) 9, B III 41; 102.4 and *passim* in 102; 112, chapter 27.3

Dacians, 112, chapter 30.2
Danube R., 19.10; 112, chapter 30.1
Delos, 9.7,14,17; 28.2,25; 47 B2,3,D3; 71 C; 84 C1
Delphi, 6 E; 12 n.1; 15.1,5; 16.2,17–18; 19.12,30; 52.6
Diospolis, 93.4
Dyme, 6 B; 11.1; 50.3
Dyrrachium, 36 n.1

Egypt, 3 A–B; 31 n.1; 55 A (B) 9, B III 40; 93.2 (prefect of); 94.20; 100, col. 2.5; 110.10 (mines of); 112, chapter 27.1
Elaea, 44 n.1
Elateia, 17 *passim*
Eleutherolakones, 74 n.1
Ephesus, 42 n.1; 47 C3,D6; 65.5; 77.44; 85.5 (M. Antonius in); 86.78 (Octavian in)
Epidauros, 51.6
Epikteteis, 69.3
Eretria, 56.10
Ethiopia, 93.7,9; 112, chapter 26.5
Euboia, 56.10; 66.23

Galatians, 5.49
Gangra, 105.4

Gaul, 11.8; 48.10,21; 52 n.; 100.4; 112, chapter 28.1 and 29.1
Greece, 63.76,85,110
Gytheates, 6 C

Hadriatic Sea, 112, chapter 27.3
Hellespont, 71 A
Heraia, 11.2
Herakleia (in Karia), 14.2
Herakleia (in Lynkos), 78.35
Herakleia (in Pontos), 68.5; 71 A
Hypopleistia, 12 B3

Iberia, 56.4; 112, chapter 31.2
Ilium, 98 C
Illyricum, 112, chapter 30.1
India, 112, chapter 31.1
Isaura Vetus, 67 B
Isaurians, 67 A
Ismaros, 64.20
Issa, 76.4
Isthmus (of Corinth), 54.4
Italy, 55 A (B) 6, B III 33; 112, chapter 32.2

Kaineik Chersonese, 55 A (B) 28 and *passim* in 55
Kallistai, 11.3
Karneia,11.6
Keramos, 63.53
Kibyra, 25.3,7,14
Kleitor, 11.3
Knidos, 55; 103.5; 109.16 (Games in)
Kolophonians, 38.56
Koroneia, 20.4; 21.58
Kos, 59b B14
Kyme (in Asia), 95.12,23

Lakedaimonians, 35.10
Lampsakos, 5 *passim*
Laodikeia, 59a B1; 59b B21
Larisa, 38.2
Leontion, 11.4
Lesbos, 97, col. d 22
Lete, 48.2
Lycia, 18.67,70; 67 A
Lydia, 13.7
Lykaonia, 55 A (B) 4, B III 23,25

Macedonia, 4 n.1; 5 n.9; 20 n.1; 22 n.2; 23.19; 24.2; 35 n.5; 36 (Via Egnatia in); 37.2; 39.4; 46 n.1; 48.5,7,24; 55 A (B) 28, (C) 4,8, B II 15,19, B IV 8,26; 66.29; 78.34
Maeander R., 96.1
Maedi, 48.22
Magna, 93.4
Magnesia (in Ionia), 34.36; 38.57; 77.59

III. Index of geographical names

Magnesia (in Lydia), 13 n.1 (battle of);
    18 nn. 2,4 (battle of)
Marcomanians, 112, chapter 32.1
Mariba, 112, chapter 26.5
Masdyenoi, 39.16
Massaliotes, 5.6,26,44,51,62
Medes, 56.4; 112, chapter 27.2 and 31.2
Melitaia, 38.14,34,45
Meroe, 112, chapter 26.5
Messenians, 7.3
Methymna, 33.8 and *passim* in 33
Miletus, 41 n.1; 71 D–E
Mylasa, 34.36; 77.45; 91.3
Mysia, 39.14; 43 A4; 69.2
Mytilene, 47 G1; 83.8; 97 (treaty with)

Nabata, 112, chapter 26.5
Narthakion, 38.2 and *passim* in 38
Nikomedia, 71 A–B
Nile R., 93.5,9
Norace, 95.12,24
Nysa, 60 A1; 107

Oenoanda, 25 n.1
Olympus (in Lycia), 67 A
Olynthos, 75 A9
Ophion, 93.4
Oropos, 70.2,36,64; 84 B1

Pamphylia, 67 A
Pannonians, 112, chapter 30.1
Paphlagonia, 56.6; 104.6
Parthia, 56.4; 91n.; 112, chapter 29.2 and
    32.1–2
Patrai, 11.1,9; 50.11
Peiraios, 23.7
Pelasgians, 96.1
Pellana, 11.5
Peparethians, 64.18
Pergamum, 7 n.2; 29.3; 35.8; 40.5(?); 45.2,7;
    56 n.6; 77.45; 80 A1; 101 IV 29, VI 58
Perrhaibians, 19.25
Pessinus, 29 nn.2–3
Pharai, 11.1
Phaselis, 67 A
Phasis, 56.3
Pheneos, 11.6
Pherai, 38.7
Philae, 93.7
Phoenicia, 3 B
Phokis, 21.57,59; 35.9
Phrygia, 49 n.
Phrygius R., 13.8
Pisidia, 112, chapter 28.1

Pitane, 44 n.1
Plarasa-Aphrodisias, 59a–b; 87.8
Pontos, 56.1; 71 A–B
Priene, 32.1; 34.35 and *passim* in 34
Propontis, 71 A
Psophis, 11.2
Pydna (battle of), 23 nn.1,4

Rhodes, 19 n.; 43 n.1; 55 A 13,17; 56.8; 96 C
Rhosos, 86.4 and *passim* in 86

Sabaei, 112, chapter 26.5
Samē, 16.11
Samos, 38.56; 46.1
Samothrace, 27 (Mysteries of); 78.19 (gods of)
Sardinia, 112, chapter 27.3
Sardis, 57.43; 77.45; 104.3; 109.21 (Games in)
Sarmatians, 112, chapter 31.2
Scordisci, 48 n.3; 52.3 (Scordisti)
Scythians, 56.4; 112, chapter 31.2
Sicily, 112, chapter 27.3
Side, 54.5
Skamandros R., 98 C
Skiathians, 64.18
Smyrna, 45 n.1; 77.45; 101 VI 41
Spain, 71 A–B; 112, chapter 29.1
Stratonikeia (in Karia), 43 n.1; 63.2 and *passim*
    in 63
Stymphalians, 17.3
Suebians, 112, chapter 32.1
Sugambrians, 112, chapter 32.1
Syria, 3 B; 19 n.; 55.9; 112, chapter 28.1

Tanais R., 112, chapter 31.2
Taurus Mts, 67 A
Tenedos, 71 B
Teos, 8.3; 26.10; 109.20 (Games in)
Termessus Maior, 72 *passim*
Thasos, 64.1
Thebaid, 93.3,6
Thebes, 19.17; 21.48
Thebes (in Egypt), 94.20
Thelphousa, 11.2
Themessos, 63.53
Thessalonike, 64.4
Thessaly, 12.8; 19.26; 38.1 and *passim* in 38
Thisbai, 21.18,49
Thracians, 19.15; 26.6; 52.4; 78.23
Thrious, 11.2
Tolostoagioi, 5.49
Tragurion, 76.7
Tralles, 65.11; 77.44; 85 n.1; 96.1
Triakontaschoinos, 93.8
Tritaia, 11.4

IV. Index of subjects and terms

IV. Subjects and terms

Actian Games, 109.3

Advisory Board, 45.21,23; 50.11; 60 A6; 62 B2; 63.96; 70.6,29,39,43,55,57; 102.86. *See also* Glossary

Advocate, 102.102

Aisymnetes, 41 B29,33

Alliances and treaties: Aetolian League, 2; Astypalaia, 53; Kibyra, 25; Methymna, 33; Mytilene, 97; mention of: 19.18 (envoys from Thebes); 51.7 (envoys from Epidaurus); 61.5 (with Mithridates VI). *See also* Friendship and Alliance

Ambassadors, *see* Envoys

Apellaios (month), 22.26; 86.1,85; 101 VI 68

Apollonia (Delian festival), 9.10

Arbitrator, 34.48,49,51; 55 B IV 36; 57.55; 74.12

Archives (Greek), 5.40–1; 50.7,22; 51.9; 77.53; 86.6–8; 87.51; 103.38; 107.10

Archives (Roman), 45 n.9; 87.30

Archon, 41 B39

Artabai, 106 *passim*

Artemitios (month), 76.5; 101 VI 70

Artists, *see* Dionysiac Artists

Assembly (Greek), 53.14; 58.11; 65.16; 74.41

Assembly (Roman), 55 A (C) 9

Association (of Victors in Sacred Games), 85.8

Atrium, 26.26–7

Auditors of Public Accounts, 44.23

Audnaios (month), 101 VI 69

Auspices, 112, chapter 26.5

Autonomous, 2.21; 5.75; 15.4; 80 B5; 86.4,74,86

Autonomy (of Greek cities), 5.34; 12.10

Bankers (Roman), 47 D3

Barbarians, 19.10,26,33; 30.14; 48.23

Basilica Porcia, 70.6

Benefactor, 9.3; 22.11,18; 43 B41,H6; 48.39; 74.2,46; 75 E2; 79 B; 98 A5 and D3 (Agrippa); 98 B4 (Julia); 101 VI 44; 110.16. *See also* Savior and Benefactor; Glossary

Billeting (of Roman troops), 37.5 (immunity from); 62 B12 (immunity from); 85.16 (freedom from); 86 n.9

Bireme, 71 D–F

Birthday (of Augustus), 101 *passim*

Boiedromion (month), 41 B38

Book, 45.20 (Record Book); 70.31 (Book of minutes of a senatorial meeting); 70.58 (Book One of Senatorial Proceedings)

Boule, 5.8 (Lampsakos); 8.3 (Teos); 9.7 and 10.2 (Delos); 14.2 (Herakleia in Karia); 23.11,28,31 (Athens); 26.27 (Abdera); 28.3 (Athens); 34.37 and 9.13 (Mylasa); 36.49 and 48.3 (Lete); 44.4 and 80 A2 (Pergamum; Hall of, in Pergamum: 44.30); 57.27 (Ephesus); 59a–b (Aphrodisias); 60 A1 (Nysa); 61.18 (Ephesus); 62 A3 (Kos); 63.2 (Stratonikeia); 64.1 (Thasos); 70.2 (Oropos); 73 (Mesambria in Thrace); 78.44 (Dionysopolis in Thrace); 79 C Chios; 83.8 (Mytilene); 86 *passim* (Rhosos in Syria); 86.7 (Tarsus); 86.7 (Antioch); 86.8 (Seleukeia (?)); 87.8 (Plarasa-Aphrodisias); 100 n.1 (no Boule at Alexandria); 104 A16 and B23 (Sardis); 103.5 (Knidos). *See also* Glossary.

Breakwater, 47 B2

Bronze plaque (tablet), 44.24,27,34,59; 51.8; 53.6,20,21; 55 A24; 66.25; 72 n.1; 83.18,23; 85.27

Calendar (in Greek cities), 101

Censor, 59.4. *See also* Glossary

Census, 102.6,17,20

Centurion, 90.9; 110 n.4

Chrematisteria, 77.54

Citharist, 62 A5

Citizen

   Greek, 39.9,11; 61 n.3; 65.10 (Tralles); 72 *passim* (Termessus Maior); 74.13,25,29 (Gytheion); 78.11,18 (Dionysopolis in Thrace); 80 A4 (Pergamum); 82.5; 87.43; 91 B2; 95.14,24; 98 C (Ilium); 102.36

   Roman, 47 G1; 55 B II 5 and *passim* here; 102 *passim*

Cohort, 110.20

Colonies, 112, chapter 28.2; 112, chapter 28.1 (of soldiers)

Colonist, 47 B3

Comitium, 38.10; 45.21; 63.20. *See also* Glossary

Commander (Roman; 'strategos' in Greek), 5.17; 16.11; 21.41,51; 43 A2; 55 A (B) 11; 112, chapter 31.1 (Latin 'dux')

Commissioners (Roman), 5.59; 35.9; 38.53; 49 n.3

Common enemies of all (= Romans), 60 C7

Common saviors (of mankind; = Romans), 61.2

Consul

   consul designate, 47 G5; 86.2; 87.3; 91.2; 103.3

   ex-consul, 67 A

   functions: asked to send letters abroad, 55 A (B) 5 and B III 28; 66.29;

IV. Index of subjects and terms

writes letters to Greek cities, *see* Letters
communicates information to senate, 45.9
forbidden to introduce motion of special
nature, 55 B II 30
must send treaty to Mytilene, 97 C23
sees to erection of bronze plaque in
Rome, 53.6; 97 C25
name on milestones, 42 A–B
name used for dating, 53.15; 55 A (B) 21;
66.1; 72 *passim*; 76.1; 79 A–E (Julius
Caesar); 82.9 (Julius Caesar); 86.73,85
(Octavian); 92; 95 A2; 97 b37,c26;
98 A4; 99.3,5; 105.2; 107.5; 108.12
See also Glossary
Contest (athletic), 41 B1,5,10,13; 48.39
(equestrian)
Contract (Greek), 74.34; 77.38
Contracts (Roman), 45.16; 55 B II 30; 59.8;
66.23; 70.19,25,32,66; 72 II 35; 83.24
Conventus (judiciary district), 77.47; 101 VI 65
Crowns (awarded by Greek states), 9.8,15;
21.32–4; 23.34; 26.30; 48.37,45;
63.30,124; 65.25; 78.46; 86.79 (to
Augustus); 101 VI 43,55,59
Curator (of a Roman cohort), 110.20
Curia Iulia, 97 b39
Customs duties, 72 II 31ff.
Cynoscephalae (battle of), 5 n.9

Daisios (month), 30.31; 48.39; 101 VI 70
Dalmatia, 112, chapter 29.1
Debts, 19.23; 50.14; 66 *passim*; 77.37
Deme, 23.4 (Kephisia), 7 (Kolonos), 8 (Phyle);
47 B1 (Acharnai). *See also* Glossary
Demiourgoi (Greek magistrates), 50.21; 103.1
Democracy (Greek), 5.34; 30.23; 35.9; 44.31
(statue of); 81.5
Denarii, 102.6,18. *See also* Glossary
Dictator, 61 A3 (Sulla); 63.1 and *passim* in 63
(Sulla); 80 A1,B (Julius Caesar); 82.10
(Julius Caesar); 83.7 (Julius Caesar)
Dionysiac Artists, 37 nn.2–3; 44.46; 62 A6;
62 A7 (Dionysos our Leader)
Drachma, 41 B26; 74.10,35–6,38. *See also*
Glossary
Dystros (month), 86.73; 101 VI 69,76

Edict, 55 A (C) 16,18,21,26
Education (Supervisor of Children's), 41 B18;
44.57
Egypt (emblem for a boat), 106.4
Ekdikoi, 101 VI 59
Ekklesia, 23.6,29. *See also* Assembly; Glossary
Elections (in Greek cities), 101 VII 82
Embassies (and envoys), 5 *passim*; 8.5; 10.5;
12.8; 14.2ff.; 15.2ff.; 16.3ff.; 18.62ff.;
19.17; 22.6; 26.5ff.; 30.11; 34.34ff.;

38.37,70; 45.3; 48.40,49; 51.3;
53.4,10,20; 55 A17, A (B) 13,18; 57.46;
59a B3,5; 59b B11; 62 A11; 63.13,17 and
passim in 63; 64.2; 65.5 and *passim* in 65;
66.27ff.; 68.6; 70.19; 73.7,9; 76.7;
78.30,34; 80.7; 83.14,28; 86.62,76;
87.14; 91.8–9,B7; 93.7; 96.3; 100.4,52;
102.8; 103 A15,17,20, B23; 103.6; 108.2;
111.33; 112, chapter 31.1
Ephebe, 41.22,25,26. *See also* Glossary
Ephor, 74.47, and *passim* in 74
Epimeletes, 47 B1 (Athenian governor of
Delos); 51.15 (magistrate)
Epopta, 27 A2; 27 B2 (epoptes)
Era, 30.31 and n.1 (Pontos); 31.1 (Ptolemaic
kings); 48 n.1 (Macedonian); 51 n.2
(Achaian); 86.1 (Rhosos); 88 and 90.13
(Cleopatra VII); 105.3 (Paphlagonia);
106.5 (Caesar Augustus, also 110.1 and
11.29)
Eumeneios (month), 39.2
Evocatio, 67 n.2
Excellence (of Greek and Roman aristocrats
praised in documents), 6 B3,E3,F3;
8.10; 7 B1; 11.9; 13.2; 26.33; 46.6;
47 A6,B5; 58.7,13; 65.14,29; 75 C7;
80 B3; 98 B4; 101.27,35
Exegetes, 100.2,1
Exemption
from levy, 74.28
from 'public duty', 102.104
from taxation, 51.16; 86.10,20; 107.11
from war contribution, 37.6
sacred territory exempt from Roman
revenue contracts, 59 *passim*; 70.20 and
passim in 70
See also Immunity
Extortion, 102.91ff. (recovery of extorted
money)

Festival, 6 G; 18.11 ff.; 19.8 (Pythian); 26.29
(of Dionysios); 51.17; 58.4–5 (Soteria
and Moukieia); 85.16 (truce during);
101 VI 58,61 (for Augustus). *See also*
Games
Founder, 80 C6. *See also* Savior and Founder
Freedom (of Greek cities), 14.10; 15.3,5;
19.25; 61.13; 66.19 (free city); 72.7 and
passim in 72; 76.12; 86.5
Friendship and Alliance (Friends and
Allies) of the Roman People: Achaians,
22.7–8; Alexandria, 55 A (B) 10;
Aphrodisias, 59b B28; Chersonesos (in
the Crimea), 30.26; Cyprus, 55 A (B) 10;
Cyrene 55 A (B) 10; Delos, 10.8; Egypt,
55 A (B) 10; Ephesus, 57.28; Epidaurus,
51.3,5; Lampsakos, 5.19; Magnesia (in

IV. Index of subjects and terms

Friendship and Alliance (*cont.*)
    Ionia), 34.41; Massalia, 5.27,54;
    Melitaia, 38.17,19; Mytilene, 83.12 and
    passim in 83; Narthakion, 38.41; Parthia
    ('suppliants for friendship'), 112,
    chapter 29.2; Pergamum, 44.12 and
    passim in 44; Priene, 34.44; Ptolemaios
    VIII, 31.16; Rhosos in Syria, 86.77;
    Stratonikeia in Karia, 63.11 and *passim*
    in 63; Syria, 55 A (B) 10; Termessus
    Maior in Pisidia, 72.7; Thasos, 64.3;
    Thisbai, 21.7
    'entering into Friendship' with the Roman
    People, 20.1; 21.22; 34.54; 38.47;
    55 A (B) 7; 108.16
    'Register of Friends' of the Roman People,
    57 n.2; 58.3; 66.24
    'remaining in Friendship with the Roman
    People', 64.29; 66.20; 70.52

Games
    Greek, 57.30; 70.47; 74.49; 78.45; 109
    passim
    Roman, 41 B20
    See also Festival
Gerousia, 98 E (Elder Citizens), n.2
Gifts, *see* Proquaestor; Quaestor
Glad tidings, 101 VI 40; 104 A14
Gorpiaios (month), 101 VI 70; 107.4
Governor (Roman), 35.10; 55 A (C) 11, B II 15,
    B IV 20
Greeks in Asia, 101 VI 50. *See also* Koinon;
    People and Tribes
Guilds, *see* Glossary under Koinon and
    Dionysiac Artists
Gymnasiarch, 6 A6; 41 A20,25,26,B10. *See also*
    Glossary
Gymnasium, 41 B20. *See also* Glossary

Hathyr (month), 106.8,11
Herakleios (month), 30.6
Herald (Greek), 9.11; 26.31; 104.12
Hieromnemones, 6 G; 76.4. *See also* Glossary
Holy writings, 107.11
Hyperberetaios (month), 101 VI 71

Ides, 21.3,14; 27 A2; 28.16; 55 B III 6; 70.5;
    107.5. *See also* Appendix
Idios Logos, 100, col. 2.6
Immunity: 15.3,5; 17.6–7; 22.13; from billeting,
    37.5; from liturgies, 37.5; 62 B4; 66.12;
    83.28, 33 (?); 86.22; from military
    service, 62 B9; from war contributions,
    37.6. *See also* Exemption
Imperator: 47 F2; 52.2; 67 B; Sulla, 63.105;
    Lucullus, 73.5,7; Pompey, 75 A–E;
    78.33; Julius Caesar, 76.11; 79 A–E; 80

    A–B; 83.7; Octavian (Augustus),
    86.2,73,85; 91.1; 92; 95.9; 98 B2; 100.1;
    102 *passim*; 104 B22; 105.1; 107.2;
    Antonius, 89 A–B. *See also* Glossary
Imperial family, 109.3 and *passim* in 109
    (Games of)
Imperium, 99 n.5
Inhabited world, 75 A6
Inheritance, 66.16
Intercalated day, 101 VI 71,76
Inviolability, 8.20; 15.2; 22.13; 70.45; 85.17;
    86.4,74,86; 107.11
Italian War, 66.7

Judiciary district, *see* Conventus
Justice, 77.51; 79 B6; 95 A11

Kalends, 45.21; 63.19; 66.4; 70.60; 72.4;
    97 C9,D22; 101 IV 23, V4;
    VI 51,55,74,77. *See also* Appendix
Knight (eques), 93.1
Koinon
    of Dionysiac Artists, 62 A6
    of Greeks in Asia, 58 n.1; 65.4,21; 77.43;
    79 n.3; 85.2; 101 IV 26, VI 30,50, VII 78;
    103.1; 109.6
    See also Glossary

Latin Allies, 55 A (B) 6, B II 8, B III 33
Laurel (crown of), 9.11,15
Laws (Roman), 53.12 (Rubrian and Acilian);
    55 *passim* (on pirates); 70.19,25,32,66 (of
    state contracts); 72 (Antonian); 72 II 16
    (Porcian); 86.10 (Munatian and
    Aemilian); 99.10; 101 VII 83
    (Cornelian); 102 *passim*; 102.117 (Julian
    Judiciary)
Leaders ('Roman leaders'), 65.6; 65.19; 74.23
Leadership ('Roman leadership'), 59a B14;
    61.13; 63.4,33; 70.49; 83.11
Leagues (Greek): Achaian, 22.2,10; 35 n.5;
    6 B; 7 n.; Aetolian, 2; Amphictionic, 15
    (second letter); Delphian, 16.15;
    Lycian, 18; Thessalian, 38 n.1; 'con-
    federacies', 35.9
Legate, 27 A4; 47 C1; 49.6; 63.77; 69.2 (legatus
    pro praetore); 71 D–F; 112, chapter 30.1
Legion, 106.2 (XXII Deiotariana); 110.4
    (III Cyrenaica)
Letters (from non-Romans to Greek states):
    5.48; 29; 60 B–C
Letters (notice of official letters to Greek
    states from Rome or Roman officials):
    5.39,64,76; 16.10,15; 21.43,56ff.; 32.7;
    34.61; 55 A5ff.; and *passim* in 55; 63.75;

64.18; 107.13; 108.6

Letters (official, from Roman magistrates):
4 (T. Quinctius Flamininus); 8 (M.
Valerius Messalla); 12 (M'. Acilius
Glabrio); 14 (L. Cornelius Scipio and
brother); 15 (Sp. Postumius); 16 (C.
Livius Salinator ?); 19 (to Delphian
Amphictiones); 34 (praetor M.
Aemilius); 37 (to Dionysiac Artists);
50 (Q. Fabius Maximus); 57 (Q. Mucius
Scaevola); 59a–b (Q. Oppius); 60 A (C.
Cassius); 62 (Sulla); 63 (Sulla); 64 (Cn.
Cornelius Dolabella); 70 (M. Terentius
Varro Lucullus and C. Cassius
Longinus); 77 (unknown Roman); 80 A
and 83 (Julius Caesar); 85 (M.
Antonius); 86–7 and 91 (Octavian);
95 B (Vinicius); 98 E (Agrippa); 100,
104 B and 103 (Augustus); 108
(unknown Roman)

Library (Roman), 111.32

Liturgy, 18.9; 37.5; 62 B4,9; 102.53,136. *See
also* Glossary

Loan, 74.8 and *passim* in 74

Loos (month), 31.1; 101 VI 70

Luck
'for the good luck', 44.44
'Good Luck', 111.53
'with good luck', 41 A1; 62 A1; 101 VI 49;
110.2

Magistrate (Roman), 55 A (B) 11,16;
55 A (C) 7,10,24; 55 B III 9; 58 n.3 (cult
of Roman magistrates); 62 B6;
63.61,66,131; 66.19.23,29; 72.36, II 6;
86.55,62,68; 102.100,105,120,137;
108.17

Market Square, 47 B3,D1; 68.5 (market
privileges)

Merchants, 47 D1

Metageitnion (month), 41 A9, B31

Military service (for Greeks), 43.25 (forced to
soldier for Rome); 85.14 (freedom
from); 86.22 (free from)

Military standards (Roman), 112, chapter
29.1–2

Mina, 74.37

Mines (superintendent of), 110.7–8

Modius, 60 A10

Moukieia (festival), 58.5

Muses, 62 B5

Mustae (mystai), 27 A5,C5; 78.21

Mysteries (Samothracian), 27

Negotiator (Roman businessman), 21 n.5;
47 G2, n.; 105.6; 'Italians' (i.e.
negotiatores): 47 C1, E1 and F2

Nikephoria, 7 n.2

Nome, 106.1 (Oxyrhynchite, in Egypt)

Nomophylakia, 77.53

Nones 15 (the decree), 1; 38.10; 76.3; 105.4;
See also Appendix

Nymphaion, 1.3

Oath, 5.10; 25.5; 30.6,25; 53.44;
55 A (C) 9,12,17; 56.1; 87.26; 105 (of
Gangra)

Odeion, 47 H4

Palaestra, 41 B14

Panemos (month), 48.1,49; 101 VI 70

Pankration, 109.17

Patron, 26.23; 46.3; 47 G5; 59b B51ff.; 73.8;
75 E2; 79 B (patron and benefactor);
79 C (patron of the city); 98 D2
(Agrippa)

Payni (month), 110.1

Pentathlon, 109.2 and *passim* in 109

'Peoples and Tribes in Asia', 57.29; 58.1;
65.1,24,27; 79 D1. *See also* Greeks in
Asia

Peritios (month), 101 VI 69,73

Phamenoth (month), 90.13

Pilot (of a boat), 106.2

Pirates, 47 n.8; 54 n.1; 55 A (B) 11–12, n.1;
71 C

Plebiscite, 55 A (B) 19,28; 55 BII 13,25;
55 BIV 7

Plebs, 72.2

Politarchai, 48.2,48

Pontifex Maximus, 3 C–D; 79 A–E and
80 A1,B2 (Julius Caesar as).
Augustus as, 100.1; 102.1,40,55,62,72;
104 B22; 103.2

Praefectus civitatis, 73 n.2

Praetor
as provincial governor, 48.13; 55 *passim*;
102.33
assigns judge or court, 55 A (C) 29
communicates information to senate, 45.10
concerned with passage of a law, 55 B III 5;
59b A3 (?)
consults the senate, 28.16; 40.2,11
grants free state as arbitrator,
34.47,49,58,62 (sends letter)
peregrine praetor, 50.26; 53.18; 66.2
urban praetor, 45.10; 53.16; 66.2
See also Glossary

Prefect, 47 G4 (of a Roman fleet); 90.1; 93.2
(of Egypt); 110.5 (of Berenike in Egypt)

Priest, 41 A4,7,11,27; 41 B9,23,30,36; 44.41;
78.10,14; 80 C2–3; 85.8 (eponymous);
101 VI 31 (introduces a motion); 107.1

IV. Index of subjects and terms

Priest (*cont.*)
    (of Roma and Augustus), 4 (of Jupiter
    Capitolinus); 107.7 (of Tiberius)
Priesthood, 39.1; 41 A2 (of the People of the
    Romans and Roma); 50.1; 86.30
Princeps, 102.85; 112, chapter 30.1 ('leader'),
    32.3
Prisoners of war, 63.118; 91 B2
Privileges, 8.22; 22.15; 62 A10,B3; 74.46;
    83.10,18,21,29; 85.11; 86.30,66,81,90;
    87.38.45
Proconsul, 36.3,5; 47 G2; 50.3; 54.3; 55 *passim*;
    57.27; 63.114; 64.1; 95.12;
    101 VI 41,44,58; 107.12; 108.3
Procurator, 110.15 (of mines)
Proedroi, 23.7,28; 65.1,11. *See also* Glossary
Promagistrate, 55 A (B) 16, A (C) 7.25, B III 9;
    62 B8; 72.36,II 6; 86.56,62,68; 108.17.
    See also Proconsul; Propraetor;
    Proquaestor; Glossary
Property (Greek)
    restored by Rome, 4.8ff.; 12 n.1; 16.13;
    20.4–8
    Rome permits Greeks to keep, 21.25ff.
    wealthy prohibited from acquiring
    additional, 35.9
Propraetor, 55 A (B) 20, 27, B III 14; pro
    praetore: 43 A16; 54.6
Proquaestor, 55 B IV 41; 63.90 (gives gifts to
    envoys)
Prosetairoi, 41 B34
Providence, 101 VI 3
Province, 48.32; 55 *passim*; 63 *passim*; 65.8;
    66.29; 77.50; 86.48,68; 95 A4; 99.9;
    101 VI 44,46; 102 *passim*; 112,
    chapter 27.3
Proxenos, 6 n.6; 9.4; 22.11; 43 B41; 74.2,46.
    See also Glossary
Prytany, 23.3,6,39 (secretary for); 41 B25
    (treasurer for); 95.23
Publicans, 45.8 (?); 22 n.; 59 n.2; 65.2; 68.5;
    70.5 and *passim* in 70; 72 II 36;
    86.52,n.9. *See also* Glossary
Pythia (festival), 19.8

Quaestor
    provincial, 42 B3,6 (restores road); 47 E4;
    48.4 and 37 (actions after death of
    governor); 55 A (C) 3, B IV 41
    urban: lets contracts for accommodations
    of envoys to Rome, 45.18; 53.10; 66.26;
    83.24
    See also Proquaestor; Glossary

Republic (Roman), 45.13,19,19; 53.8;
    55 A (B) 15; 59b B19; 63.9,81,121; 64.5;
    66 and *passim* in 66; 70.68; 83.25; 86.17;

    87.5; 92; 97 C8,C19; 99.9; 102.45,47
Resident aliens, 39.12–13,20; 47 B4
Revenues
    Greek, 63.54,98,106,108; 64.16; 70.47;
    83.81
    Roman, 45.15 (Asia); 55 *passim*
    (Macedonia); 70.21; 72 II 35
Romaion (sacred enclosure), 41 B22

Sanctuaries, 38.44,49
Sarapieion, 28.6
Savior, 75 A2; 101 VI 35–6
Savior and Benefactor, 6 A; 59a B4 (Romans
    as); 75 C4; 79 A–B (Julius Caesar);
    80 B1 (Julius Caesar); 81.3 (P. Servilius
    Isauricus); 84 B4 (M. Iunius Brutus).
    See also Glossary
Seal (official), 104 A19; 106.8ff.; 108.12 (sealed
    copy)
Secretary (Greek), 50.1; 51.18 (sees to the
    engraving of decree); 61.18 (should
    introduce decree); 65.1 (of Koinon);
    107.6
Senate (Roman), decree of (quoted): 15; 20; 32;
    38; 40; 53; 63; 66; 70; 70.55 (partial);
    83; 97; 102.84ff. *See also* Glossary
Sesterces, 38.69; 55 A (C) 21
Ship, name of: 71 D–F
Ship-Captain, 71 F
Shipowners and merchants, 47 A1,B3
Sitologi, 106.6
Six Hundred (Boule of), 5.49 (Massalia)
Skirophorion (month), 23.5
Slaves, interrogation of, 103.11ff.
Slave War,112, chapter 27.3
Soteria (festival), 58.4
Statues
    of Greeks: 7 B1 (King Eumenes); 11.8; 13.1;
    47 A5; 47 B1; 65.27; 78.46
    of Romans: 6 A–F (T. Quinctius
    Flamininus); 46.1 (Cn. Domitius
    Ahenobarbus); 47 C (Marius); 47 D
    (Roman banker); 47 E (quaestor); 47 F
    (Q. Caecilius Metellus); 47 G (pro-
    consul); 59.2 and 79 A–E (Julius
    Caesar); 75 A–E (Pompey); 84 A–B (M.
    Iunius Brutus); 84 C (Q. Hortensius);
    98 A–B,D (Agrippa); 98 B (Julia);
    102.53 (Augustus)
    other: 25.15 (of Roma); 44.31 (of
    Democracy); 71 C (of gods)
Stele, 17.7; 22.16,20;23.40,44; 44.35,38;
    48.46–7; 55 A25; 62.9,15; 74.53; 86.6;
    101 VI 63,65. *See also* Glossary
Stephanephoros, 41 A 10, n.2; 43 B 36 (?), n.1;
    44.40; 59a B9; 107.3. *See also* Glossary
Strategos (Greek magistrate), 22.20 (sees to

erection of stele); 28.1 (Athenian);
38.1,6 (head of Thessalian League);
39.3 and 44.10 (makes a motion to
People of Pergamum); 59a A8 (of a
territory); 61.18 (is to introduce decree
at Ephesus); 104.6 (introduces motion
at Sardis); 107.9 (Nysa's board of
generals). *See also* Glossary
Supervisor, *see* Education
Synhedrion, 50.2 ('Council' at Dyme)

Tablet (of bronze), 25.12–13. *See also* Bronze
plaque
Tagoi, 4.2; 38.3
Taureon (month), 41 A18
Taxes
    Greek, 8.21; 15.3,5; 62 B10; 66.12; 102.59
    (Greek?)
    Roman, 66.23; 68.5–6; 70.23,67; 86.10 and
    passim in 86
Testament (of King Attalus III), 39.7
Thargelion (month), 41 B27
Titieia (Games of Titus), 6 G
Toga, 104.7, n.3
Toparchy, 106.7
Torch race, 41 B14
Trainer (in Gymnasium), 85.7
Treasurer (Greek), 41 A5,15,B25; 44.60; 48.48;
    51.13
Treasurer of Military Fund (Athens), 23.44
Treasury (Roman), 21 n.1 (Aerarium); 51.7
Treasury (Greek), 12.7
Treaties, 30 (King Pharnakes and city of
    Chersonesos); 57 n. (Sardis and

Ephesus). *See also* Alliances and
Treaties
Tribes (Greek), 23.2 (Attalis, at Athens)
Tribes (Roman): Aniensis, 45.23; Arnensis,
70.7,10,13; Claudia, 70.61; Crustumina,
28.22, 97 C15; Cornelia, 38.12, 70.12,
86.24; Fabia, 34.39(?), 76.12; Falerna,
38.13, 97 B41; Horatia, 70.15; Lemonia,
70.15,16,60; Menenia, 45.23; Palatina,
97 B40, 97 C11; Papiria, 34.39, 70.11,
97 B41, 97 C15; Pomptina, 70.8,9;
Quirina, 70.12,63; Romilia, 70.13;
Stellatina, 36 n.2, 70.9; Teretina, 70.14;
Voltinia, 21.5. *See also* Glossary
Tribune (of plebs), 8.3; 16.1–2; 55 A (C) 11
Tribunician power, 99.1 n.1; 100.2;
102.1,41,55,63,73; 104 B22; 105.4
Tribute (assigned by Rome in 146 BC),
35.9, n.1
Trireme, 68.5; 71 B
Triumvir (for the constitution of the Republic),
85.2 (Antonius); 86.9 and 87.4
(Octavian); 89 A–B (Antonius). *See also*
Glossary

Via Egnatia, 36
Votive offering, 53.48

Wintering-over, 72 II 9ff.; 73.11; 78.16; 86 n.9
Worshippers of Pompey (Society of), 75.1–2

Xandikos (month), 101 VI 69,71,.77

Young Men (educational age-group in the
gymnasia), 41 B 11,21; 44.56

V. Translated passages

Those marked with an asterisk (*) are only partially translated.

INSCRIPTIONS

CIL I²
    588: 66
    589: 72
    622: 24
    692: 52
    743: 69
    746: 47 F
    845: 47 C
    2662: 54
CIL III
    455: 47 G
    7177: 42 C
    7183: 42 A
    14147.5: 93
    14202.4: 42 B
Corinth VIII 1
    72: 6 B
Corinth VIII 2

1: 54
Durrbach, *Choix*
    64: 9
    65: 10
    95: 47 B
    105: 47 A
    138: 47 D
    159: 71 E
    160: 71 D
    162: 75 B
FIRA I²
    9: 55
    11: 72
    31: 21
    35: 66
    36: 70
    *55: 86
    68: 102

FIRA III
  185: 103
Fouilles de Delphes III
  4.37: 55
  4.75: 19
Fraser, *Samothrace*
  28 a: 27 A
  30: 27 B
  32: 27 C
IC III
  4.18: 1
I. Délos
  1526: 47A
  1622: 84 C
  1641: 75 B
  1645: 47 B
  1699: 47 C
  1725: 47 D
  1855: 71 D
  1856: 71 E
  1857: 71 F
IG II^2
  3426: 47 H
  4122: 98 A
IG IV^2
  1.63: 51
IG V
  1.1146: 74
  1.1165: 6 C
IG VII
  383: 84 B
  *2413: 37
IG IX
  2.89: 38
IG IX^2
  2.241: 2
IG XI
  4.756: 10
IG XII
  2.35 col. b 6–36: 83
  2.35 b–d: 97
  2.202: 75 A
  2.204: 98 B
  2.510: 33
  3.173: 53
  3.174: 103
  5.557: 79 E
  9.233: 6 D
  9.931: 6 A
IG Bulg I^2
  13: 78
  314 a: 73
IGLS III
  1.718: 86
IGRR I
  118: 66

  401: 69
  1293: 93
  1300: 90
IGRR III
  137: 105
IGRR IV
  33 col. b: 83
  33 b–d: 97
  54: 75 A
  64: 98B
  179: 5
  188: 58
  194: 59
  204: 98D
  262: 45
  264: 42A
  *289: 39
  *297: 57
  301: 40
  305: 79B
  433: 81
  752: 49
  880: 42C
  928: 79C
  943: 108
  968: 46
  1028: 53
  1031: 103
  1064: 109
  1557: 8
  1558: 26
  1659: 42B
  1677: 80B
  1682: 80C
  1692: 44
  *1756: 104A–B
I. Ilion
  71: 59
ILLRP
  323: 24
  337: 52
  342: 54
  343: 47C
  370: 47E
  372: 69
  374: 47F
  433: 47G
  455: 42A
  456: 42B
  513: 66
I. Lampsakos
  4: 45
ILS
  27: 42A
  37: 69
  38: 72

867: 47F
891: 47G
5814: 42B
8766: 6C
8770: 59
8774: 71D
8776: 75A
8779: 81
8781: 105
8884: 24
8887: 52
8995: 93
9458: 1
9459: 75C
9460: 84C

IOSPE I²
   691: 82

Milet I 7
   203: 41
   253: 75E

OGIS
   135: 47
   315 C VI: 29
   *338: 39
   *351: 32
   354: 47H
   435: 40
   436: 49
   437: 57
   438: 58
   440: 59
   *441: 63
   445: 69
   447: 71D
   449: 81
   453–54: 87
   *458: 101
   532: 105
   654: 93
   762: 25

RDGE
   1: 15
   2: 21
   3: 20
   5: 28
   6 B: 32
   7: 34
   9: 38
   11: 40
   *12: 45
   13: 49
   16 A–B: 53
   18: 63
   *21: 64
   22: 66
   23: 70

24 A: 76
*26: 83; 97
28 A: 87
31: 102
33: 4
34: 8
35: 14
37 A: 12
38: 16
40 B: 19
43: 50
*44: 37
*47: 57
48: 60
49: 62
*52: 77
*54: 80A
57: 85
*58: 86
60: 91
61: 95
63: 98E
*65: 101
67: 103
68: 104
69 I: 107
70: 108

Sardis VII 1
   8, 1–27: 103A–B

Schmitt, *Staatsverträge* III
   536: 2

SEG IX
   7: 31
   8: 102

SEG XI
   73: 6B

SEG XIV
   121: 79A

SEG XV
   254: 11

SEG XVI
   255: 22

SEG XVII
   75: 84A
   209: 84B
   525: 75D

SEG XVIII
   555: 95
   570: 18

SEG XIX
   374: 20

SEG XX
   670: 110

SEG XXII
   214: 6B
   *266: 6G

V. Index of translated passages

SEG XXII (*cont.*)
   507: 108
SEG XXIII
   412: 6F
SEG XXV
   118: 23
   *445: 17
SIG^3
   591: 5
   592: 6C
   593: 4
   595 A–B: 7
   601: 8
   606: 13
   *609: 12
   611: 16
   612: 15
   616: 6E
   618: 14
   643: 19
   646: 21
   652 a: 24
   *656: 26
   664: 28
   674: 38
   679 IIB: 34
   684: 50
   693: 33
   694: 44
   700: 48
   710 C: 52
   741: 60
   *742: 61
   747: 70
   748: 74
   749 A: 75B
   751: 75A
   760: 79
   764: 83
   768: 91
   776: 98D
   780: 105
   781 I: 107
   785: 108
   1065: 109
Sokolowski, *Lois*
   15: 44
   49: 41

Moretti, *IGUR* I
   1: 65
Moretti, *ISE*
   1.35: 23
   1.42: 22
   1.55: 17
   1.60: 11
   2.87: 2
Welles, *RC*
   61: 29
   73–74: 60

BCH
   78 (1954) 84: 47E
   96 (1972) 444: 65
   98 (1974) 814: 36

JRS
   44 (1954) 65f: 79A
   44 (1954) 68: 80B
   *64 (1974) 201ff.: 55

ZPE
   5 (1970) 226: 99
   24 (1977) 229: 92
Hall, A., in *Akten des VI. Internationalen Kongresses für Griechischen und Lateinischen Epigraphik*, Vestigia 17, (Munich 1973)
   p. 570: 67B
Holleaux, *Études* II
   *179–98: 43
Laffi, U., *Studi Classici e Orientali* 16 (1967)
   *18–23: 101
Maier, *Griechische Mauerbauinschriften* I
   41: 71E
   42: 71F
Reynolds, *Rome and Aphrodisias*
   Document 2: 59a
   Document 3: 59b
   Document 6: 87
Robert, *Opera* I
   p. 559: 46
   p. 614 : 80C
   p. 614 B: 80 B

RES GESTAE DIVI AUGUSTI
   Chapters 26–33: 112

LITERARY TEXTS

Agathias
  Historiae (Keydell)
    2.17: 96
Eusebius (Karst)
   Arm. p. 79: 88

Eutropius
   6.3: 67A
Justin
   30.2,8: 3A
   31.1,2: 3B

V. Index of translated passages

Memnon
  FGrHist 434
    F 22.1–10: 56
    F 27.5–6: 68
    F 29.5: 71A
    F 33.1–2: 71B
Nikolaos of Damascus
  FGrHist 90

F 134: 98 C
Pausanias
  7.16.7–10: 35
Phlegon of Tralles
  FGrHist 257
    F 12.13: 71C
Valerius Maximus
  6.6.1: 3C

PAPYRI

Journal of Juristic Papyrology 4 (1950)
  101-11: 106
P. Köln
  10: 99

P. Oxy.
  2435: 111
  2820: 94
  3020: 100